CROWDING
AND
BEHAVIOR

Edited by
Chalsa M. Loo
University of California
at Santa Cruz

MSS INFORMATION CORPORATION

Distributed by **ARNO PRESS**
3 Park Avenue, New York, N.Y. 10016

This is a custom-made book of readings prepared for the courses taught by the editor, as well as for related courses and for college and university libraries. For information about our program, please write to:

MSS INFORMATION CORPORATION

MSS wishes to express its appreciation to the authors of the articles in the collection for their cooperation in making their work available in this format.

Library of Congress Cataloging in Publication Data

Loo, Chalsa M   comp.
    Crowding and behavior.

    1. Personal space — Addresses, essays, lectures.
2. Crowds — Addresses, essays, lectures. 3. Crowding
stress — Addresses, essays, lectures. I. Title.
[DNLM: 1. Crowding — Collected works. HM291 L863c
1974]
HM291.L63   301.18'2'08   74-8362
ISBN 0-8422-5180-4
ISBN 0-8422-0415-6 (pbk.)

CONTENTS

PREFACE

"I would rather have a pumpkin all to myself, than be crowded on a velvet cushion."

Henry David Thoreau

The focus of this book of readings is on the phenomena of crowding and its effect on human behavior. The first series of articles deal with population and urbanization, two social forces that have had a significant impact on the present concern over the effects of crowding on human beings. The next two series of articles cover the theoretical, empirical, and anthropological approaches to understanding the phenomena of crowding. The last series of articles deals with the area of personal space, as related to seating patterns and body buffer zones, a concept which is integral to a full consideration of crowding.

In keeping with the interdisciplinary nature of Environmental Psychology, this book combines writings from various disciplines, although the primary focus is psychological. This book represents an attempt to compile the more recent articles on crowding, a topic of great social importance and of recent theoretical and empirical investigation.

POPULATION AND URBANIZATION

The Tragedy of the Commons

Garrett Hardin

At the end of a thoughtful article on the future of nuclear war, Wiesner and York (*1*) concluded that: "Both sides in the arms race are . . . confronted by the dilemma of steadily increasing military power and steadily decreasing national security. *It is our considered professional judgment that this dilemma has no technical solution.* If the great powers continue to look for solutions in the area of science and technology only, the result will be to worsen the situation."

I would like to focus your attention not on the subject of the article (national security in a nuclear world) but on the kind of conclusion they reached, namely that there is no technical solution to the problem. An implicit and almost universal assumption of discussions published in professional and semipopular scientific journals is that the problem under discussion has a technical solution. A technical solution may be defined as one that requires a change only in the techniques of the natural sciences, demanding little or nothing in the way of change in human values or ideas of morality.

In our day (though not in earlier times) technical solutions are always welcome. Because of previous failures in prophecy, it takes courage to assert that a desired technical solution is not possible. Wiesner and York exhibited this courage; publishing in a science journal, they insisted that the solution to the problem was not to be found in the natural sciences. They cautiously qualified their statement with the phrase, "It is our considered professional judgment. . . ." Whether they were right or not is not the concern of the present article. Rather, the concern here is with the important concept of a class of human problems which can be called "no technical solution problems," and, more specifically, with the identification and discussion of one of these.

It is easy to show that the class is not a null class. Recall the game of tick-tack-toe. Consider the problem, "How can I win the game of tick-tack-toe?" It is well known that I cannot, if I assume (in keeping with the conventions of game theory) that my opponent understands the game perfectly. Put another way, there is no "technical solution" to the problem. I can win only by giving a radical meaning to the word "win." I can hit my opponent over the head; or I can drug him; or I can falsify the records. Every way in which I "win" involves, in some sense, an abandonment of the game, as we intuitively understand it. (I can also, of course, openly abandon the game—refuse to play it. This is what most adults do.)

The class of "No technical solution problems" has members. My thesis is that the "population problem," as conventionally conceived, is a member of this class. How it is conventionally conceived needs some comment. It is fair to say that most people who anguish over the population problem are trying to find a way to avoid the evils of overpopulation without relinquishing any of

SCIENCE, Dec. 13, 1968, vol. 162, pp. 1243-1248.

the privileges they now enjoy. They think that farming the seas or developing new strains of wheat will solve the problem—technologically. I try to show here that the solution they seek cannot be found. The population problem cannot be solved in a technical way, any more than can the problem of winning the game of tick-tack-toe.

What Shall We Maximize?

Population, as Malthus said, naturally tends to grow "geometrically," or, as we would now say, exponentially. In a finite world this means that the per capita share of the world's goods must steadily decrease. Is ours a finite world?

A fair defense can be put forward for the view that the world is infinite; or that we do not know that it is not. But, in terms of the practical problems that we must face in the next few generations with the foreseeable technology, it is clear that we will greatly increase human misery if we do not, during the immediate future, assume that the world available to the terrestrial human population is finite. "Space" is no escape (2).

A finite world can support only a finite population; therefore, population growth must eventually equal zero. (The case of perpetual wide fluctuations above and below zero is a trivial variant that need not be discussed.) When this condition is met, what will be the situation of mankind? Specifically, can Bentham's goal of "the greatest good for the greatest number" be realized?

No—for two reasons, each sufficient by itself. The first is a theoretical one. It is not mathematically possible to maximize for two (or more) variables at the same time. This was clearly stated by von Neumann and Morgenstern (3),

but the principle is implicit in the theory of partial differential equations, dating back at least to D'Alembert (1717–1783).

The second reason springs directly from biological facts. To live, any organism must have a source of energy (for example, food). This energy is utilized for two purposes: mere maintenance and work. For man, maintenance of life requires about 1600 kilocalories a day ("maintenance calories"). Anything that he does over and above merely staying alive will be defined as work, and is supported by "work calories" which he takes in. Work calories are used not only for what we call work in common speech; they are also required for all forms of enjoyment, from swimming and automobile racing to playing music and writing poetry. If our goal is to maximize population it is obvious what we must do: We must make the work calories per person approach as close to zero as possible. No gourmet meals, no vacations, no sports, no music, no literature, no art. . . . I think that everyone will grant, without argument or proof, that maximizing population does not maximize goods. Bentham's goal is impossible.

In reaching this conclusion I have made the usual assumption that it is the acquisition of energy that is the problem. The appearance of atomic energy has led some to question this assumption. However, given an infinite source of energy, population growth still produces an inescapable problem. The problem of the acquisition of energy is replaced by the problem of its dissipation, as J. H. Fremlin has so wittily shown (4). The arithmetic signs in the analysis are, as it were, reversed; but Bentham's goal is still unobtainable.

The optimum population is, then, less than the maximum. The difficulty of defining the optimum is enormous; so far as I know, no one has seriously tackled this problem. Reaching an acceptable and stable solution will surely require more than one generation of hard analytical work—and much persuasion.

We want the maximum good per person; but what is good? To one person it is wilderness, to another it is ski lodges for thousands. To one it is estuaries to nourish ducks for hunters to shoot; to another it is factory land. Comparing one good with another is, we usually say, impossible because goods are incommensurable. Incommensurables cannot be compared.

Theoretically this may be true; but in real life incommensurables *are* commensurable. Only a criterion of judgment and a system of weighting are needed. In nature the criterion is survival. Is it better for a species to be small and hideable, or large and powerful? Natural selection commensurates the incommensurables. The compromise achieved depends on a natural weighting of the values of the variables.

Man must imitate this process. There is no doubt that in fact he already does, but unconsciously. It is when the hidden decisions are made explicit that the arguments begin. The problem for the years ahead is to work out an acceptable theory of weighting. Synergistic effects, nonlinear variation, and difficulties in discounting the future make the intellectual problem difficult, but not (in principle) insoluble.

Has any cultural group solved this practical problem at the present time, even on an intuitive level? One simple fact proves that none has: there is no prosperous population in the world today that has, and has had for some time, a growth rate of zero. Any people that has intuitively identified its optimum point will soon reach it, after

which its growth rate becomes and remains zero.

Of course, a positive growth rate might be taken as evidence that a population is below its optimum. However, by any reasonable standards, the most rapidly growing populations on earth today are (in general) the most miserable. This association (which need not be invariable) casts doubt on the optimistic assumption that the positive growth rate of a population is evidence that it has yet to reach its optimum.

We can make little progress in working toward optimum poulation size until we explicitly exorcize the spirit of Adam Smith in the field of practical demography. In economic affairs, *The Wealth of Nations* (1776) popularized the "invisible hand," the idea that an individual who "intends only his own gain," is, as it were, "led by an invisible hand to promote . . . the public interest" (5). Adam Smith did not assert that this was invariably true, and perhaps neither did any of his followers. But he contributed to a dominant tendency of thought that has ever since interfered with positive action based on rational analysis, namely, the tendency to assume that decisions reached individually will, in fact, be the best decisions for an entire society. If this assumption is correct it justifies the continuance of our present policy of laissez-faire in reproduction. If it is correct we can assume that men will control their individual fecundity so as to produce the optimum population. If the assumption is not correct, we need to reexamine our individual freedoms to see which ones are defensible.

Tragedy of Freedom in a Commons

The rebuttal to the invisible hand in population control is to be found in a

10

scenario first sketched in a little-known pamphlet (6) in 1833 by a mathematical amateur named William Forster Lloyd (1794–1852). We may well call it "the tragedy of the commons," using the word "tragedy" as the philosopher Whitehead used it (7): "The essence of dramatic tragedy is not unhappiness. It resides in the solemnity of the remorseless working of things." He then goes on to say, "This inevitableness of destiny can only be illustrated in terms of human life by incidents which in fact involve unhappiness. For it is only by them that the futility of escape can be made evident in the drama."

The tragedy of the commons develops in this way. Picture a pasture open to all. It is to be expected that each herdsman will try to keep as many cattle as possible on the commons. Such an arrangement may work reasonably satisfactorily for centuries because tribal wars, poaching, and disease keep the numbers of both man and beast well below the carrying capacity of the land. Finally, however, comes the day of reckoning, that is, the day when the long-desired goal of social stability becomes a reality. At this point, the inherent logic of the commons remorselessly generates tragedy.

As a rational being, each herdsman seeks to maximize his gain. Explicitly or implicitly, more or less consciously, he asks, "What is the utility *to me* of adding one more animal to my herd?" This utility has one negative and one positive component.

1) The positive component is a function of the increment of one animal. Since the herdsman receives all the proceeds from the sale of the additional animal, the positive utility is nearly +1.

2) The negative component is a function of the additional overgrazing created by one more animal. Since, however, the effects of overgrazing are shared by all the herdsmen, the negative utility for any particular decision-making herdsman is only a fraction of −1.

Adding together the component partial utilities, the rational herdsman concludes that the only sensible course for him to pursue is to add another animal to his herd. And another; and another. . . . But this is the conclusion reached by each and every rational herdsman sharing a commons. Therein is the tragedy. Each man is locked into a system that compels him to increase his herd without limit—in a world that is limited. Ruin is the destination toward which all men rush, each pursuing his own best interest in a society that believes in the freedom of the commons. Freedom in a commons brings ruin to all.

Some would say that this is a platitude. Would that it were! In a sense, it was learned thousands of years ago, but natural selection favors the forces of psychological denial (8). The individual benefits as an individual from his ability to deny the truth even though society as a whole, of which he is a part, suffers. Education can counteract the natural tendency to do the wrong thing, but the inexorable succession of generations requires that the basis for this knowledge be constantly refreshed.

A simple incident that occurred a few years ago in Leominster, Massachusetts, shows how perishable the knowledge is. During the Christmas shopping season the parking meters downtown were covered with plastic bags that bore tags reading: "Do not open until after Christmas. Free parking courtesy of the mayor and city council." In other words, facing the prospect of an increased demand for already scarce space, the city fathers reinstituted the system of the commons. (Cynically, we suspect that they gained more votes than they lost by this retrogressive act.)

In an approximate way, the logic of the commons has been understood for a long time, perhaps since the discovery of agriculture or the invention of private property in real estate. But it is understood mostly only in special cases which are not sufficiently generalized. Even at this late date, cattlemen leasing national land on the western ranges demonstrate no more than an ambivalent understanding, in constantly pressuring federal authorities to increase the head count to the point where overgrazing produces erosion and weed-dominance. Likewise, the oceans of the world continue to suffer from the survival of the philosophy of the commons. Maritime nations still respond automatically to the shibboleth of the "freedom of the seas." Professing to believe in the "inexhaustible resources of the oceans," they bring species after species of fish and whales closer to extinction (9).

The National Parks present another instance of the working out of the tragedy of the commons. At present, they are open to all, without limit. The parks themselves are limited in extent—there is only one Yosemite Valley—whereas population seems to grow without limit. The values that visitors seek in the parks are steadily eroded. Plainly, we must soon cease to treat the parks as commons or they will be of no value to anyone.

What shall we do? We have several options. We might sell them off as private property. We might keep them as public property, but allocate the right to enter them. The allocation might be on the basis of wealth, by the use of an auction system. It might be on the basis of merit, as defined by some agreed-upon standards. It might be by lottery. Or it might be on a first-come, first-served basis, administered to long queues. These, I think, are all the reasonable possibilities. They are all objectionable. But we must choose—or acquiesce in the destruction of the commons that we call our National Parks.

Pollution

In a reverse way, the tragedy of the commons reappears in problems of pollution. Here it is not a question of taking something out of the commons, but of putting something in—sewage, or chemical, radioactive, and heat wastes into water; noxious and dangerous fumes into the air; and distracting and unpleasant advertising signs into the line of sight. The calculations of utility are much the same as before. The rational man finds that his share of the cost of the wastes he discharges into the commons is less than the cost of purifying his wastes before releasing them. Since this is true for everyone, we are locked into a system of "fouling our own nest," so long as we behave only as independent, rational, free-enterprisers.

The tragedy of the commons as a food basket is averted by private property, or something formally like it. But the air and waters surrounding us cannot readily be fenced, and so the tragedy of the commons as a cesspool must be prevented by different means, by coercive laws or taxing devices that make it cheaper for the polluter to treat his pollutants than to discharge them untreated. We have not progressed as far with the solution of this problem as we have with the first. Indeed, our particular concept of private property, which deters us from exhausting the positive resources of the earth, favors pollution. The owner of a factory on the bank of a stream—whose property extends to the middle of the stream—often has difficulty seeing why it is not his natural right to muddy the waters flowing past his door. The law, always behind the times, requires elaborate stitching and fitting to adapt it to this newly perceived aspect of the commons.

The pollution problem is a consequence of population. It did not much matter how a lonely American frontiersman disposed of his waste. "Flowing water purifies itself every 10 miles," my grandfather used to say, and the myth was near enough to the truth when he was a boy, for there were not too many people. But as population became denser, the natural chemical and biological recycling processes became overloaded, calling for a redefinition of property rights.

How To Legislate Temperance?

Analysis of the pollution problem as a function of population density uncovers a not generally recognized principle of morality, namely: *the morality of an act is a function of the state of the system at the time it is performed* (*10*). Using the commons as a cesspool does not harm the general public under frontier conditions, because there is no public; the same behavior in a metropolis is unbearable. A hundred and fifty years ago a plainsman could kill an American bison, cut out only the tongue for his dinner, and discard the rest of the animal. He was not in any important sense being wasteful. Today, with only a few thousand bison left, we would be appalled at such behavior.

In passing, it is worth noting that the morality of an act cannot be determined from a photograph. One does not know whether a man killing an elephant or setting fire to the grassland is harming others until one knows the total system in which his act appears. "One picture is worth a thousand words," said an ancient Chinese; but it may take 10,000 words to validate it. It is as tempting to ecologists as it is to reformers in general to try to persuade others by way of the photographic shortcut. But the essense of an argument cannot be photographed: it must be presented rationally —in words.

That morality is system-sensitive escaped the attention of most codifiers of ethics in the past. "Thou shalt not . . ." is the form of traditional ethical directives which make no allowance for particular circumstances. The laws of our society follow the pattern of ancient ethics, and therefore are poorly suited to governing a complex, crowded, changeable world. Our epicyclic solution is to augment statutory law with administrative law. Since it is practically impossible to spell out all the conditions under which it is safe to burn trash in the back yard or to run an automobile without smog-control, by law we delegate the details to bureaus. The result is administrative law, which is rightly feared for an ancient reason—*Quis custodiet ipsos custodes?*—"Who shall watch the watchers themselves?" John Adams said that we must have "a government of laws and not men." Bureau administrators, trying to evaluate the morality of acts in the total system, are singularly liable to corruption, producing a government by men, not laws.

Prohibition is easy to legislate (though not necessarily to enforce); but how do we legislate temperance? Experience indicates that it can be accomplished best through the mediation of administrative law. We limit possibilities unnecessarily if we suppose that the sentiment of *Quis custodiet* denies us the use of administrative law. We should rather retain the phrase as a perpetual reminder of fearful dangers we cannot avoid. The great challenge facing us now is to invent the corrective feedbacks that are needed to keep custodians honest. We must find ways to legitimate the needed authority of both the custodians and the corrective feedbacks.

Freedom To Breed Is Intolerable

The tragedy of the commons is involved in population problems in another way. In a world governed solely by the principle of "dog eat dog"—if indeed there ever was such a world— how many children a family had would not be a matter of public concern. Parents who bred too exuberantly would leave fewer descendants, not more, because they would be unable to care adequately for their children. David Lack and others have found that such a negative feedback demonstrably controls the fecundity of birds (11). But men are not birds, and have not acted like them for millenniums, at least.

If each human family were dependent only on its own resources; *if* the children of improvident parents starved to death; *if*, thus, overbreeding brought its own "punishment" to the germ line— *then* there would be no public interest in controlling the breeding of families. But our society is deeply committed to the welfare state (12), and hence is confronted with another aspect of the tragedy of the commons.

In a welfare state, how shall we deal with the family, the religion, the race, or the class (or indeed any distinguishable and cohesive group) that adopts overbreeding as a policy to secure its own aggrandizement (13)? To couple the concept of freedom to breed with the belief that everyone born has an equal right to the commons is to lock the world into a tragic course of action.

Unfortunately this is just the course of action that is being pursued by the United Nations. In late 1967, some 30 nations agreed to the following (14):

The Universal Declaration of Human Rights describes the family as the natural and fundamental unit of society. It follows that any choice and decision with regard to the size of the family must irrevocably rest with the family itself, and cannot be made by anyone else.

It is painful to have to deny categorically the validity of this right; denying it, one feels as uncomfortable as a resident of Salem, Massachusetts, who denied the reality of witches in the 17th century. At the present time, in liberal quarters, something like a taboo acts to inhibit criticism of the United Nations. There is a feeling that the United Nations is "our last and best hope," that we shouldn't find fault with it; we shouldn't play into the hands of the archconservatives. However, let us not forget what Robert Louis Stevenson said: "The truth that is suppressed by friends is the readiest weapon of the enemy." If we love the truth we must openly deny the validity of the Universal Declaration of Human Rights, even though it is promoted by the United Nations. We should also join with Kingsley Davis (15) in attempting to get Planned Parenthood-World Population to see the error of its ways in embracing the same tragic ideal.

Conscience Is Self-Eliminating

It is a mistake to think that we can control the breeding of mankind in the

14

long run by an appeal to conscience. Charles Galton Darwin made this point when he spoke on the centennial of the publication of his grandfather's great book. The argument is straightforward and Darwinian.

People vary. Confronted with appeals to limit breeding, some people will undoubtedly respond to the plea more than others. Those who have more children will produce a larger fraction of the next generation than those with more susceptible consciences. The difference will be accentuated, generation by generation.

In C. G. Darwin's words: "It may well be that it would take hundreds of generations for the progenitive instinct to develop in this way, but if it should do so, nature would have taken her revenge, and the variety *Homo contracipiens* would become extinct and would be replaced by the variety *Homo progenitivus*" (*16*).

The argument assumes that conscience or the desire for children (no matter which) is hereditary—but hereditary only in the most general formal sense. The result will be the same whether the attitude is transmitted through germ cells, or exosomatically, to use A. J. Lotka's term. (If one denies the latter possibility as well as the former, then what's the point of education?) The argument has here been stated in the context of the population problem, but it applies equally well to any instance in which society appeals to an individual exploiting a commons to restrain himself for the general good—by means of his conscience. To make such an appeal is to set up a selective system that works toward the elimination of conscience from the race.

Pathogenic Effects of Conscience

The long-term disadvantage of an appeal to conscience should be enough to condemn it; but has serious short-term disadvantages as well. If we ask a man who is exploiting a commons to desist "in the name of conscience," what are we saying to him? What does he hear?—not only at the moment but also in the wee small hours of the night when, half asleep, he remembers not merely the words we used but also the nonverbal communication cues we gave him unawares? Sooner or later, consciously or subconsciously, he senses that he has received two communications, and that they are contradictory: (i) (intended communication) "If you don't do as we ask, we will openly condemn you for not acting like a responsible citizen"; (ii) (the unintended communication) "If you *do* behave as we ask, we will secretly condemn. you for a simpleton who can be shamed into standing aside while the rest of us exploit the commons."

Everyman then is caught in what Bateson has called a "double bind." Bateson and his co-workers have made a plausible case for viewing the double bind as an important causative factor in the genesis of schizophrenia (*17*). The double bind may not always be so damaging, but it always endangers the mental health of anyone to whom it is applied. "A bad conscience," said Nietzsche, "is a kind of illness."

To conjure up a conscience in others is tempting to anyone who wishes to extend his control beyond the legal limits. Leaders at the highest level succumb to this temptation. Has any President during the past generation failed to call on labor unions to moderate voluntarily their demands for higher wages, or to steel companies to honor voluntary guidelines on prices? I can recall none. The rhetoric used on such occasions is designed to produce feel-

15

ings of guilt in noncooperators.

For centuries it was assumed without proof that guilt was a valuable, perhaps even an indispensable, ingredient of the civilized life. Now, in this post-Freudian world, we doubt it.

Paul Goodman speaks from the modern point of view when he says: "No good has ever come from feeling guilty, neither intelligence, policy, nor compassion. The guilty do not pay attention to the object but only to themselves, and not even to their own interests, which might make sense, but to their anxieties" (18).

One does not have to be a professional psychiatrist to see the consequences of anxiety. We in the Western world are just emerging from a dreadful two-centuries-long Dark Ages of Eros that was sustained partly by prohibition laws, but perhaps more effectively by the anxiety-generating mechanisms of education. Alex Comfort has told the story well in *The Anxiety Makers* (19); it is not a pretty one.

Since proof is difficult, we may even concede that the results of anxiety may sometimes, from certain points of view, be desirable. The larger question we should ask is whether, as a matter of policy, we should ever encourage the use of a technique the tendency (if not the intention) of which is psychologically pathogenic. We hear much talk these days of responsible parenthood; the coupled words are incorporated into the titles of some organizations devoted to birth control. Some people have proposed massive propaganda campaigns to instill responsibility into the nation's (or the world's) breeders. But what is the meaning of the word responsibility in this context? Is it not merely a synonym for the word conscience? When we use the word responsibility in the absence of substantial sanctions are we not trying to browbeat

a free man in a commons into acting against his own interest? Responsibility is a verbal counterfeit for a substantial *quid pro quo*. It is an attempt to get something for nothing.

If the word responsibility is to be used at all, I suggest that it be in the sense Charles Frankel uses it (20). "Responsibility," says this philosopher, "is the product of definite social arrangements." Notice that Frankel calls for social arrangements—not propaganda.

Mutual Coercion

Mutually Agreed upon

The social arrangements that produce responsibility are arrangements that create coercion, of some sort. Consider bank-robbing. The man who takes money from a bank acts as if the bank were a commons. How do we prevent such action? Certainly not by trying to control his behavior solely by a verbal appeal to his sense of responsibility. Rather than rely on propaganda we follow Frankel's lead and insist that a bank is not a commons; we seek the definite social arrangements that will keep it from becoming a commons. That we thereby infringe on the freedom of would-be robbers we neither deny nor regret.

The morality of bank-robbing is particularly easy to understand because we accept complete prohibition of this activity. We are willing to say "Thou shalt not rob banks," without providing for exceptions. But temperance also can be created by coercion. Taxing is a good coercive device. To keep downtown shoppers temperate in their use of parking space we introduce parking meters for short periods, and traffic fines for longer ones. We need not

16

actually forbid a citizen to park as long as he wants to; we need merely make it increasingly expensive for him to do so. Not prohibition, but carefully biased options are what we offer him. A Madison Avenue man might call this persuasion; I prefer the greater candor of the word coercion.

Coercion is a dirty word to most liberals now, but it need not forever be so. As with the four-letter words, its dirtiness can be cleansed away by exposure to the light, by saying it over and over without apology or embarrassment. To many, the word coercion implies arbitrary decisions of distant and irresponsible bureaucrats; but this is not a necessary part of its meaning. The only kind of coercion I recommend is mutual coercion, mutually agreed upon by the majority of the people affected.

To say that we mutually agree to coercion is not to say that we are required to enjoy it, or even to pretend we enjoy it. Who enjoys taxes? We all grumble about them. But we accept compulsory taxes because we recognize that voluntary taxes would favor the conscienceless. We institute and (grumblingly) support taxes and other coercive devices to escape the horror of the commons.

An alternative to the commons need not be perfectly just to be preferable. With real estate and other material goods, the alternative we have chosen is the institution of private property coupled with legal inheritance. Is this system perfectly just? As a genetically trained biologist I deny that it is. It seems to me that, if there are to be differences in individual inheritance, legal possession should be perfectly correlated with biological inheritance—that those who are biologically more fit to be the custodians of property and power should legally inherit more. But genetic recombination continually makes a mockery of the doctrine of "like father, like son" implicit in our laws of legal inheritance. An idiot can inherit millions, and a trust fund can keep his estate intact. We must admit that our legal system of private property plus inheritance is unjust—but we put up with it because we are not convinced, at the moment, that anyone has invented a better system. The alternative of the commons is too horrifying to contemplate. Injustice is preferable to total ruin.

It is one of the peculiarities of the warfare between reform and the status quo that it is thoughtlessly governed by a double standard. Whenever a reform measure is proposed it is often defeated when its opponents triumphantly discover a flaw in it. As Kingsley Davis has pointed out (21), worshippers of the status quo sometimes imply that no reform is possible without unanimous agreement, an implication contrary to historical fact. As nearly as I can make out, automatic rejection of proposed reforms is based on one of two unconscious assumptions: (i) that the status quo is perfect; or (ii) that the choice we face is between reform and no action; if the proposed reform is imperfect, we presumably should take no action at all, while we wait for a perfect proposal.

But we can never do nothing. That which we have done for thousands of years is also action. It also produces evils. Once we are aware that the status quo is action, we can then compare its discoverable advantages and disadvantages with the predicted advantages and disadvantages of the proposed reform, discounting as best we can for our lack of experience. On the basis of such a comparison, we can make a rational decision which will not involve the unworkable assumption that only perfect systems are tolerable.

Recognition of Necessity

Perhaps the simplest summary of this analysis of man's population problems is this: the commons, if justifiable at all, is justifiable only under conditions of low-population density. As the human population has increased, the commons has had to be abandoned in one aspect after another.

First we abandoned the commons in food gathering, enclosing farm land and restricting pastures and hunting and fishing areas. These restrictions are still not complete throughout the world.

Somewhat later we saw that the commons as a place for waste disposal would also have to be abandoned. Restrictions on the disposal of domestic sewage are widely accepted in the Western world; we are still struggling to close the commons to pollution by automobiles, factories, insecticide sprayers, fertilizing operations, and atomic energy installations.

In a still more embryonic state is our recognition of the evils of the commons in matters of pleasure. There is almost no restriction on the propagation of sound waves in the public medium. The shopping public is assaulted with mindless music, without its consent. Our government is paying out billions of dollars to create supersonic transport which will disturb 50,000 people for every one person who is whisked from coast to coast 3 hours faster. Advertisers muddy the airwaves of radio and television and pollute the view of travelers. We are a long way from outlawing the commons in matters of pleasure. Is this because our Puritan inheritance makes us view pleasure as something of a sin, and pain (that is, the pollution of advertising) as the sign of virtue?

Every new enclosure of the commons involves the infringement of somebody's personal liberty. Infringements made in the distant past are accepted because no contemporary complains of a loss. It is the newly proposed infringements that we vigorously oppose; cries of "rights" and "freedom" fill the air. But what does "freedom" mean? When men mutually agreed to pass laws against robbing, mankind became more free, not less so. Individuals locked into the logic of the commons are free only to bring on universal ruin; once they see the necessity of mutual coercion, they become free to pursue other goals. I believe it was Hegel who said, "Freedom is the recognition of necessity."

The most important aspect of necessity that we must now recognize, is the necessity of abandoning the commons in breeding. No technical solution can rescue us from the misery of overpopulation. Freedom to breed will bring ruin to all. At the moment, to avoid hard decisions many of us are tempted to propagandize for conscience and responsible parenthood. The temptation must be resisted, because an appeal to independently acting consciences **selects for the disappearance of all conscience in the long run, and an increase in anxiety in the short.**

The only way we can preserve and nurture other and more precious freedoms is by relinquishing the freedom to breed, and that very soon. "Freedom is the recognition of necessity"—and it is the role of education to reveal to all the necessity of abandoning the freedom to breed. Only so, can we put an end to this aspect of the tragedy of the commons.

References

1. J. B. Wiesner and H. F. York, *Sci. Amer.* **211** (No. 4), 27 (1964).
2. G. Hardin, *J. Hered.* **50**, 68 (1959); S. von Hoernor, *Science* **137**, 18 (1962).
3. J. von Neumann and O. Morgenstern, *Theory of Games and Economic Behavior* (Princeton Univ. Press, Princeton, N.J., 1947), p. 11.
4. J. H. Fremlin, *New Sci.*, No. 415 (1964), p. 285.
5. A. Smith, *The Wealth of Nations* (Modern Library, New York, 1937), p. 423.
6. W. F. Lloyd, *Two Lectures on the Checks to Population* (Oxford Univ. Press, Oxford, England, 1833), reprinted (in part) in *Population, Evolution, and Birth Control*, G. Hardin, Ed. (Freeman, San Francisco, 1964), p. 37.
7. A. N. Whitehead, *Science and the Modern World* (Mentor, New York, 1948), p. 17.
8. G. Hardin, Ed. *Population, Evolution, and Birth Control* (Freeman, San Francisco, 1964), p. 56.
9. S. McVay, *Sci. Amer.* **216** (No. 8), 13 (1966).
10. J. Fletcher. *Situation Ethics* (Westminster, Philadelphia, 1966).
11. D. Lack, *The Natural Regulation of Animal Numbers* (Clarendon Press, Oxford, 1954).
12. H. Girvetz, *From Wealth to Welfare* (Stanford Univ. Press, Stanford, Calif., 1950).
13. G. Hardim, *Perspec. Biol. Med.* **6**, 366 (1963).
14. U. Thant, *Int. Planned Parenthood News*, No. 168 (February 1968), p. 3.
15. K. Davis, *Science* **158**, 730 (1967).
16. S. Tax, Ed., *Evolution after Darwin* (Univ. of Chicago Press, Chicago, 1960), vol. 2, p. 469.
17. G. Bateson, D. D. Jackson, J. Haley, J. Weakland, *Behav. Sci.* **1**, 251 (1956).
18. P. Goodman, *New York Rev. Books* **10**(8), 22 (23 May 1968).
19. A. Comfort, *The Anxiety Makers* (Nelson, London, 1967).
20. C. Frankel, *The Case for Modern Man* (Harper, New York, 1955), p. 203.
21. J. D. Roslansky, *Genetics and the Future of Man* (Appleton-Century-Crofts, New York, 1966), p. 177.

19

U.S.

POPULATION

DATA SHEET

(population figures in thousands)

POPULATION

REFERENCE

BUREAU, INC.

	Area (Sq. Mi.)	Date of Admission	First Census After Admission [1]	1900
United States	3,615,122	—	3,929	76,212
Alabama	51,609	1819	128	1,829
Alaska	586,412	1959	226	64
Arizona	113,909	1912	334	123
Arkansas	53,104	1836	98	1,312
California	158,693	1850	93	1,485
Colorado	104,247	1876	194	540
Connecticut	5,009	1788	238	908
Delaware	2,057	1787	59	185
D. of Columbia	67	—	8	279
Florida	58,560	1845	87	529
Georgia	58,876	1788	83	2,216
Hawaii	6,450	1959	633	154
Idaho	83,557	1890	89	162
Illinois	56,400	1818	55	4,822
Indiana	36,291	1816	147	2,516
Iowa	56,290	1846	192	2,232
Kansas	82,264	1861	364	1,470
Kentucky	40,395	1792	221	2,147
Louisiana	48,523	1812	153	1,382
Maine	33,215	1820	298	694
Maryland	10,577	1788	320	1,188
Massachusetts	8,257	1788	379	2,805
Michigan	58,216	1837	212	2,241
Minnesota	84,068	1858	172	1,751
Mississippi	47,716	1817	75	1,551
Missouri	69,686	1821	140	3,107
Montana	147,138	1889	143	243
Nebraska	77,227	1867	123	1,066
Nevada	110,540	1864	42	42
New Hampshire	9,304	1788	142	412
New Jersey	7,836	1787	184	1,884
New Mexico	121,666	1912	360	195
New York	49,576	1788	340	7,269
North Carolina	52,586	1789	394	1,894
North Dakota	70,665	1889	191	319
Ohio	41,222	1803	231	4,158
Oklahoma	69,919	1907	1,657	790
Oregon	96,981	1859	52	414
Pennsylvania	45,333	1787	434	6,302
Rhode Island	1,214	1790	69	429
South Carolina	31,055	1788	249	1,340
South Dakota	77,047	1889	349	402
Tennessee	42,244	1796	106	2,021
Texas	267,338	1845	213	3,049
Utah	84,916	1896	277	277
Vermont	9,609	1791	154	344
Virginia	40,817	1788	692	1,854
Washington	68,192	1889	357	518
West Virginia	24,181	1863	442	959
Wisconsin	56,154	1848	305	2,069
Wyoming	97,914	1890	63	93
Puerto Rico	3,435	—	—	953[2]

1910	1920	1930	1940	1950	1960	1970	Percent of Change 1960-1970
92,228	106,022	123,203	132,165	151,326	179,323	203,235	13.3
2,138	2,348	2,646	2,833	3,062	3,267	3,444	5.4
64	55	59	73	129	226	302	32.8
204	334	436	499	750	1,302	1,772	36.0
1,574	1,752	1,854	1,949	1,909	1,786	1,923	7.7
2,378	3,427	5,677	6,907	10,586	15,717	19,953	27.0
799	940	1,036	1,123	1,325	1,754	2,207	25.8
1,115	1,381	1,607	1,709	2,007	2,535	3,032	19.6
202	223	238	267	318	446	548	22.8
331	438	487	663	802	764	757	− 1.0
753	968	1,468	1,897	2,771	4,952	6,789	37.1
2,609	2,896	2,909	3,124	3,445	3,943	4,590	16.4
192	256	368	423	500	633	770	21.5
326	432	445	525	589	667	713	6.8
5,639	6,485	7,631	7,897	8,712	10,081	11,114	10.2
2,701	2,930	3,239	3,428	3,934	4,662	5,194	11.4
2,225	2,404	2,471	2,538	2,621	2,758	2,825	2.4
1,691	1,769	1,881	1,801	1,905	2,179	2,249	3.1
2,290	2,417	2,615	2,846	2,945	3,038	3,219	5.9
1,656	1,799	2,102	2,364	2,684	3,257	3,643	11.8
742	768	797	847	914	969	994	2.4
1,295	1,450	1,632	1,821	2,343	3,101	3,922	26.5
3,366	3,852	4,250	4,317	4,691	5,149	5,689	10.5
2,810	3,668	4,842	5,256	6,372	7,823	8,875	13.4
2,076	2,387	2,564	2,792	2,982	3,414	3,805	11.5
1,797	1,791	2,010	2,184	2,179	2,178	2,217	1.8
3,293	3,404	3,629	3,785	3,955	4,320	4,677	8.3
376	549	538	559	591	675	694	2.9
1,192	1,296	1,378	1,316	1,326	1,411	1,484	5.1
82	77	91	110	160	285	489	71.3
431	443	465	492	553	607	738	21.5
2,537	3,156	4,041	4,160	4,835	6,067	7,168	18.2
327	360	423	532	681	951	1,016	6.8
9,114	10,385	12,588	13,479	14,830	16,782	18,241	8.7
2,206	2,559	3,170	3,572	4,062	4,556	5,082	11.5
577	647	681	642	620	632	618	− 2.3
4,767	5,759	6,647	6,908	7,947	9,706	10,652	9.7
1,657	2,028	2,396	2,336	2,233	2,328	2,559	9.9
673	783	954	1,090	1,521	1,769	2,091	18.2
7,665	8,720	9,631	9,900	10,498	11,319	11,794	4.2
543	604	687	713	792	859	950	10.1
1,515	1,684	1,739	1,900	2,117	2,383	2,591	8.7
584	637	693	643	653	681	666	− 2.2
2,185	2,338	2,617	2,916	3,292	3,567	3,924	10.0
3,897	4,663	5,825	6,415	7,711	9,580	11,197	16.9
373	449	508	550	689	891	1,059	18.9
356	352	360	359	378	390	445	14.0
2,062	2,309	2,422	2,678	3,319	3,967	4,648	17.2
1,142	1,357	1,563	1,736	2,379	2,853	3,409	19.5
1,221	1,464	1,729	1,902	2,006	1,860	1,744	− 6.2
2,334	2,632	2,939	3,138	3,435	3,952	4,418	11.8
146	194	226	251	291	330	332	0.7
1,118	1,300	1,544	1,869	2,211	2,350	2,712	15.4

	Net Migration 1960-1970 (Percent) [3]	Percent Urban 1970 [4]	Annual Births per 1,000 Population 1971	Annual Deaths per 1,000 Population 1971	Total Infant Mortality 1971 [5]	Population Estimates Mid-1972 [6]	Population Projections 1980 [7]
United States	1.7	73.5	17.3	9.3	19.2	208,232	226,934
Alabama	−7.1	58.4	19.1	9.7	23.6	3,510	3,565
Alaska	7.1	48.4	22.9	5.0	18.3	325	352
Arizona	17.5	79.6	21.0	8.6	18.3	1,945	2,164
Arkansas	−4.0	50.0	18.1	10.6	19.9	1,978	2,052
California	13.4	90.9	16.8	8.5	16.8	20,468	24,226
Colorado	12.3	78.5	18.1	8.1	18.0	2,357	2,636
Connecticut	8.5	77.4	14.6	8.5	15.5	3,082	3,551
Delaware	8.5	72.2	17.7	9.0	14.4	565	655
D. of Columbia	−13.1	100.0	33.8	13.9	28.5	748	—
Florida	26.8	80.5	16.5	11.2	20.7	7,259	8,280
Georgia	1.3	60.3	20.4	9.0	21.3	4,720	5,191
Hawaii	1.7	83.1	20.1	5.7	18.1	809	874
Idaho	−6.2	54.1	19.1	8.4	16.6	756	761
Illinois	−0.4	83.0	17.2	9.6	20.7	11,251	12,256
Indiana	−0.3	64.9	18.3	9.3	18.0	5,291	5,782
Iowa	−6.6	57.2	16.1	10.3	17.0	2,883	2,908
Kansas	−6.0	66.1	15.1	9.6	19.8	2,258	2,334
Kentucky	−5.0	52.3	18.1	10.3	20.4	3,299	3,372
Louisiana	−4.0	66.1	20.1	9.2	22.1	3,720	3,975
Maine	−7.2	50.8	17.3	10.7	16.3	1,029	1,016
Maryland	12.4	76.6	14.3	7.9	18.0	4,056	4,782
Massachusetts	1.4	84.6	15.7	9.9	17.1	5,787	6,277
Michigan	0.3	73.8	17.9	8.5	19.2	9,082	10,031
Minnesota	−0.7	66.4	16.3	8.9	17.8	3,896	4,245
Mississippi	−12.3	44.5	21.7	10.4	26.6	2,263	2,245
Missouri	—	70.1	17.1	10.9	19.0	4,753	5,070
Montana	−8.6	53.4	17.2	9.5	20.7	719	721
Nebraska	−5.2	61.5	17.0	10.2	17.2	1,525	1,570
Nevada	50.4	80.9	18.9	8.3	22.9	527	673
New Hampshire	11.3	56.4	16.6	9.8	15.6	771	878
New Jersey	8.0	88.9	15.1	9.2	18.0	7,367	8,300
New Mexico	−13.6	69.8	21.6	7.5	20.9	1,065	1,088
New York	−0.6	85.6	15.5	10.1	18.6	18,366	19,789
North Carolina	−2.1	45.0	18.6	8.8	22.2	5,214	5,482
North Dakota	−14.9	44.3	17.5	9.2	15.3	632	600
Ohio	−1.3	75.3	17.7	9.2	18.2	10,783	11,675
Oklahoma	0.6	68.0	17.2	9.6	18.4	2,634	2,787
Oregon	9.0	67.1	15.8	9.3	18.1	2,182	2,421
Pennsylvania	−3.3	71.5	15.2	10.5	18.1	11,926	12,157
Rhode Island	1.5	87.1	15.8	9.8	18.9	968	1,027
South Carolina	−6.3	47.6	20.2	8.8	22.5	2,665	2,731
South Dakota	−13.9	44.6	17.0	9.9	17.1	679	658
Tennessee	−1.3	58.8	19.1	10.0	21.6	4,031	4,259
Texas	1.5	79.7	20.1	8.1	19.5	11,649	12,812
Utah	−1.2	80.4	25.8	6.8	14.1	1,126	1,234
Vermont	3.8	32.2	17.1	9.7	15.0	462	504
Virginia	3.6	63.1	16.9	8.2	20.8	4,764	5,229
Washington	8.7	72.6	15.7	8.8	18.6	3,443	3,958
West Virginia	−14.2	39.0	18.0	11.5	21.9	1,781	1,634
Wisconsin	0.1	65.9	16.0	9.1	15.7	4,520	4,930
Wyoming	−11.9	60.5	17.4	8.9	21.1	345	342
Puerto Rico	—	58.1	25.4	7.5[2]	24.5[2]	—	—

22

Population totals to the nearest thousand.

1790-1970 data from U.S. Bureau of the Census, U.S. Census of Population: 1970 Number of Inhabitants, Final Report PC(1)-A1 United States Summary, U.S. Government Printing Office, Washington, D. C. 1971. (1970 Official Counts as corrected.)

Provisional statistics for state and national birth, death, and total infant mortality rates for 1971 are from U.S. Department of Health, Education and Welfare, Public Health Service, Health Services and Mental Health Administration, National Center for Health Statistics, Rockville, Maryland, Monthly Vital Statistics Report, Provisional Statistics, Annual Summary for the United States, 1971 (HSM) 73-1121, Vol. 20, No. 13, August 30, 1972.

[1] 1812 admission date would mean 1820 Census population, etc., United States population is for 1790, the first National Census; District of Columbia data is for 1800; California, Idaho, Maine, Rhode Island, Wyoming population is the year of admission; Florida and Texas, 1850.

Territorial population data for Alaska (1900-1950), Arizona (1900), Hawaii (1900-1950), New Mexico (1900), Oklahoma (1900).

[2] Population: 1899 figure; birth and death rates: 1970 figures.

[3] Net inmigration and outmigration as a percentage of the 1960 population, U.S. Department of Commerce News, Release CB71-85, May 17, 1971.

[4] Urban population comprises all persons living in urbanized areas (usually containing at least one city of 50,000 or more and that portion of surrounding territory which meet specified criteria relating to population density) and places of 2,500 inhabitants or more outside urban areas. (1970 Census definition.) U.S. Bureau of the Census, U.S. Census of Population: 1970, Number of Inhabitants, Final Report PC(1)-A1 United States Summary, U.S. Government Printing Office, Washington, D. C. 1971.

[5] Annual deaths to infants under one year of age per 1,000 live births.

[6] July 1, 1972 population estimates from U.S. Bureau of the Census, Estimates of the Population of States: July 1, 1971 and 1972, Series P-25, No. 488, September 1972, U.S. Government Printing Office, Washington, D. C. 1972.

[7] 1980 population projections (Series I-E) from U.S. Bureau of the Census, Population Estimates and Projections, March 1972, Series P-25, No. 488, U.S. Government Printing Office, Washington, D. C. 1972.

POPULATION DENSITY AND THE STYLE OF SOCIAL LIFE

Nathan Keyfitz

To see how population density can occur at a rudimentary level of culture and what its effects may be, think of hunting groups with given apparatus, say spears or bows and arrows. Following Clifford Geertz (1963) and Julian Steward (1955) we observe that if the animals which they hunt move in herds, as do caribou, then large groups of hunters can pursue them. When they find a herd and attack successfully, there will be food for all. This herding of the animal prey is reflected in the gathering together of men, and communities can be large. If on the other hand the prey consists of small animals spread through a forest and caught one at a time, then men will have to spread out correspondingly; the large community cannot come into existence; human life will be lived out in isolated families. This latter condition, says Steward, applies to the Bushman and Eskimo, who have little in common but the dispersion of their game. Larger groups appeared among the Athabaskans and Algonkians of Canada and probably the prehorse plains' bison hunters.

This primary fact of dispersion or concentration will determine other circumstances. Isolated families cannot evolve the division of labor that is possible in bigger communities. In larger groups, specialization is likely to arise as some individuals become more adept at making spears, others at sighting herds, others at the tasks of surrounding the prey. Specialization will mean a variety of occupations, and, insofar as men are made by their work, a variety of men. Some of the occupations will have more prestige than others, perhaps because they require rarer skills. Even at this primitive level, where money may not exist in any form, the notion of a market for talent and a corresponding prestige hierarchy has a possible bearing.

Prestige is a source of power. Ambitious individuals can use occupational prestige to gain further power, especially if they have organizational ability. This suggests an interaction of economic and political phases, never entirely separated in real life. My only point here is that both the economy and the polity are more elaborated in large communities than in small, and hence more to be looked for in tribes living off herds of big game than in those living on dispersed small animals. The sociability of the animal, so to speak, permits a higher degree of sociability in the men; density causes density. To go one step more, and exaggerate somewhat, the animals have created the economic and political structures in the human group.

Human history and ecology did not stop at the hunting culture. The great change in society was the invention of agriculture, which even in the form of neolithic shifting cultivation permits much higher density than does hunting. Is the discovery of planting and tilling the cause of greater human density? Or was the causation the other

BIOSCIENCE, 1966, Vol. 16, pp. 868-873.

way, the density coming first and forcing men to utilize their environment more intensively. Fortunately we do not need to stop here to investigate this question of meta-history. The important fact is that agriculturalists can produce a surplus, which hunters can rarely manage. Robert M. Adams (1965) has described the agricultural base of the early cities. The farmer can grow enough for himself and his family and have, let us say, 5% left over. Once this technological achievement occurs, then 5% of the population can live in cities. It becomes worthwhile for a ruler to dominate the farmer, to collect the food as booty or taxes, and use it to support an army and a court. The patriarch becomes a prince.

Some of the troubles, as well as the glories, of civilization are implicit in the first cities, however small they may have been by modern standards. The total number of people which could congregate was limited, because strong political organization was needed to dominate a countryside, and an organization that tried to spread too far would be diluted and lose its control; the ancient empires often did outreach themselves in this way and fell apart. Physically, the area of control could not be too extended, since the transport of grain by ox-cart, the means used in the land empires of Asia, has natural limits set by the fact that the ox has to be fueled from the cargo. Among premachine cities, Rome did attain a population of nearly a million, but this was by virtue of extraordinarily competent, and harsh, organization of the lands around the Mediterranean, and by the use of sea transport for the movement of North African and Balkan grain.

Long before ecology or sociology became formal studies, a North African writer and politician called Ibn Khaldhun described with the utmost clarity how the population that could be concentrated in the capital city of an empire increased when the skill of the ruler and the discipline of his army and tax collectors enabled him to dominate a larger area of countryside, and how the population of the same city diminished when the rule was weaker so that the outlying provinces could successfully revolt from the exactions of the capital.

I have referred, then, to several levels of density — the dispersed hunters, the larger hunting group, the agriculturalists, the preindustrial city of landlords and princes organizing the countryside and living off the proceeds.

The city which constituted the capital of a despotic empire or of one of its provinces is not the only historical type. In Europe cities grew up specifically released from feudal ties, exempted from the domination of princes or landholders, their sustenance obtained by trade, religious, or entertainment functions, their independence assured by a sworn brotherhood of armed merchants. Not having to oppress a peasantry in order to secure their food, they could be loose in their internal arrangements; a medieval proverb says that "City air makes men free." The typical modern western city lives by a great extension of these same nonpolitical functions, and especially by manufacturing with mechanical power. Far from having to squeeze its food from the countryside, the city has become an autonomous economic force. Today, the countryside wants city goods more than the city wants food. The concentrated population of cities, which in the preindustrial empires was parasitic, has now become incredibly productive. Exploitation, if that is the right word, goes the other way from that of Ibn Khaldhun's account; rural legislators tax the cities to maintain support prices for grains, butter and other foods. Today's pattern, at least in the United States, England, and other western countries, is that men are more productive in dense settlements than in sparse ones.

The increase of cities, especially the increase of very large cities, is to be seen on all continents. Not only in the rich countries as foci of industry and trade, but in the poorest, to which industry has hardly come, the cities are expanding. In fact, during the 1950's the urban populations of developed countries increased by 25%, while those of underdeveloped countries increased by 55%. The increase of poor, dense populations was twice as rapid as that of rich ones, Bourgeois-Pichat (1966) tells us.

How could that 55% increase occur, if what I have said about the preindustrial city being dependent on the limited surplus of a countryside is true? The surplus food of the Asian peasantry did not increase by 55% in the 1950's; it hardly increased at all. How can Djakarta be five times as populous as it was before World War II, and three times as populous as ancient Rome at the highest point of its imperial power? Djakarta has not much more industry than Rome had. Its weak civil or military domination of an island territory, in some degree democratic, cannot compare in extractive power with the iron rule of Rome. The answer, of course, is that it draws food from foreign territories, including the United States; some of it paid for with the export of raw materials; some of it borrowed; some as gifts.

Unable or unwilling to exploit its own peasantry, the large contemporary non-industrial city more and more bases itself ecologically on the fields of the American west, together with the ships and harbors which link those fields with its massive populations. Population in the Asian countryside itself is growing beyond food supplies; far from having a surplus to ship to the city, the peasant is himself hungry.

Once the local countryside can no longer produce enough food for its own inhabitants so that these must be supported by foreign food, they tend naturally to gather into such seaport cities as Djakarta, Calcutta, and Rio de Janeiro, as close as possible to the spot where the boats will discharge their cargoes of American, or occasionally Burmese or Cambodian, grain. If people are to be fed from abroad it is cheaper

to have them at the seaports than dispersed through the countryside. At the present time the United States is shipping about 800,000 tons of grain per month to India alone. At the Asian standard of about one pound per person per day, this is enough for 40,000,000 people to live on; that number happens to be about equal to all the citizens of India living in the seacoast cities. If population continues to increase in the countryside and food does not, one can expect further flight to those cities.

One could say much about what density and size will do to the condition of dependence of those cities. We know that their inhabitants tend to perform services rather than make goods. The services have the function of distributing the claim to the food shipments, the dominant ideal being to give employment rather than to get work done. Some studies have indicated that the new migrants to the cities retain links with the countryside. Others show that the simple and traditional patterns of association in the countryside are transferred to the city, which thereby seems like a number of contiguous villages, lacking only their fields and their crops. These dense cities of rural culture are a new phenomenon in the world.

For some quite different concomitants of density, shown in their most accentuated form, we must go to those world cities of the 19th century which were ecological consequences of the railroad and steamship — New York, London, Paris, Berlin. In the 20th-century West a process of dispersal has occurred; cities produced by the automobile are less dense than those produced by the railroad and street car. We are getting strip cities, of which the best known is Megalopolis, the name Jean Gottman (1961) gave to Boston-New York-Washington.

The industrial city of the 19th century as well as the strip city of the late 20th century intensifies competition on many levels. We must not only find a

26

livelihood, we must find a life, each of us for himself, in the crowded city. This search for a tolerable physical and moral existence preoccupies every city dweller, and it has drastic consequences for urban society as a whole. Just as Darwin saw the animal or plant adapting to a niche in which it is partly sheltered from competition, so the sociologist Durkheim (1960) sees the city man restlessly searching for, and adapting to, a niche constituted by a specialized occupation and specialized personality. During the strike of airplane mechanics I was part of an undifferentiated mass seeking tickets at an airline counter. If one had to face daily the direct competition of millions of people, the struggle would so weigh on each of us that existence would be impossible for our spirits as well as our bodies. One's niche may be teacher, stock broker, or truck driver; it requires skills that others lack, or involves work that others do not want to do. It gives each a place with a certain minimum of predictable security. We are under constant inducement to better our position, and we seek to do so by further specialization.

Now the electronics engineer in Chicago, say, has to concern himself, at most, with the competition of other electronics engineers. But he does not even have to cope with them, at least in the short run. There are a hundred specialties within the field of electronics, and within each of these recognized specialties an individual practitioner, through his own tastes and capacities, can make himself unique. People in a particular plant come to depend on him. If the city is, on the one side, a jungle of potentially infinite and destroying competition, on the other, it shows a nearly infinite capacity of its members to differentiate themselves, to become useful to one another, to become needed.

The differentiated citizen can afford to be tolerant of those he meets, even to like them. This could not be true if competition were more direct, with individuals as personally ambitious as we know them to be in western countries. The struggle for upward mobility, characterizing all developed societies, can only through the process of specialization avoid the harshness of personal character that the blast of full competition would create.

The differentiation is only possible within an economic space that is honeycombed with organizations that are themselves competing, at a supra-individual level, and have their own lives, usually longer than those of individual men. The plants and firms live among a host of other organizations which serve varied interests — trade unions, professional societies, sporting clubs.

Corresponding to the infinite shades and gradations of personalities and types of work, spread through a complex social space, an unprecedented sensitivity to symbol systems comes into existence in the city. The contemporary mathematician, or biologist, or sociologist, along with such other products of city culture as the banker, the store manager, or the traffic analyst, each has his own characteristic set of symbols and has to cope with unprecedented variety, subtlety, and sheer mass of material. Typically 8 or 10 years of intense training, for most of us only possible between the ages of about 15 and 25, are the necessary means to develop the sensitivity, the awareness of issues, the minimum basic storehouse of facts in a given field. You only put up with me, if you do, because you suppose that I have an extensive and powerful storehouse of facts in my own field, which is the mathematics of population. This reciprocal imputation of subtle, mysterious, and extensive knowledge is what permits mutual respect in the more·specialized residents of the city. We do not know just what it is that the other man knows, but we assume he knows something and is capable of doing his own job with reasonable competence, whether it is embryology or pants cutting.

Such a basis of respect is characteristically metropolitan. In a society of smaller volume such as a village, each gets to know all about the few score or the few hundred people with whom he will have contact in the course of a lifetime. He knows them as whole people, is concerned with literally everything about them.

Each of us as city people has contact in a day with as many individuals as the villager meets in the course of a lifetime; this includes store clerks, bus conductors, taxi drivers, students, colleagues, theatre ushers, not to mention those we pass as we walk or drive along the street. It would destroy us if we had to react to every one of them as people. We want to know about each of them only enough to cover his particular relationship with us. We care only that the bus conductor is an authorized employee of the company and will take our fare and drop us at the corner of Madison and 42nd Street. Whether he is happily married with four children or a debauched bachelor, whether he is Presbyterian or Catholic, we never inquire. His uniform tells us everything about him that we need to know. It is mere personal whim on our part if we even look at his face.

The well adapted citizen of the high income metropolis has learned to protect himself against its potentially infinitely varied stimulation. In some measure he becomes blasé; whatever happens he has seen something more exciting. He becomes absent-minded and dulls his recollection of gross stimuli and even his perception of them in order to accentuate his capacity to react to the subtler issues and symbols of his own business, professional, technical, or scholarly life. He goes out of his way to cultivate ignorance of fields outside his own. Whereas constant full exposure to what the city offers and demands would weary and frustrate him, by protecting himself sufficiently against stimuli he need show only a slight antipathy or even be perfectly good-natured. This is the nature of urban contacts, suggestively portrayed by Georg Simmel (1964). Note that this characterization applies only to those members of the city who have adapted to city life over two or three generations, and as a result are suitably educated, and are productive enough to command the facilities of the city. They do not apply to the recent migrant to Chicago from the rural south, or to Calcutta from inland Bengal.

The ultimate refuge against the pressures of the metropolis is flight. A quiet place in the country becomes the ideal of all and, in one form or another, the seasonal recuperation of most. But with the acceleration of the population growth, and especially with the improvement of transport through the private automobile, that quiet place in the country, the most precious of resources, is bound to become scarcer. We not only are a larger population, and able to get out of the city more easily, but a larger fraction of us has the means to travel. We are 197 million people in the 3.6 million square miles of the United States. Deducting the areas of the cities, superhighways, lakes, deserts (both natural and those made by man, for instance by mining operations), we could still each have 4 acres of countryside — which means just enough to get out of the sight of one another. But not very long ago the United States was growing at 1.5% per year, a pace which would double our numbers each 45 years. It would halve the 4 acres in 45 years, quarter it in 90 years. I mention these figures only to show that within the lifetime of children now born, at an increase of 1.5% per year, dispersion would become impossible; no amount of redeployment would enable us to get out of sight of one another.

Simultaneous with the increase in numbers, the advance of technology makes each of us more mobile, and requires more space — especially highways — to be set aside merely for facilitating our movement. Aside from this, if effective density is counted in units of potential contact rather than in people per square mile, we increase our effective density merely in improving transportation. Man is unlike other creatures in drastically remaking his means of locomotion. United States' automobile and truck registrations were 86 million in 1964, and will pass the 100 million mark by the end of the 1960's. Nearly 10 million new vehicles are being put on the road each year, offset by only two-thirds that number of scrappings; this fact alone would tend to crowd us even if we were the same number of people. Year by year we are both more in numbers *and* are moving faster, always within a fixed people-container, the terrestrial area of the United States. The result is rising pressure and temperature, apparently under the operation of laws analogous to those governing the behavior of gases.

I do not know how we shall respond. Will we build up higher capacity for discretion and reserve? Will we develop the sort of etiquette of noninterference with our neighbors — silence, dignity, and good humor — that helps make life tolerable on a long submarine voyage? I knew a charming family in Paris during the housing shortage who had two and a half rooms, counting the bathroom, for five people. They managed the situation well, and despite proximity each was able to have his private thoughts without interference. The life required a degree of self-discipline that not all of us could furnish. Events on the city streets this hot summer do not suggest that our civilization is moving toward those standards of reserve, discretion, and respect for the rights of others that would make greater density acceptable.

In fact, the response of society to higher density is usually the very opposite of reserve and respect for the privacy of individuals; it is rather interference and planning. The frontier had no traffic lights or parking regulations. People did not have to regulate their activities by the activities of others. If the clocks and watches of frontier families were randomly in error, little inconvenience would have resulted; but

if those of a modern city were wrong, say by 2 hours, all its activities would be brought to a halt. Everything we do interlocks with what others do. The frontier needed no zoning bylaws or building standards. The necessity for all these forms of planning has come with density. Richard Meier (1962) describes an arrangement of the city of Madras in South India, one of the growing harbor cities I have spoken of, such that 100 million people could live in it, but life would have to be planned in the most excruciating detail. People would not even be allowed to own bicycles, simply because parking individually owned bicycles would tie up the streets. Movement would be restricted, and all that was necessary would be provided by mass transportation.

The density continuum from the frontier to Meier's imaginary Madras is also a planning continuum; density and planning seem to be positively correlated.

Less clear is the degree in which freedom in the West has declined with planning, and hence with density. George Orwell's *1984* is inconceivable without high population density, supplemented by closed circuit television and other devices to eliminate privacy. It exhibits in extreme form an historical process by which the State has been extending its power at the expense of the Church, the Family, and the Local Community, a process extending over 150 years.

Though the trend to State power has accompanied the increase of density, I do not know whether, up to now, density, even combined with the march of technology, and combined with State control, has diminished the individual's effective freedom on balance. After all, the individual benefits from the State and from the increasing wealth that has gone along with density and with planning, including clocks and traffic lights. In the United States the gain to freedom through rising average wealth may offset the attack on freedom through State measures. In the USSR increasing wealth seems to be bringing about a loosening of totalitarian structures.

A convincing account of the relation between sparseness and abundance on the one side and national character on the other is presented by David Potter (1954). The wealth of the economy, first on the frontier and then in the cities, encouraged mobility and individual success as an ideal. The real wealth of the country — and this arose from spaciousness in the largely agricultural epoch when national character was being formed — was great enough that a mobile, optimistic, ambitious, and generous attitude would have scope for success and would often succeed. One man who succeeded with these traits encouraged the growth of similar qualities in others. In the United States, sparsely settled during most of its history, when men were scarce and resources plentiful, labor was sought after by employers rather than the other way round. This gave the common man confidence in himself; self-confidence made him open-handed and he taught his children open-handedness.

Plenty also encouraged freedom — if there are enough goods for everyone, let each one take the part of the patrimony he wants or can earn. If there are enough seats on the train each passenger can choose the one he wants without supervision; a shortage of seats compels a system of reservations, which is to say planning. Abundance brings men to potential economic equality — at least in the sense that each can hope to find the resources that will make his labor fruitful. By virtue of the same fact, it inclines them to political equality. Density and poverty make for the opposite of democracy—as Wittfogel (1957) argues in his study of hydraulic civilization.

If density tends to shackle us, and wealth to free us, then the question of what will happen in the United States in the 21st century that is only 34 years away is still an open question. I do not know enough of the conditions of the present race between exhaustion of raw materials on the one hand and technology on the other to make a firm statement, but suppose technology wins and we become much denser but also much richer. For us the wealth worked counter to the density. But what about those dense societies which have little prospect of attaining the wealth of the United States and whose density, combined with their traditional agricultural techniques, already places them near the point of starvation?

I started this discussion with the preindustrial environment, and went on to those contemporary preindustrial cities clustered around the coasts of the underdeveloped world in which ports, built for the export of now obsolete colonial tropical products, are operating at capacity to unload cargoes of food. Here are larger cities than Ibn Khaldhun contemplated. If those city dwellers oppress any peasantry it is that of the United States. But it is not that of the United States either, since American productivity has increased faster in agriculture than in industry these last years. The labor cost of that food to the American farmer is at an all-time low, and in any case, the city-dweller is paying for PL480 shipments, for which the Prairie farmer gets spendable cash. I said that if poor peasant populations are to be fed by imported grain rather than by grain from their own countryside, then it is convenient for them to bring their mouths to the harbors where the grain is unloaded, rather than having the grain carried to them dispersed over the countryside, and that this is the basis for much contemporary urban growth.

How different the case would be if the United States had given fertilizer factories rather than wheat. Then more grain could sprout throughout the South Asian mainland, and there would be no reason for the peasants to accumulate in the city in numbers beyond the industrial jobs available.

I have spoken of the problem of privacy in the dense industrial city. The problem is accentuated in the cities of

30

Asia, where millions of similiar beings exist in close contact, without the shelter provided to each through specialization and the division of labor. In the West we each come to have a special claim on the production of others through our own specialized production, especially through the voluminous contribution which each of us can make in our highly capitalized society. We have some degree of uniqueness of personality through all those devices by which we differentiate ourselves, some of them arising out of our work, but others quite separate: sports and hobbies, for instance, which the affluent society lavishly supports and equips. Education, also a result of our wealth, inducts us into elaborate, differentiated symbol systems and into that etiquette of restraint and reserve which mitigates the closeness of city living.

The citizen of the poor crowded city is in all these respects disadvantaged. He has neither specialized work, nor capital to make his work productive, nor hobbies to reinforce a personal identity, nor education to make him sensitive to complex symbol systems. Here is the hurt of density without its benefits.

The only defense for the poverty-stricken urbanite in the tropics is through the retention of some of his rural habits; he may manage a kind of village existence, with village ecological relations complete in all respects except that the village fields are absent. The village within the city of Calcutta or Madras may well have its own temple and traditional service occupations: sweepers, watchmen, priests, headmen. Some physical production by village methods goes on, and there are tanners, potters, and makers of bullock-carts — but very few farmers. Each compressed village in the city may have some residue of the administrative structure of the village its inhabitants have left, and village factionalism need not be forgotten on the move to the city. The village in the city may have a rate of growth more rapid than the old village, be-cause its death rate may be low, its birth rate remains almost up to rural levels, and the city is swelled by new entrants from the countryside. It is hungry, as the rural village often was, but now its hunger is a matter of high political importance, affecting both national and international politics.

Our picture now is of two dense agglomerations of mankind facing one another, both urban, one rich and one poor. America takes its cities into the countryside — it becomes an urban society through and through. Asia remains rural, even to parts of the dense agglomerations at the seaports — it brings its rural culture into the cities. In a sense, the rich city has called the poor one into existence, first by DDT and medicine which lower the death rate of India from perhaps 35 per thousand to 20 per thousand, and then by the provision of food.

In a quite different sense, Europe had earlier contributed to Asian population. The industrial revolution of Europe and America demanded raw materials, and this demand was translated into a demand for people who would produce its goods. The needs of Europe for sugar, spices, and rubber brought into existence large populations, for example in Indonesia; Java grew from under 5 million in 1815 to 40 million by World War II. And when our technical advance, especially western synthetics, enabled us to make the things that formerly could only be produced by tropical sunshine and tropical labor, those populations were left high and dry. They are functionless in relation to the Western industrial machine which brought them into existence, but they keep growing nonetheless.

Western governments and electorates sense the tragic state of affairs, and, at least vaguely, feel responsible for this aftermath of colonialism; therefore we provide food and other kinds of aid. But such are the dilemmas of doing good in this difficult world that each shipment of food draws more people to the seaports, and we arrive at nothing more constructive than a larger population than before dependent on shipments of food. If the need for food is a temporary emergency, philanthropy is highly recommended, but the condition of tropical agriculture and population seems to be chronic rather than acute.

And yet the aid cannot be stopped. As the populations of these port cities grow so does the problem of producing and shipping food to them. But so also do the economic, political, and moral problems of cutting off the aid. When famine was the work of God, whose acts man lacked the technical capacity to offset, such issues did not arise.

The only escape is through the economic development of the countries of Asia, Africa, and Latin America. With increase of income arises the sort of communication system through which people can receive and act on signals in regard to the size of their families. Americans since 1957 have come to understand that their families had been too large — signals reach them to this effect through the price system and through the difficulties of placing children in college and in a job. For underdeveloped people such a signalling system of prices and costs is not in existence, and messages that create a desirable feedback and permit automatic control do not carry.

On the other hand, the growth of population for many reasons itself inhibits the development process which could solve the population problem. That is why some students of the matter think that the control of population should be tackled directly. Each point by which the birth rate falls makes the process of saving and investment and hence development that much easier.

I have spoken of two sorts of dense agglomerations of people looking at one another across the oceans. The one is wealthy, modern, productive, highly differentiated by occupation, handling complex symbol systems, dominating the environment. The other is poor, traditional, nonproductive except for services that are not badly wanted, less differentiated by occupation, illiterate or barely literate, highly dependent on the environment. Our rich American cities contain a minority which is taking refuge from rural poverty. Some Asian cities consist of a majority of such refugees.

I have refrained from reference to the individual human tragedy of the multiplying homeless sidewalk-dwellers of Calcutta and other cities of the tropics. No one can say that their plight is irremediable; evidently a number of countries are achieving development today, including Hong Kong, Taiwan, Mexico, Turkey. On the other hand, I see no grounds for the facile optimism that declares that development is inevitable for all. To turn the despairing kind of density into the affluent kind requires that three issues be squarely met: food supplies must be assured, industry established, population controlled. Only in some of the underdeveloped countries are these seen as key issues and seriously tackled.

Is the hardship of life in the crowded and poor city itself a stimulus to effective action? Do density and poverty make for greater sensitivity to the real problems, and greater judiciousness in their treatment? Not necessarily; especially not for the miserable newcomers, the first ill-adapted migrant generation to the city. In the slums of first settlement, whether in 19th century London and Paris or 20th century Chicago and Calcutta, city mobs can be readily aroused by their troubles to action and to violence, but they do not necessarily see the root of their frustrations and the way to overcome them. Penetrating analysis does not guide mob action. The crowd, mobilized by some incident, acts with a violence out of all proportion to the event that excited its anger. It streams through a city street, stops to throw bottles at the police who reply with tear gas, overturns automobiles, is finally dispersed by a National Guard armed with bayonets. Far from being a disappearing relic of the past, it is with us both in the temperate zone and in the tropics, in wealthy countries and in poor ones. Food riots occur in Bombay and civil rights riots in Chicago, New York and Cleveland. This ultimate manifestation of population density, which colors the social history of all continents, is a challenge to learn more about the causes of tension and frustration in city life.

References

Adams, R. M. 1965. *Land Behind Baghdad*. University of Chicago Press, Chicago, Ill.

Bourgeois-Pichat, Jean. 1966. *Population Growth and Development*. International Conciliation, No. 556, January. Carnegie Endowment for International Peace.

Durkheim, Emile. 1960. *De la division du travail social*. 7th ed. Chap. III, La solidarité due à la division du travail ou organique, Presses Universitaires de France, Paris. pp. 79-102.

Geertz, Clifford. 1963. *Agricultural Involution: The Process of Ecological Change in Indonesia*. University of California Press, Berkeley, Calif.

Gottman, Jean. 1961. *Megalopolis: The Urbanized Northeastern Seaboard of the United States*. Twentieth Century Fund, New York.

Hawley, Amos H. 1950. *Human Ecology: A Theory of Community Structure*. Ronald Press, New York.

Meier, R. L. 1962. Relations of technology to the design of very large cities. In *India's Urban Future* (Roy Turner Ed.). University of California Press, Berkeley, Calif. pp. 299-323.

Potter, David M. 1954. *People of Plenty: Economic Abundance and the American Character*. University of Chicago Press, Chicago, Ill.

Riesman, David. 1950. *The Lonely Crowd: A Study of the Changing American Character*. University of Chicago Press, Chicago, Ill.

Simmel, Georg. 1964. The Metropolis and Mental Life. In *The Sociology of Georg Simmel* (edited and translated by Kurt H. Wolff). Free Press of Glencoe, Collier-Macmillan, London. pp. 409-424.

Steward, J. 1955. *Theory of Culture Change*. University of Illinois Press, Urbana, Ill.

Wirth, Louis. 1964. Urbanism as a Way of Life. In *On Cities and Social Life*. University of Chicago Press, Chicago, Ill. pp. 60-83.

Wittfogel, Karl A. 1957. *Oriental Despotism: A Comparative Study of Total Power*. Yale University Press, New Haven, Conn.

Wolff, Kurt H. (Ed.) 1964. *The Sociology of Georg Simmel*. Collier-Macmillan, London.

THE MISUNDERSTOOD CHALLENGE OF POPULATION CHANGE

by Dudley Kirk

The popular emphasis today is on population growth. I would like to draw attention to the larger problem of population *change,* a problem that includes other dimensions besides growth.

In the United States much attention has been given to the population "crisis," usually described in terms of the menace of population growth. Much of this discussion has been superficial and cast in the language of doomsday rhetoric. To many well-meaning people it is "obvious" that national population size and growth are the chief causes of the deterioration in the quality of life that they see around them—pollution, crowding, traffic congestion, urban sprawl, crime, corruption, and many other aspects of social disorganization.

This is an oversimplified interpretation of what is actually occurring. We are not a densely populated country but we are a crowded one, because so many of us have gravitated to a few great metropolitan areas; we are not a rapidly growing population but with our mobility and affluence we have created major problems of urban sprawl, pollution, and crowding of our recreational areas.

I would like to consider four aspects of population change in the United States—size, growth, distribution, and mobility—and some of the economic and social consequences of each.

The size of our population

The United States has a large population, at the moment some 210 million people. But we also have

Dudley Kirk is Morrison Professor of Population Studies at the Food Research Institute and Department of Sociology, Stanford University. This Selection *is adapted with the author's permission from an address Dr. Kirk gave at the May 1973 convention of the American Institute of Architects in San Francisco.*

PRB (Population Reference Bureau, Inc.), November 1973, Selection No. 44.

34

a very large area and our population is very unevenly distributed. Anyone on a transcontinental flight who has been able to look out the window realizes that vast areas of our continental country are very thinly populated, or indeed uninhabited.

Many of us might prefer a country of 150 million or 100 million rather than our present 200-plus million, but this is an academic question. Barring a major cataclysm, or unless we are prepared to encourage wholesale euthanasia, we are going to have our present population size and almost certainly a somewhat larger population in the foreseeable future.

It is doubtless true that a larger population in the same environment contributes more to the depletion of resources and to pollution than a smaller one. But our present population size and overall density are not in themselves the chief cause of our pollution, crime, racial strife, and other social ills. Countries like Great Britain, with ten times our density of population, or the Netherlands, with eighteen times, have far less crime and social disorganization, and have had more success in protecting their environments. Dramatic examples of the latter are the reduction of smog in London and the purification of the Thames. By contrast, Sydney, Australia, a city and metropolitan complex not unlike our own San Francisco Bay Area, has many of the same problems that we have: pollution of Botany Bay, pollution of beaches near Sydney, traffic jams at rush hours, rising crime, and many of the social ills that we are confronted with in the United States. This is in a continent occupied by 13 million people compared with our 210 million. The problems are not so much those of sheer numbers or density as they are of *where* and *how* we choose to live.

National population growth

Nor is our *present* rate of national growth a major threat to our quality of life. Our national birth rate and rate of reproduction are the lowest in our history and portend zero population growth, though, it is true, not until after the turn of the century. There is a great deal of inertia in national population change simply because we live a long time—on the average 70 years.

But the birth rate and the reproduction rate have been declining continuously since 1957 and are still going down. If we earlier had a national population "bomb" or "crisis" we certainly do not have it now. This in no way denigrates the efforts of those who

35

have worked so valiantly for voluntary parenthood to prevent unwanted pregnancies and births. On the contrary it is a tribute to their success.[1]

True, the upper middle class that forms the chief constituency of the ZPG movement has experienced invasion of its residential and recreational areas, an invasion that it understandably continues to interpret as a population explosion. Indeed, for members of this class there *was* a population explosion. First, they experienced the "baby boom" in the 1950s more acutely than did the rest of the population, especially when large numbers of children put great pressure on schools and other facilities in the suburbs. Second, and even more important, this group formerly had close to a monopoly on the better residential areas in the suburbs, the universities, the better beaches, and access to the national parks because of widespread ownership of autos. What is seen as urban sprawl is the result of the growing affluence of the mass of the American people who now have sufficient income to buy homes in the suburbs, to go to the universities, to travel, and to visit the favored recreational areas such as our wilderness and our national parks.

Let me illustrate the relative impact of population growth and of affluence with two examples.

When I was growing up, our household of five persons produced one barrel of trash a week. Today my household of five produces *four* barrels of trash each week. The same population—four times as much solid waste. More paper, more disposable cartons, cans, bottles, built-in obsolescence, that we only fractionally counter by recycling.

A second example relates to crowding. In 1950 there were 33 million visitors to our national parks and national monuments. Had the number of visitors simply increased with population growth, by 1971 there would have been 45 million or a bit over one-third.[2] Of course there were not—there were some 200 million visitors. The difference is the result of the greater accessibility of the national parks to the majority of our population through better roads, ownership of automobiles, and money to

---

[1] The birth rate has fallen from 25.3 per 1,000 population in 1957 to 15.6 in 1972, the rate of natural increase (births minus deaths) from 16.7 in 1957 to 5.9 in 1972, or about 6 per 1,000. This is a modest rate of increase (0.6 percent per year) by almost any standard. The reproduction rate is presently below the level of replacement of the childbearing generation; if continued the population will decline. We continue to have some population growth only because of (1) the heavy concentration in our population of young adults who produce most of the births but very few deaths and (2) immigration.

[2] Strictly speaking, the comparison should also take into account the increase in park acreage from 23 million to 30 million acres in this period. The combined effect of population growth and increase in park acreage (pro rata) would have meant an attendance of 69 million in 1971.

36

travel. Had population growth alone been involved, one would have scarcely noticed the difference.

One could of course multiply such examples many times. Our population is now growing at about 10 percent per decade while our power needs are doubling each decade. Roughly 10 percent of the greater demand is now due to population growth and 90 percent due to greater affluence.[3]

At the national level, population control is a slow and inefficient way to meet such problems, which are created by affluence more than population growth. We would continue to have all of them without *any* population growth (i.e., if we had ZPG tomorrow). Of course we don't need more people. But, happily, since 1957 the American people themselves have been making the adjustment in population growth in the direction of a lower or no-growth population in the long run.

Population distribution

Most experts now are convinced that the *distribution* of our population is a more serious problem than our population size or growth. The rural heartland of our country in the Mississippi-Missouri Valley is being deserted. Over one-third of the counties of the United States *lost* population between 1960 and 1970 and are being *de*populated. The vast majority of counties in the U.S. lost population by migration. As a people we are being drawn to regions of sun and sand and water.

Above all, of course, we have been drawn into the great metropolitan areas. By now some 70 percent of our population are concentrated in somewhat less than 2 percent of our total area. The resulting congestion is not typical of the country as a whole and is something new in American life. Historically we have not been an urban people. Perhaps the most significant single social index of the change in America is this: A century ago, in 1870, the average American lived on a farm. A generation later, in 1900, he still lived in a rural area, but in a village. After another generation, about 1930, the average American lived in a small town. Today he lives in a suburb of a large metropolitan area. We have become an overwhelmingly urban people and have not yet made an adjustment to this new kind of life. This is especially true of our inner city residents

---

[3] It will be said that we cannot continue to have even less than 1 percent population growth in the United States over any long historical period. This is true—any geometric rate of growth, no matter how small, ultimately leads to disaster. But this is also true of a host of economic and social indices, many of which if continued indefinitely would be quite as menacing as population growth; for example, increases in the number of automobiles, in the number of murders, or indeed in the production of artichokes.

37

many of whom come directly from southern rural areas or from rural areas in other parts of the world.

Within the metropolitan areas themselves we have the other phenomenon of urban sprawl and the tentacles of the great metropolises reaching out toward each other. If we have a population explosion today, it isn't in our national population; it is in the rapid spatial expansion of our metropolitan areas. Again this is because more and more of our people have the affluence to demand and to get more living space.

Mobility

Let us carry this one step further to the question of population mobility. We are a highly mobile people and always have been. But the effects have been intensified in at least two ways. Thanks to our much greater physical mobility, especially in automobiles, we travel farther, faster, and more often. Many people own mobile homes or perhaps two homes. Also, we increasingly live segmented lives and in segregated communities. I have in mind not so much the more spectacular forms of segregation by race as segregation by age and by stages in the life cycle.

The majority of us now live in age-graded communities. A very large percentage of our young adults who by virtue of their abilities and education would be expected to be leaders in the next generation have been moved about as children and do not really think of themselves as seriously committed to a "home community." Most of them after graduation from college or professional schools expect to find jobs somewhere other than in the suburbs in which they were raised. As young adults they commonly drift to the larger cities. After marriage and starting a family they are likely to seek lower-cost suburban housing in the urban sprawl. If they are successful they will move to higher income suburbs. Higher ranking employees of large firms take it as a matter of course that they will be shifted from one city to another and hence from Scarsdale to Shaker Heights to Beverly Hills to Hillsborough, or vice versa. After their own children have grown they no longer need the large houses, now "empty nests," that they often cannot afford on lower retirement incomes. So they move again, often to a more favorable climate.

We are becoming a rootless people, without the stability of a lasting community life. For some of us in such occupations as university teaching, the profession in a sense becomes our surrogate community—a community of interest for the professional man or woman, but our spouses and children must make frequent adjustments as we move from position to position. More and more we live in these segregated communities—not just in terms of class and race but even more importantly in terms of age and stage in the life cycle. More and more we are becoming a people without longstanding personal relationships, without the informal sanctions of shared values that keep us in line without the coercion of the law and the police. All too often we no longer live in a community of friends and relatives; all too many of us live in a community of strangers.

Most of our ancestors didn't have to worry about who they were. They knew. Nor did they have to worry so much about changing and conflicting values because they were well seated in a community life that was a true "home." One could argue at length about the relative merit of the stimulating qualities of life in a modern urban environment versus the quieter and less stimulating life that our grandparents had in smaller communities. But I think this fact is unassailable: our present life style puts a very great strain on the individual and on the society in which he lives. Many of our young people, especially the most idealistic, are turning to life styles in which they attempt to recreate the more human personal communities of the past. They are reaching for roots and for the deeper levels of human association that characterized more stable communities.

I have given a hasty and perhaps arbitrary analysis of the effects of population changes on our society. Now, the question is, "Well, what can we do about it?"

Obviously no single professional group, such as architects or demographers or any other, can do the whole job itself. But I do think that architects could have a vital role in meeting some of the problems I have outlined here. Already we have seen a major revolt against the high-rise apartment building, whether in slum clearance or in the provision of other housing. We see architects designing much more human types of living arrangements, smaller units in which people will *know* their neighbors, as well as recognize intruders and strangers, buildings that bring people together rather than divide them. One sees some efforts, not too sophisticated, to replace Main Street with shopping malls that are accessible on foot or bicycle from residential areas and where the pedestrian is king.

I would like to see this carried much further. We need communities or subcommunities that include very different types of housing that appeal to people at all stages in the life cycle: small apartments, perhaps for the elderly and newly married, with easy access to some shopping facilities; small houses for small families—all together. Old people are needed and need to be babysitters and companions for the young. Young adults, perhaps even more desperately, need relief from the problems of child care. Children need comfort and a sense of continuity and history by contact with the experience, the patience, and the wisdom of older people. We need architecture that brings all ages together in such complementary ways.

Architects today are being challenged to think more and more in terms of the social and communal impact of the structures they are designing. It is true that in our living and physical arrangements we must continue to contend with problems arising from our large population size, our modest population growth, and especially from our concentration in great metropolitan aggregations. But we must also contend with the loss of community and stability arising from *mobility*. The challenge of population *change* in the United States is broader than the problems of national population growth. If it were only the latter, one could say we were doing very well at the present time.

The Experience of Living in Cities

Adaptations to urban overload create characteristic qualities of city life that can be measured.

Stanley Milgram

"When I first came to New York it seemed like a nightmare. As soon as I got off the train at Grand Central I was caught up in pushing, shoving crowds on 42nd Street. Sometimes people bumped into me without apology; what really frightened me was to see two people literally engaged in combat for possession of a cab. Why were they so rushed? Even drunks on the street were bypassed without a glance. People didn't seem to care about each other at all."

This statement represents a common reaction to a great city, but it does not tell the whole story. Obviously cities have great appeal because of their variety, eventfulness, possibility of choice, and the stimulation of an intense atmosphere that many individuals find a desirable background to their lives. Where face-to-face contacts are important, the city offers unparalleled possibilities. It has been calculated by the Regional Plan Association (1) that in Nassau County, a suburb of New York City, an individual can meet 11,000 others within a 10-minute radius of his office by foot or car. In Newark, a moderate-sized city, he can meet more than 20,000 persons within this radius. But in midtown Manhattan he can meet fully 220,000. So there is an order-of-magnitude increment in the communication possibilities offered by a great city. That is one of the bases of its appeal and, indeed, of its functional necessity. The city provides options that no other social arrangement permits. But there is a negative side also, as we shall see.

Granted that cities are indispensable in complex society, we may still ask what contribution psychology can make to understanding the experience of liv-ing in them. What theories are relevant? How can we extend our knowledge of the psychological aspects of life in cities through empirical inquiry? If empirical inquiry is possible, along what lines should it proceed? In short, where do we start in constructing urban theory and in laying out lines of research?

Observation is the indispensable starting point. Any observer in the streets of midtown Manhattan will see (i) large numbers of people, (ii) a high population density, and (iii) heterogeneity of population. These three factors need to be at the root of any sociopsychological theory of city life, for they condition all aspects of our experience in the metropolis. Louis Wirth (2), if not the first to point to these factors, is nonetheless the sociologist who relied most heavily on them in his analysis of the city. Yet, for a psychologist, there is something unsatisfactory about Wirth's theoretical variables. Numbers, density, and heterogeneity are demographic facts but they are not yet psychological facts. They are external to the individual. Psychology needs an idea that links the individual's *experience* to the demographic circumstances of urban life.

SCIENCE, March 13, 1970, Vol. 167, pp. 1461-1468.

One link is provided by the concept of overload. This term, drawn from systems analysis, refers to a system's inability to process inputs from the environment because there are too many inputs for the system to cope with, or because successive inputs come so fast that input *A* cannot be processed when input *B* is presented. When overload is present, adaptations occur. The system must set priorities and make choices. *A* may be processed first while *B* is kept in abeyance, or one input may be sacrificed altogether. City life, as we experience it, constitutes a continuous set of encounters with overload, and of resultant adaptations. Overload characteristically deforms daily life on several levels, impinging on role performance, the evolution of social norms, cognitive functioning, and the use of facilities.

The concept has been implicit in several theories of urban experience. In 1903 George Simmel (3) pointed out that, since urban dwellers come into contact with vast numbers of people each day, they conserve psychic energy by becoming acquainted with a far smaller proportion of people than their rural counterparts do, and by maintaining more superficial relationships even with these acquaintances. Wirth (2) points specifically to "the superficiality, the anonymity, and the transitory character of urban social relations."

One adaptive response to overload, therefore, is the allocation of less time to each input. A second adaptive mechanism is disregard of low-priority inputs. Principles of selectivity are formulated such that investment of time and energy are reserved for carefully defined inputs (the urbanite disregards the drunk sick on the street as he purposefully navigates through the crowd). Third, boundaries are redrawn in certain social transactions so that the overloaded system can shift the burden to the other party in the exchange; thus, harried New York bus drivers once made change for customers, but now this responsibility has been shifted to the client, who must have the exact fare ready. Fourth, reception is blocked off prior to entrance into a system; city dwellers increasingly use unlisted telephone numbers to prevent individuals from calling them, and a small but growing number resort to keeping the telephone off the hook to prevent incoming calls. More subtly, a city dweller blocks inputs by assuming an unfriendly countenance, which discourages others from initiating contact. Additionally, social screening devices are interposed between the individual and environmental inputs (in a town of 5000 anyone can drop in to chat with the mayor, but in the metropolis organizational screening devices deflect inputs to other destinations). Fifth, the intensity of inputs is diminished by filtering devices, so that only weak and relatively superficial forms of involvement with others are allowed. Sixth, specialized institutions are created to absorb inputs that would otherwise swamp the individual (welfare departments handle the financial needs of a million individuals in New York City, who would otherwise create an army of mendicants continuously importuning the pedestrian). The interposition of institutions between the individual and the social world, a characteristic of all modern society, and most notably of the large metropolis, has its negative side. It deprives the individual of a sense of direct contact and spontaneous integration in the life around him. It simultaneously protects and estranges the individual from his social environment.

Many of these adaptive mechanisms apply not only to individuals but to institutional systems as well, as Meier (4) has so brilliantly shown in connection with the library and the stock exchange.

In sum, the observed behavior of the urbanite in a wide range of situations appears to be determined largely by a variety of adaptations to overload. I now deal with several specific consequences of responses to overload, which make for differences in the tone of city and town.

Social Responsibility

The principal point of interest for a social psychology of the city is that moral and social involvement with individuals is necessarily restricted. This is a direct and necessary function of excess of input over capacity to process. Such restriction of involvement runs a broad spectrum from refusal to become involved in the needs of another person, even when the person desperately needs assistance, through refusal to do favors, to the simple withdrawal of courtesies (such as offering a lady a seat, or saying "sorry" when a pedestrian collision occurs). In any transaction more and more details need to be dropped as the total number of units to be processed increases and assaults an instrument of limited processing capacity.

The ultimate adaptation to an overloaded social environment is to totally disregard the needs, interests, and demands of those whom one does not define as relevant to the satisfaction of personal needs, and to develop highly efficient perceptual means of determining whether an individual falls into the category of friend or stranger. The disparity in the treatment of friends and strangers ought to be greater in cities than in towns; the time allotment and willingness to become involved with those who have no personal claim on one's time is likely to be less in cities than in towns.

Bystander intervention in crises. The most striking deficiencies in social responsibility in cities occur in crisis situations, such as the Genovese murder in Queens. In 1964, Catherine Genovese, coming home from a night job in the early hours of an April morning, was stabbed repeatedly, over an extended period of time. Thirty-eight residents of a respectable New York City neighborhood admit to having witnessed at least a part of the attack, but none went to her aid or called the police until after she was dead. Milgram and Hollander, writing in *The Nation* (5), analyzed the event in these terms:

Urban friendships and associations are not primarily formed on the basis of physical proximity. A person with numerous close friends in different parts of the city may not know the occupant of an adjacent apartment. This does not mean that a city dweller has fewer friends than does a villager, or knows fewer persons who will come to his aid; however, it does mean that his allies are not constantly at hand. Miss Genovese required immediate aid from those physically present. There is no evidence that the city had deprived Miss Genovese of human associations, but the friends who might have rushed to her side were miles from the scene of her tragedy.

Further, it is known that her cries for help were not directed to a specific person; they were general. But only individuals can act, and as the cries were not specifically directed, no particular person felt a special responsibility. The crime and the failure of community response seem absurd to us. At the time, it may well have seemed equally absurd to the Kew Gardens residents that not one of the neighbors would have called the police. A collective paralysis may have developed from the belief of each of the witnesses that someone else must surely have taken that obvious step.

Latané and Darley (6) have reported laboratory approaches to the study of bystander intervention and have established experimentally the following principle: the larger the number of bystanders, the less the likelihood that any one of them will intervene in an emergency. Gaertner and Bickman (7) of The City University of New York have extended the bystander studies to an examination of help across ethnic lines. Blacks and whites, with clearly identifiable accents, called strangers (through what the caller represented as an error in telephone dialing), gave them a plausible story of being stranded on an outlying highway without more dimes, and asked the stranger to call a garage. The experimenters found that the white callers had a significantly better chance of obtaining assistance than the black callers. This suggests that ethnic allegiance may well be another means of coping with overload: the city dweller can reduce excessive demands and

Table 1. Percentage of entries achieved by investigators for city and town dwellings (see text).

Experimenter	Entries achieved (%)	
	City*	Small town†
Male		
No. 1	16	40
No. 2	12	60
Female		
No. 3	40	87
No. 4	40	100

* Number of requests for entry, 100. † Number of requests for entry, 60.

screen out urban heterogeneity by responding along ethnic lines; overload is made more manageable by limiting the "span of sympathy."

In any quantitative characterization of the social texture of city life, a necessary first step is the application of such experimental methods as these to field situations in large cities and small towns. Theorists argue that the indifference shown in the Genovese case would not be found in a small town, but in the absence of solid experimental evidence the question remains an open one.

More than just callousness prevents bystanders from participating in altercations between people. A rule of urban life is respect for other people's emotional and social privacy, perhaps because physical privacy is so hard to achieve. And in situations for which the standards are heterogeneous, it is much harder to know whether taking an active role is unwarranted meddling or an appropriate response to a critical situation. If a husband and wife are quarreling in public, at what point should a bystander step in? On the one hand, the heterogeneity of the city produces substantially greater tolerance about behavior, dress, and codes of ethics than is generally found in the small town, but this diversity also encourages people to withhold aid for fear of antagonizing the participants or crossing an inappropriate and difficult-to-define line.

Moreover, the frequency of demands present in the city gives rise to norms of noninvolvement. There are practical limitations to the Samaritan impulse in a major city. If a citizen attended to every needy person, if he were sensitive to and acted on every altruistic impulse that was evoked in the city, he could scarely keep his own affairs in order.

Willingness to trust and assist strangers. We now move away from crisis situations to less urgent examples of social responsibility. For it is not only in situations of dramatic need but in the ordinary, everyday willingness to lend a hand that the city dweller is said to be deficient relative to his small-town cousin. The comparative method must be used in any empirical examination of this question. A commonplace social situation is staged in an urban setting and in a small town—a situation to which a subject can respond by either extending help or withholding it. The responses in town and city are compared.

One factor in the purported unwillingness of urbanites to be helpful to strangers may well be their heightened sense of physical (and emotional) vulnerability—a feeling that is supported by urban crime statistics. A key test for distinguishing between city and town behavior, therefore, is determining how city dwellers compare with town dwellers in offering aid that increases their personal vulnerability and requires some trust of strangers. Altman, Levine, Nadien, and Villena (8) of The City University of New York devised a study to compare the behaviors of city and town dwellers in this respect. The criterion used in this study was the willingness of householders to allow strangers to enter their home to use the telephone. The student investigators individually rang doorbells, explained that they had misplaced the address of a friend nearby, and asked to use the phone. The investigators (two males and two females) made 100 requests for entry into homes in the city and 60 requests in the small towns. The results for middle-income housing developments in Manhattan were compared with data for several small towns (Stony Point, Spring Valley, Ramapo, Nyack, New City, and West

44

Clarkstown) in Rockland County, outside of New York City. As Table 1 shows, in all cases there was a sharp increase in the proportion of entries achieved by an experimenter when he moved from the city to a small town. In the most extreme case the experimenter was five times as likely to gain admission to homes in a small town as to homes in Manhattan. Although the female experimenters had notably greater success both in cities and in towns than the male experimenters had, each of the four students did at least twice as well in towns as in cities. This suggests that the city-town distinction overrides even the predictably greater fear of male strangers than of female ones.

The lower level of helpfulness by city dwellers seems due in part to recognition of the dangers of living in Manhattan, rather than to mere indifference or coldness. It is significant that 75 percent of all the city respondents received and answered messages by shouting through closed doors and by peering out through peepholes; in the towns, by contrast, about 75 percent of the respondents opened the door.

Supporting the experimenters' quantitative results was their general observation that the town dwellers were noticeably more friendly and less suspicious than the city dwellers. In seeking to explain the reasons for the greater sense of psychological vulnerability city dwellers feel, above and beyond the differences in crime statistics, Villena (8) points out that, if a crime is committed in a village, a resident of a neighboring village may not perceive the crime as personally relevant, though the geographic distance may be small, whereas a criminal act committed anywhere in the city, though miles from the city-dweller's home is still verbally located within the city; thus, Villena says, "the inhabitant of the city possesses a larger vulnerable space."

Civilities. Even at the most superficial level of involvement—the exercise of everyday civilities—urbanites are reputedly deficient. People bump into each other and often do not apologize. They knock over another person's packages and, as often as not, proceed on their way with a grumpy exclamation instead of an offer of assistance. Such behavior, which many visitors to great cities find distasteful, is less common, we are told, in smaller communities, where traditional courtesies are more likely to be observed.

In some instances it is not simply that, in the city, traditional courtesies are violated; rather, the cities develop new norms of noninvolvement. These are so well defined and so deeply a part of city life that *they* constitute the norms people are reluctant to violate. Men are actually embarrassed to give up a seat on the subway to an old woman; they mumble "I was getting off anyway," instead of making the gesture in a straightforward and gracious way. These norms develop because everyone realizes that, in situations of high population density, people cannot implicate themselves in each others' affairs, for to do so would create conditions of continual distraction which would frustrate purposeful action.

In discussing the effects of overload I do not imply that at every instant the city dweller is bombarded with an unmanageable number of inputs, and that his responses are determined by the excess of input at any given instant. Rather, adaptation occurs in the form of gradual evolution of norms of behavior. Norms are evolved in response to frequent discrete experiences of overload; they persist and become generalized modes of responding.

Overload on cognitive capacities: anonymity. That we respond differently toward those whom we know and those who are strangers to us is a truism. An eager patron aggressively cuts in front of someone in a long movie line to save time only to confront a friend; he then behaves sheepishly. A man is involved in an automobile accident caused by another driver, emerges from his car shouting in rage, then moderates his behavior on discovering a friend driving the other car. The city dweller, when walking through the midtown streets, is in a state of continual anonymity vis-à-vis the other pedestrians.

Anonymity is part of a continuous spectrum ranging from total anonymity to full acquaintance, and it may well be that measurement of the precise degrees of anonymity in cities and towns would help to explain important distinctions between the quality of life in each. Conditions of full acquaintance, for example, offer security and familiarity, but they may also be stifling, because the individual is caught in a web of established relationships. Conditions of complete anonymity, by contrast, provide freedom from routinized social ties, but they may also create feelings of alienation and detachment.

Empirically one could investigate the proportion of activities in which the city dweller or the town dweller is known by others at given times in his daily life, and the proportion of activities in the course of which he interacts with individuals who know him. At his job, for instance, the city dweller may be known to as many people as his rural counterpart. However, when he is not fulfilling his occupational role—say, when merely traveling about the city—the urbanite is doubtless more anonymous than his rural counterpart.

Limited empirical work on anonymity has begun. Zimbardo (9) has tested whether the social anonymity and impersonality of the big city encourage greater vandalism than do small towns. Zimbardo arranged for one automobile to be left for 64 hours near the Bronx campus of New York University and for a counterpart to be left for the same number of hours near Stanford University in Palo Alto. The license plates on the two cars were removed and the hoods were opened, to provide "releaser cues" for potential vandals. The New York car was stripped of all movable parts within the first 24 hours, and by the end of 3 days was only a hunk of metal rubble. Unexpectedly, however, most of the destruction occurred during daylight hours, usually under the scrutiny of observers, and the leaders in the vandalism were well-dressed, white adults. The Palo Alto car was left untouched.

Zimbardo attributes the difference in the treatment accorded the two cars to the "acquired feelings of social anonymity provided by life in a city like New York," and he supports his conclusions with several other anecdotes illustrating casual, wanton vandalism in the city. In any comparative study of the effects of anonymity in city and town, however, there must be satisfactory control for other confounding factors: the large number of drug addicts in a city like New York; the higher proportion of slum-dwellers in the city; and so on.

Another direction for empirical study is investigation of the beneficial effects of anonymity. The impersonality of city life breeds its own tolerance for the private lives of the inhabitants. Individuality and even eccentricity, we may assume, can flourish more readily in the metropolis than in the small town. Stigmatized persons may find it easier to lead comfortable lives in the city, free of the constant scrutiny of neighbors. To what degree can this assumed difference between city and town be shown empirically? Judith Waters (10), at The City University of New York, hypothesized that avowed homosexuals would be more likely to be accepted as tenants in a large city than in small towns, and she dispatched letters from homosexuals and from normal individuals to real estate agents in cities and towns across the country. The results of her study were inconclusive. But the general idea of examining the protective benefits of city life to the stigmatized ought to be pursued.

Role behavior in cities and towns. Another product of urban overload is the adjustment in roles made by urbanites in daily interactions. As Wirth has said (2): "Urbanites meet one another in highly segmental roles. ... They are less dependent upon particular persons, and their dependence upon others is confined to a highly fractionalized aspect of the other's round of activity." This tendency is particularly noticeable in transactions between customers and individuals offering professional or sales services. The owner of a country store has time to become well acquainted with his dozen-or-so daily customers, but the girl at the checkout counter of a busy A & P, serving hundreds of customers a day, barely has time to toss the green stamps into one customer's shopping bag before the next customer confronts her with his pile of groceries.

Meier, in his stimulating analysis of the city (4), discusses several adaptations a system may make when confronted by inputs that exceed its capacity to process them. Meier argues that, according to the principle of competition for scarce resources, the scope and time of the transaction shrink as customer volume and daily turnover rise. This, in fact, is what is meant by the "brusque" quality of city life. New standards have developed in cities concerning what levels of services are appropriate in business transactions (see Fig. 1).

McKenna and Morgenthau (11), in a seminar at The City University of New York, devised a study (i) to compare the willingness of city dwellers and small-town dwellers to do favors for strangers that entailed expenditure of a small amount of time and slight inconvenience but no personal vulnerability, and (ii) to determine whether the more compartmentalized, transitory relationships of the city would make urban salesgirls less likely than small-town salesgirls to carry out, for strangers, tasks not related to their customary roles.

To test for differences between city dwellers and small-town dwellers, a simple experiment was devised in which persons from both settings were asked (by telephone) to perform increasingly onerous favors for anonymous strangers. Within the cities (Chicago, New York, and Philadelphia), half the calls were to housewives and the other half to salesgirls in women's apparel shops; the division was the same for the 37 small towns of the study, which were in the same states as the cities. Each experimenter represented herself as a long-distance caller who had, through error, been connected with the respondent by the operator. The experimenter began by asking for simple information about the weather for purposes of travel. Next the experimenter excused herself on some pretext (asking the respondent to "please hold on"), put the phone down for almost a full minute, and then picked it up again and asked the respondent to provide the phone number of a hotel or motel in her vicinity at which the experimenter might stay during a forthcoming visit. Scores were assigned the subjects on the basis of how helpful they had been. McKenna summarizes her results in this manner:

People in the city, whether they are engaged in a specific job or not, are less helpful and informative than people in small towns; . . . People at home, regardless of where they live, are less helpful and informative than people working in shops.

However, the absolute level of cooperativeness for urban subjects was found to be quite high, and does not accord with the stereotype of the urbanite as aloof, self-centered, and unwilling to help strangers. The quantitative differences obtained by McKenna and Morgenthau are less great than one might have expected. This again points up the need for extensive empirical research in rural-urban differences, research that goes far beyond that provided in the few illustrative pilot studies presented here. At this point we have very limited objective evidence on differences in the quality of social encounters in city and small town.

But the research needs to be guided by unifying theoretical concepts. As I have tried to demonstrate, the concept of overload helps to explain a wide variety of contrasts between city behavior and town behavior: (i) the differences in role enactment (the tendency of urban dwellers to deal with one another in highly segmented, functional terms, and of urban sales personnel to devote limited time and attention to their customers); (ii) the evolution of urban norms quite different from traditional town values (such as the acceptance of noninvolvement, impersonality, and aloofness in urban life); (iii) the adaptation of the urban dweller's cognitive processes (his inability to identify most of the people he sees daily, his screening of sensory stimuli, his development of blasé attitudes toward deviant or bizarre behavior, and his selectivity in responding to human demands); and (iv) the competition for scarce facilities in the city (the subway rush; the fight for taxis; traffic jams; standing in line to await services). I suggest that contrasts between city and rural behavior probably reflect the responses of similar people to very different situations, rather than intrinsic differences in the personalities of rural and city dwellers. The city is a situation to which individuals respond adaptively.

Further Aspects of Urban Experience

Some features of urban experience do not fit neatly into the system of analysis presented thus far. They are no less important for that reason. The issues raised next are difficult to treat in quantitative fashion. Yet I prefer discussing them in a loose way to excluding them because appropriate language and data have not yet been developed. My aim is to suggest how phenomena such as "urban atmosphere" can be pinned down through techniques of measurement.

The "atmosphere" of great cities. The contrast in the behavior of city and town dwellers has been a natural starting point for urban social scientists. But even among great cities there are marked differences in "atmosphere." The tone, pacing, and texture of social encounters are different in London and New York, and many persons willingly make financial sacrifices for the privilege of living within a specific urban atmosphere which they find pleasing or stimulating. A second perspective in the study of cities, therefore, is to define exactly what is meant by the atmosphere of a city and to pinpoint the factors that give rise to it. It may seem that urban atmosphere is too evanescent a quality to be reduced to a set of measurable variables, but I do not believe the matter can be judged before substantial effort has been made in this direction. It is obvious that any such approach must be comparative. It makes no sense at all to say that New York is "vibrant" and "frenetic" unless one has some specific city in mind as a basis of comparison.

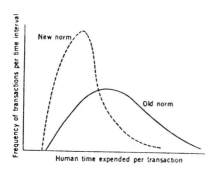

Fig. 1. Changes in the demand for time for a given task when the overall transaction frequency increases in a social system. [Reprinted with permission from R. L. Meier, *A Communications Theory of Urban Growth*, 1962. Copyrighted by M.I.T. Press, 1962]

In an undergraduate tutorial that I conducted at Harvard University some years ago, New York, London, and Paris were selected as reference points for attempts to measure urban atmosphere. We began with a simple question: Does any consensus exist about the qualities that typify given cities? To answer this question one could undertake a content analysis of travel-book, literary, and journalistic accounts of cities. A second approach, which we adopted, is to ask people to characterize (with descriptive terms and accounts of typical experiences) cities they have lived in or visited. In advertisements placed in the *New York Times* and the *Harvard Crimson* we asked people to give us accounts of specific incidents in London, Paris, or New York that best illuminated the character of that particular city. Questionnaires were then developed, and administered to persons who were familiar with at least two of the three cities.

Some distinctive patterns emerged (*12*). The distinguishing themes concerning New York, for example, dealt with its diversity, its great size, its pace and level of activity, its cultural and entertainment opportunities, and the heterogeneity and segmentation ("ghettoization") of its population. New York elicited more descriptions in terms of physical qualities, pace, and emotional impact than Paris or London did, a fact which suggests that these are particularly important aspects of New York's ambiance.

A contrasting profile emerges for London; in this case respondents placed far greater emphasis on their interactions with the inhabitants than on physical surroundings. There was near unanimity on certain themes: those dealing with the tolerance and courtesy of London's inhabitants. One respondent said:

When I was 12, my grandfather took me to the British Museum . . . one day by tube and recited the *Aeneid* in Latin for my benefit. . . . He is rather deaf, speaks very loudly and it embarrassed the hell out of me, until I realized that nobody was paying any attention. Londoners are extremely worldly and tolerant.

In contrast, respondents who described New Yorkers as aloof, cold, and rude referred to such incidents as the following:

I saw a boy of 19 passing out anti-war leaflets to passersby. When he stopped at a corner, a man dressed in a business suit walked by him at a brisk pace, hit the boy's arm, and scattered the leaflets all over the street. The man kept walking at the same pace down the block.

We need to obtain many more such descriptions of incidents, using careful methods of sampling. By the application of factor-analytic techniques, relevant dimensions for each city can be discerned.

The responses for Paris were about equally divided between responses concerning its inhabitants and those regarding its physical and sensory attributes. Cafés and parks were often mentioned as contributing to the sense that Paris is a city of amenities, but many respondents complained that Parisians were inhospitable, nasty, and cold.

We cannot be certain, of course, to what degree these statements reflect actual characteristics of the cities in question and to what degree they simply tap the respondents' knowledge of widely held preconceptions. Indeed, one may point to three factors, apart from the actual atmospheres of the cities, that determine the subjects' responses.

1) A person's impression of a given city depends on his implicit standard of comparison. A New Yorker who visits Paris may well describe that city as "leisurely," whereas a compatriot from Richmond, Virginia, may consider Paris too "hectic." Obtaining reciprocal judgment, in which New Yorkers judge Londoners, and Londoners judge New Yorkers, seems a useful way to take into account not only the city being judged but also the home city that serves as the visitor's base line.

2) Perceptions of a city are also af-

fected by whether the observer is a tourist, a newcomer, or a longer-term resident. First, a tourist will be exposed to features of the city different from those familiar to a long-time resident. Second, a prerequisite for adapting to continuing life in a given city seems to be the filtering out of many observations about the city that the newcomer or tourist finds particularly arresting; this selective process seems to be part of the long-term resident's mechanism for coping with overload. In the interest of psychic economy, the resident simply learns to tune out many aspects of daily life. One method for studying the specific impact of adaptation on perception of the city is to ask several pairs of newcomers and old-timers (one newcomer and one old-timer to a pair) to walk down certain city blocks and then report separately what each has observed.

Additionally, many persons have noted that when travelers return to New York from an extended sojourn abroad they often feel themselves confronted with "brutal ugliness" (13) and a distinctive, frenetic atmosphere whose contributing details are, for a few hours or days, remarkably sharp and clear. This period of fresh perception should receive special attention in the study of city atmosphere. For, in a few days, details which are initially arresting become less easy to specify. They are assimilated into an increasingly familiar background atmosphere which, though important in setting the tone of things, is difficult to analyze. There is no better point at which to begin the study of city atmosphere than at the moment when a traveler returns from abroad.

3) The popular myths and expectations each visitor brings to the city will also affect the way in which he perceives it (see 14). Sometimes a person's preconceptions about a city are relatively accurate distillations of its character, but preconceptions may also reinforce myths by filtering the visitor's perceptions to conform with his expectations. Preconceptions affect not only a person's perceptions of a city but what he reports about it.

The influence of a person's urban base line on his perceptions of a given city, the differences between the observations of the long-time inhibitant and those of the newcomer, and the filtering effect of personal expectations and stereotypes raise serious questions about the validity of travelers' reports. Moreover, no social psychologist wants to rely exclusively on verbal accounts if he is attempting to obtain an accurate and objective description of the cities' social texture, pace, and general atmosphere. What he needs to do is to devise means of embedding objective experimental measures in the daily flux of city life, measures that can accurately index the qualities of a given urban atmosphere.

Experimental Comparisons of Behavior

Roy Feldman (15) incorporated these principles in a comparative study of behavior toward compatriots and foreigners in Paris, Athens, and Boston. Feldman wanted to see (i) whether absolute levels and patterns of helpfulness varied significantly from city to city, and (ii) whether inhabitants in each city tended to treat compatriots differently from foreigners. He examined five concrete behavioral episodes, each carried out by a team of native experimenters and a team of American experimenters in the three cities. The episodes involved (i) asking natives of the city for street directions; (ii) asking natives to mail a letter for the experimenter; (iii) asking natives if they had just dropped a dollar bill (or the Greek or French equivalent) when the money actually belonged to the experimenter himself; (iv) deliberately overpaying for goods in a store to see if the cashier would correct the mistake and return the excess money; and (v) determining whether taxicab drivers overcharged strangers and whether they took the most direct route available.

Feldman's results suggest some interesting contrasts in the profiles of the three cities. In Paris, for instance, certain stereotypes were borne out. Parisian cab drivers overcharged foreigners significantly more often than they overcharged compatriots. But other aspects of the Parisians' behavior were not in accord with American preconceptions: in mailing a letter for a stranger, Parisians treated foreigners significantly better than Athenians or Bostonians did, and, when asked to mail letters that were already stamped, Parisians actually treated foreigners better than they treated compatriots. Similarly, Parisians were significantly more honest than Athenians or Bostonians in resisting the temptation to claim money that was not theirs, and Parisians were the only citizens who were more honest with foreigners than with compatriots in this experiment.

Feldman's studies not only begin to quantify some of the variables that give a city its distinctive texture but they also provide a methodological model for other comparative research. His most important contribution is his successful application of objective, experimental measures to everyday situations, a mode of study which provides conclusions about urban life that are more pertinent than those achieved through laboratory experiments.

Tempo and Pace

Another important component of a city's atmosphere is its tempo or pace, an attribute frequently remarked on but less often studied. Does a city have a frenetic, hectic quality, or is it easygoing and leisurely? In any empirical treatment of this question, it is best to start in a very simple way. Walking speeds of pedestrians in different cities and in cities and towns should be measured and compared. William Berkowitz (16) of Lafayette College has undertaken an extensive series of studies of walking speeds in Philadelphia, New York, and Boston, as well as in small and moder-

ate-sized towns. Berkowitz writes that "there does appear to be a significant linear relation between walking speed and size of municipality, but the absolute size of the difference varies by less than ten percent."

Perhaps the feeling of rapid tempo is due not so much to absolute pedestrian speeds as to the constant need to dodge others in a large city to avoid collisions with other pedestrians. (One basis for computing the adjustments needed to avoid collisions is to hypothesize a set of mechanical manikins sent walking along a city street and to calculate the number of collisions when no adjustments are made. Clearly, the higher the density of manikins the greater the number of collisions per unit of time, or, conversely, the greater the frequency of adjustments needed in higher population densities to avoid collisions.)

Patterns of automobile traffic contribute to a city's tempo. Driving an automobile provides a direct means of translating feelings about tempo into measurable acceleration, and a city's pace should be particularly evident in vehicular velocities, patterns of acceleration, and latency of response to traffic signals. The inexorable tempo of New York is expressed, further, in the manner in which pedestrians stand at busy intersections, impatiently awaiting a change in traffic light, making tentative excursions into the intersection, and frequently surging into the street even before the green light appears.

Visual Components

Hall has remarked (17) that the physical layout of the city also affects its atmosphere. A gridiron pattern of streets gives the visitor a feeling of rationality, orderliness, and predictability but is sometimes monotonous. Winding lanes or streets branching off at strange angles, with many forks (as in Paris or Greenwich Village), create feelings of surprise and esthetic pleasure, while forcing greater decision-making in plotting one's course. Some would argue that the visual component is all-important—that the "look" of Paris or New York can almost be equated with its atmosphere. To investigate this hypothesis, we might conduct studies in which only blind, or at least blindfolded, respondents were used. We would no doubt discover that each city has a distinctive texture even when the visual component is eliminated.

Sources of Ambiance

Thus far we have tried to pinpoint and measure some of the factors that contribute to the distinctive atmosphere of a great city. But we may also ask, Why do differences in urban atmosphere exist? How did they come about, and are they in any way related to the factors of density, large numbers, and heterogeneity discussed above?

First, there is the obvious factor that, even among great cities, populations and densities differ. The metropolitan areas of New York, London, and Paris, for example, contain 15 million, 12 million, and 8 million persons, respectively. London has average densities of 43 persons per acre, while Paris is more congested, with average densities of 114 persons per acre (18). Whatever characteristics are specifically attributable to density are more likely to be pronounced in Paris than in London.

A second factor affecting the atmosphere of cities is the source from which the populations are drawn (19). It is a characteristic of great cities that they do not reproduce their own populations, but that their numbers are constantly maintained and augmented by the influx of residents from other parts of the country. This can have a determining effect on the city's atmosphere. For example, Oslo is a city in which almost all of the residents are only one or two generations removed from a purely rural existence, and this contributes to its almost agricultural norms.

A third source of atmosphere is the general national culture. Paris combines adaptations to the demography of cities *and* certain values specific to French culture. New York is an admixture of American values and values that arise as a result of extraordinarily high density and large population.

Finally, one could speculate that the atmosphere of a great city is traceable to the specific historical conditions under which adaptations to urban overload occurred. For example, a city which acquired its mass and density during a period of commercial expansion will respond to new demographic conditions by adaptations designed to serve purely commercial needs. Thus, Chicago, which grew and became a great city under a purely commercial stimulus, adapted in a manner that emphasizes business needs. European capitals, on the other hand, incorporate many of the adaptations which were appropriate to the period of their increasing numbers and density. Because aristocratic values were prevalent at the time of the growth of these cities, the mechanisms developed for coping with overload were based on considerations other than pure efficiency. Thus, the manners, norms, and facilities of Paris and Vienna continue to reflect esthetic values and the idealization of leisure.

Cognitive Maps of Cities

When we speak of "behavioral comparisons" among cities, we must specify which parts of the city are most relevant for sampling purposes. In a sampling of "New Yorkers," should we include residents of Bay Ridge or Flatbush as well as inhabitants of Manhattan? And, if so, how should we weight our sample distribution? One approach to defining relevant boundaries in sampling is to determine which areas form the psychological or cognitive core of the city. We weight our samples most heavily in the areas considered by most people to represent the "essence" of the city.

The psychologist is less interested in the geographic layout of a city or in its political boundaries than in the cognitive representation of the city. Hans Blumenfeld (20) points out that the perceptual structure of a modern city can be expressed by the "silhouette" of the group of skyscrapers at its center and that of smaller groups of office buildings at its "subcenters" but that urban areas can no longer, because of their vast extent, be experienced as fully articulated sets of streets, squares, and space.

In *The Image of the City* (21), Kevin Lynch created a cognitive map of Boston by interviewing Bostonians. Perhaps his most significant finding was that,

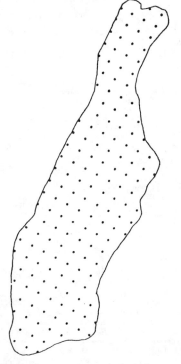

Fig. 2. To create a psychological map of Manhattan, geographic points are sampled, and, from photographs, the subjects attempt to identify the location of each point. To each point a numerical index is assigned indicating the proportion of persons able to identify its location.

while certain landmarks, such as Paul Revere's house and the Boston Common, as well as the paths linking them, are known to almost all Bostonians, vast areas of the city are simply unknown to its inhabitants.

Using Lynch's technique, Donald Hooper (22) created a psychological map of New York from the answers to the study questionnaire on Paris, London, and New York. Hooper's results were similar to those of Lynch: New York appears to have a dense core of well-known landmarks in midtown Manhattan, surrounded by the vast unknown reaches of Queens, Brooklyn, and the Bronx. Times Square, Rockefeller Center, and the Fifth Avenue department stores alone comprise half the places specifically cited by respondents as the haunts in which they spent most of their time. However, outside the midtown area, only scattered landmarks were recognized. Another interesting pattern is evident: even the best-known symbols of New York are relatively self-contained, and the pathways joining them appear to be insignificant on the map.

The psychological map can be used for more than just sampling techniques. Lynch (21) argues, for instance, that a good city is highly "imageable," having many known symbols joined by widely known pathways, whereas dull cities are gray and nondescript. We might test the relative "imagibility" of several cities by determining the proportion of residents who recognize sampled geographic points and their accompanying pathways.

If we wanted to be even more precise we could construct a cognitive map that would not only show the symbols of the city but would measure the precise degree of cognitive significance of any given point in the city relative to any other. By applying a pattern of points to a map of New York City, for example, and taking photographs from each point, we could determine what proportion of a sample of the city's inhabitants could identify the locale specified by each point (see Fig. 2). We might even take the subjects blindfolded to a point represented on the map, then remove the blindfold and ask them to identify their location from the view around them.

One might also use psychological maps to gain insight into the differing perceptions of a given city that are held by members of its cultural subgroups, and into the manner in which their perceptions may change. In the earlier stages of life, whites and Negroes alike probably have only a limited view of the city, centering on the immediate neighborhood in which they are raised. In adolescence, however, the field of knowledge of the white teen-ager probably undergoes rapid enlargement; he learns of opportunities in midtown and outlying sections and comes to see himself as functioning in a larger urban field. But the process of ghettoization, to which the black teen-ager is subjected, may well hamper the expansion of his sense of the city. These are speculative notions, but they are readily subject to precise test.

Conclusion

I have tried to indicate some organizing theory that starts with the basic facts of city life: large numbers, density, and heterogeneity. These are external to the individual. He experiences these factors as overloads at the level of roles, norms, cognitive functions, and facilities. These overloads lead to adaptive mechanisms which create the distinctive tone and behaviors of city life. These notions, of course, need to be examined by objective comparative studies of cities and towns.

A second perspective concerns the differing atmospheres of great cities, such as Paris, London, and New York. Each has a distinctive flavor, offering a differentiable quality of experience. More precise knowledge of urban atmosphere seems attainable through application of the tools of experimental inquiry.

References and Notes

1. *New York Times* (15 June 1969).
2. L. Wirth, *Amer. J. Soc.* 44, 1 (1938). Wirth's ideas have come under heavy criticism by contemporary city planners, who point out that the city is broken down into neighborhoods, which fulfill many of the functions of small towns. See, for example, H. J. Gans, *People and Plans: Essays on Urban Problems and Solutions* (Basic Books, New York, 1968); J. Jacobs, *The Death and Life of Great American Cities* (Random House, New York, 1961); G. D. Suttles, *The Social Order of the Slum* (Univ. of Chicago Press, Chicago, 1968).
3. G. Simmel, *The Sociology of Georg Simmel*, K. H. Wolff, Ed. (Macmillan, New York, 1950) [English translation of G. Simmel, *Die Grossstadte und das Geistesleben Die Grossstadt* (Jansch, Dresden, 1903)].
4. R. L. Meier, *A Communications Theory of Urban Growth* (M.I.T. Press, Cambridge, Mass., 1962).
5. S. Milgram and P. Hollander, *Nation* 25, 602 (1964).
6. B. Latané and J. Darley, *Amer. Sci.* 57, 244 (1969).
7. S. Gaertner and L. Bickman (Graduate Center, The City University of New York), unpublished research.
8. D. Altman, M. Levine, M. Nadien, J. Villena (Graduate Center, The City University of New York), unpublished research.
9. P. G. Zimbardo, paper presented at the Nebraska Symposium on Motivation (1969).
10. J. Waters (Graduate Center, The City University of New York), unpublished research.
11. W. McKenna and S. Morgenthau (Graduate Center, The City University of New York), unpublished research.
12. N. Abuza (Harvard University), "The Paris-London-New York Questionnaires," unpublished.
13. P. Abelson, *Science* 165, 853 (1969).
14. A. L. Strauss, Ed., *The American City: A Sourcebook of Urban Imagery* (Aldine, Chicago, 1968).
15. R. E. Feldman, *J. Personality Soc. Psychol.* 10, 202 (1968).
16. W. Berkowitz, personal communication.
17. E. T. Hall, *The Hidden Dimension* (Doubleday, New York, 1966).
18. P. Hall, *The World Cities* (McGraw-Hill, New York, 1966).
19. R. E. Park, E. W. Burgess, R. D. McKenzie, *The City* (Univ. of Chicago Press, Chicago, 1967), pp. 1–45.
20. H. Blumenfeld, in *The Quality of Urban Life* (Sage, Beverly Hills, Calif., 1969).
21. K. Lynch, *The Image of the City* (M.I.T. and Harvard Univ. Press, Cambridge, Mass., 1960).
22. D. Hooper (Harvard University), unpublished.
23. Barbara Bengen worked closely with me in preparing the present version of this article. I thank Dr. Gary Winkel, editor of *Environment and Behavior*, for useful suggestions and advice.

The Social Environment

René Dubos

1. PHYSIOLOGICAL RESPONSES TO POPULATION DENSITY

The word crowd has unpleasant connotations. It evokes disease, pestilence, and group-generated attitudes often irrational and either too submissive or too aggressive. Congested cities call to mind unhealthy complexions and harassed behavior; city crowds are accused of accepting despotic power and of blindly engaging in acts of violence. In contrast, rural areas and small towns are thought to foster health and freedom. The legendary Arcadia and the Utopias of all times are imagined as comfortably populated by human beings enjoying vast horizons. The nature and history of man are far too complex, of course, to justify such generalizations, but there is some truth nevertheless in the belief that crowding generates problems of disease and behavior. However, these problems are poorly understood and their formulation is rendered even more difficult by a number of oversimplified and erroneous concepts inherited from the late nineteenth century.

During the Industrial Revolution, the crowding in tenements, factories, and offices was associated with tremendous increases in morbidity and mortality rates. Along with malnutrition, the various "fevers" were the most obvious causes of ill health. Epidemic outbreaks and chronic forms of microbial disease constituted the largest medical problems of the late nineteenth century because they were extremely prevalent, not only among the economically destitute but also among the more favored classes. The new science of microbiology that developed during that period provided a theory that appeared sufficient at first sight to explain the explosive spread of infection. The germ theory made it obvious that crowding facilitates the transfer of microbes from one person to another, and this led to the reasonable conclusion that the newly industrialized communities had been caught in a web of infection, resulting from the increase in human contacts.

The expression "crowd diseases" thus became, and has remained ever since, identified with a state of affairs conducive to the rapid spread of infective agents, particularly under unsanitary conditions. Epidemiologists have built their science on the hypothesis that the pattern of microbial diseases in a given community of animals or men is determined by the channels available for the spread of microbes. In reality, however, the rise and fall of animal populations, both in confined environments and in the field, present aspects that cannot be entirely accounted for by these classical concepts of epidemiology. The reason, as we shall now see, is that crowding has several independent effects. On the one hand, it facilitates the spread of infective agents; on the other hand, it also modifies the manner in which men and animals respond to the presence of these agents and thereby increases indirectly the prevalence and severity of microbial disease. In fact, crowding affects the response of the individual and social body, not only to infection, but also to most of life's stresses.

In many species, the numbers of animals increase continuously from year to year until a maximum population density is reached; then suddenly an enormous mortality descends. This phenomenon, known as "population crash," has long been assumed to be caused by epidemics corresponding to those which have been so destructive in the

MAN ADAPTING, New Haven, Conn.: Yale University Press, 1965, pp. 100-109.

course of human history, for example plague or yellow fever. Indeed, several different kinds of pathogens have been found to attack animal populations at the time of the crash. Pasteurellae and salmonellae are among the bacterial organisms that used to be most commonly incriminated; two decades ago a particular strain of *Mycobacterium muris* (the vole bacillus), isolated from field mice in England, was thought for a while to be responsible for population crashes in these rodents. Now that viruses have taken the limelight from bacteria, they in turn have been made responsible for occurrences of widespread mortality in several animal species.

It has become apparent, however, that the relation between population crashes and microbial diseases is far less clear than was once thought. On the one hand, several different types of pathogens can be associated with crashes in a given animal species. On the other hand, there are certain crashes for which no pathogen has been found to account for the pathological picture. These puzzling observations have led to the theory that the microbial diseases associated with population crashes are but secondary phenomena, and that the primary cause is a metabolic disturbance.

Food shortages, or at least nutritional deficiencies, were long considered as a probable cause of drastic population decline. It is well known, in fact, that when wild animals multiply without check under natural conditions they exhaust their food supply, lose weight, and bear fewer young; this occurs for example when their predators are eliminated. However, a poor nutritional state can hardly account alone for population crashes. Its effect is rather to limit reproduction, either by failure of conception or by abortion; the overall result is an automatic adjustment of population size to the food supply instead of a massive crash. In fact, drastic population declines commonly occur even when the food supply is abundant.

The trend during recent years has been to explain population crashes by a "shock disease" related in some obscure way to overactivity of the adrenopituitary system. A notorious example of this type of crowd disease is the mass migration of the Norwegian lemmings from the mountaintops of Scandinavia. According to an ancient Norwegian belief, the lemmings periodically experience an irresistible "collective urge" either to commit suicide or to search for their ancestral home on the lost Atlantic Continent, and consequently they march unswervingly into the sea. In reality, such migrations take place whenever the lemmings become overcrowded, a situation that occurs every third or fourth year, as each mating pair produces 13 to 16 young annually. The migration of Norwegian lemmings was so massive in 1960–61 that a steamer entering the Trondheim Fjord took one hour to pass through a two-mile-long pack of swimming and sinking rodents!

Although the nature of the initial stimulus that prompts the lemmings to migrate is not understood, crowding is almost certainly one of its aspects. As the rodents become more and more crowded they fall victims to a kind of mass psychosis. This results in a wild scrambling about that, contrary to legend, is not necessarily a march toward the sea but merely random movement. The animals die, not by drowning, but from metabolic derangements associated with stress; lesions are commonly found in the brain and the adrenals.

Profound changes have also been observed to occur at more or less regular intervals in the population of snowshoe hares. According to a classical description, these animals observed in Minnesota during periods of crash

> . . . characteristically died in convulsive seizures with sudden onset, running movements, hind leg extension, retraction of the head and neck, and sudden leaps with clonic seizures upon alighting. Other animals were typically lethargic or comatose. . . . This syndrome was characterized primarily by decrease in liver glycogen and a hypoglycemia preceding death. Petechial or ecchymotic brain hemorrhages, and congestion and hemorrhage of the adrenals, thyroid, and kid-

neys were frequent findings (Deevey, 1960).

Interestingly enough, many of the signs and symptoms observed in wild animals dying during population crashes have been reproduced in the laboratory by subjecting experimental animals to crowding and other forms of stress. Voles placed for a few hours a day during a month in cages containing another pair of aggressive voles eventually died, but not of wounds. The main finding at necropsy was a marked increase in the weight of their adrenals and spleen and a decrease in the weight of the thymus. Similar findings have been made in captive and wild rats.

Crowding can act as a form of stress in most species of experimental animals. In chickens, mice, rats, and voles, it causes an enlargement of the adrenals chiefly through cellular hyperplasia in the cortical areas; in addition it interferes with both growth and reproductive function.

Crowding affects many other biological characteristics of animal population; for example, the reproducibility of the response to various abnormal states, such as barbiturate anaesthesia, is affected by population density. The toxicity of central nervous system stimulants such as amphetamine is remarkably enhanced when the animals are placed in a crowded environment; central depressants protect to some degree against this aggregation effect. The experimental hypertension produced in rats bearing regenerating adrenals is increased by crowding, and coronary arteriosclerosis develops more rapidly and more intensely in chickens that are grouped than in animals kept isolated.

Field studies of voles in England have revealed the puzzling fact that their population continues to fall the year after the crash. It would appear, therefore, that the reduced viability responsible for the crash is transmitted from one generation to another. This finding is compatible with other observations which indicate that crowding of the mother affects the physical development and behavior of the offspring.

The response to almost any kind of stimulus can be modified by crowding, as is illustrated by the production of experimental granuloma. Cotton pellets impregnated with turpentine were introduced subcutaneously into groups of mice that were then either caged individually or in groups. The granulomas that developed in the grouped mice weighed 19 percent less than in the other animals, a result probably due to the fact that the greater adrenocortical activity in the grouped mice had exerted a suppressive effect on the inflammatory reaction.

It is probable that the effect of crowding on tissue response accounts for the decrease in resistance to infection. In order to put this hypothesis to the test, mice were infected with a standardized dose of *Trichinella* and then were either isolated in individual jars or caged in groups immediately after infection. When these mice were sacrificed 15 days later, it was found that all the grouped animals had large numbers of worms (15 to 51) in their intestines, whereas only 3 out of 12 of the isolated animals showed any sign of infection. Although exposure to infection had been identical, crowding had therefore increased the ability of trichinella to invade the intestinal wall, probably by decreasing the inflammatory response to the parasite. Analogous observations have been made with regard to infantile diarrhea of mice. The incidence of clinical signs of this disease remains small or is nil when the population density in the animal room is low, but it increases as the colony approaches peak production. The infection is endemic in most colonies, but the disease does not become overt until the animals are crowded.

The groupings of several organisms of one given species has certainly many physiological consequences more subtle than those mentioned above. One such curious effect has been observed in male ducks kept constantly either in the dark or exposed to artificial light for periods of over two years. In both cases, these abnormal conditions of light exposure resulted in marked disturbances of the sexual cycles, which were no longer in phase with the seasonal rhythms. However, the animals within each group exhibited a remarkable synchronism of testicular evolution, thus revealing a "group effect" on sexual activity that was independent of light, of season, and of the presence of animals of the opposite sex.

2. TERRITORIALITY, DOMINANCE, AND ADAPTATION TO CROWDING

As we have just seen, the epidemiology of "crowd" diseases involves factors other than those affecting the spread of infectious agents. Association with other living things modifies the total response of the organism to the various environmental forces and thereby affects susceptibility to a multiplicity of noxious influences, including infection.

A quantitative statement of population density is not sufficient, however, to forecast the effects of crowding on human beings or animals. Even more important than numbers of specimens of a given species per unit area is the manner in which each particular person or animal responds to the other members of the group under a given set of conditions. The response to population density is determined in large part by the history of the group and of its individual members; furthermore, it may be favorable or unfavorable, depending upon the circumstances.

Many types of rodents, such as laboratory rats and mice, prefer to be somewhat crowded. In fact, individually housed rats and mice usually behave in a more "emotional" or "frightened" manner than their group-housed counterparts; they are also less able to adapt to a variety of experimental procedures such as food restriction, food selection, or cold stress. Isolated mice are less able than grouped mice to overcome the disturbances in intestinal ecology caused by antimicrobial drugs and other physiological disturbances (unpublished observations). The practice of mutual cleaning accelerates wound healing in many animal species, and isolation has unfavorable effects on the behavior and personality structure of animals and man.

In most animal species, probably in all, each group develops a complex social organization based on territoriality and on a social hierarchy comprising subordinate and dominant members, the so-called pecking order. The place of each animal in the hierarchy is probably determined in part by anatomical and physiological endowments and in part by the history of the group. In any case, the behavioral differences that result from the pecking order eventually bring about anatomical and physiological differences far more profound than those initially present. For example, the dominant animals usually have larger adrenals than the subordinates and they grow more rapidly because they have more ready access to food. It appears also that in rhesus monkeys the young males issued from females with a high social rank have a better chance than other males to become dominant in the colony.

Under a given set of conditions, the relative rank of each individual animal is fairly predictable. Social competition is often restricted to the male sex, the reproductive fortunes of the female being determined by the status of the male which selects her. Females associated with subordinate males in experimental populations may entirely fail to reproduce. However, the pecking order is valid only for well-defined environmental conditions. For example, each canary bird is dominant in the region near its nest; and similarly chickens in their home yard win more combats than strangers to that yard. The successes of animals on their own territorial grounds bring to mind the better performance of baseball teams on their home fields.

Successful competition within the group naturally confers advantages. The despot has first choice with regard to food and mates, and its position may even increase its resistance to certain forms of stress such as infection. In a particular experiment involving tenches, one fish in the group was found to dominate the whole territory and to be the first one to feed. This dominance had such profound physiological consequences that when all the tenches were infected with trypanosomes, the infection disappeared first from the dominant fish. When this fish was removed from the tank, fighting started among those remaining; the fish that became dominant in the new grouping in its turn had first access to the food, and soon got rid of its trypanosome infection.

The phenomenon of dominance has a social meaning which transcends the advantages that it gives to the dominant individuals. Acceptance of the hierarchical order reduces fighting and other forms of social tensions and thus provides a stability that is beneficial to the group as a whole. In an undisturbed organized flock of chickens, for example, the individual animals peck each other less frequently and less violently, eat more, maintain weight better, and lay more eggs than do chickens in flocks undergoing social reorganization through removal of some animals or addition of new ones. Furthermore, the subordinate animals do not suffer as much as could be expected from their low rank in the pecking order. There is no direct competition for food or for mates in the well-organized group; the subordinates readily yield their place to the dominants at the feeding box; they exhibit no sexual interest, often behaving as if they were "socially castrated." Thus, the establishment of an accepted hierarchy in a stable group of animals almost eliminates the stresses of social tension and results in a kind of social homeostasis.

Needless to say, there are limits to the protective efficacy social organization can provide against the dangers created by high population density. Excessive crowding has deleterious effects even in the most gregarious rodents. When laboratory rats are allowed to multiply without restriction in a confined space, an excess of food being available at all times, they develop abnormal behavior with regard to mating, nest building, and care of the young as soon as the population becomes too dense. However, such conditions of life are extremely artificial. Under the usual conditions of rodent life in the wild, animals migrate or are killed when the population becomes too large for the amount of food available.

Although man is a gregarious animal, sudden increases in population density can be as dangerous for him as they are for animals. The biological disturbances created during the Industrial Revolution by lack of sanitation and by crowding in tenements and factories were aggravated by the fact that most members of the new labor class had immigrated from rural areas and were totally unadapted to urban life. In contrast, the world is now becoming more and more urbanized. Constant and intimate contact with hordes of human beings has come to constitute the "normal" way of life, and men have eagerly adjusted to it. This change has certainly brought about all kinds of phenotypic adaptations that are making it easier for urban man to respond successfully to situations that in the past constituted biological and emotional threats.

There may be here an analogy with the fact that domesticated animals do not respond to various types of threatening situations in the laboratory as do wild animals of the same or related species. In any case, the effects of crowding on modern urban man are certainly very different from those experienced by the farmer and his family when they were first and suddenly exposed a century ago to the city environment of industrialized societies.

The readiness with which man adapts to potentially dangerous situations makes it unwise to apply directly to human life the results of experiments designed to test the acute effects of crowding on animals. Under normal circumstances, the dangerous consequences of crowding are mollified by a multiplicity of biological and social adaptations. In fact, crowding per se, that is, population density, is probably far less important in the long run even in animals than is the intensity of the social conflicts, or the relative peace achieved after social adjustments have been made. As already mentioned, animal populations in which status differences are clearly established are likely to reach a greater size than those in which differences in rank are less well defined.

Little is known concerning the density

of population or the intensity of stimulation that is optimum in the long run for the body and the mind of man. Crowding is a relative term. The biological significance of population density must be evaluated in the light of the past experience of the group concerned, because this experience conditions the manner in which each of its members responds to the others as well as to environmental stimuli and trauma.

Laying claim to a territory and maintaining a certain distance from one's fellow are probably as real biological needs in man as they are in animals, but their expressions are culturally conditioned. The proper distance between persons in a group varies from culture to culture. People reared in cultures where the proper distance is short appear "pushy" to those coming from social groups where propriety demands greater physical separation. In contrast, the latter will appear to the former as behaving in a cold, aloof, withdrawn, and standoffish manner. Although social anthropologists have not yet adequately explained the origin of these differences, they have provided evidence that ignorance of them in human relations or in the design of dwellings and hospitals can have serious social and pathological consequences.

The problems posed by crowding in human populations are thus more complex than those which exist in animal populations because they are so profoundly conditioned by social and cultural determinants. Indeed, there is probably no aspect of human life for which it is easier to agree with Ortega y Gasset that "man has no nature. What he has is a history." Most experimental biologists are inclined to scorn discussions of mob psychology and related problems because they feel that the time is not yet ripe for scientific studies on the mechanisms of collective behavior. Yet the phrase "mob psychology" serves at least to emphasize that the response of human beings to any situation is profoundly influenced by the structure of the social environment.

The numerous outbreaks of dancing manias that occurred in Europe from the fourteenth to sixteenth century constitute a picturesque illustration of abnormal collective behavior; such an event was witnessed by P. Breughel the Elder and became the subject of one of his most famous paintings, "The Saint Vitus Dancers," now in Vienna. Even today, revivalists, tremblers and shakers often outdo the feats of the medieval performers during the dancing manias. And millions of people can still be collectively bewitched by the antics of a Hitler or other self-proclaimed prophet, to whom they yield body and soul. What happens in the mind of man is always reflected in the diseases of his body. The epidemiology of crowd diseases cannot be completely understood without knowledge of mob psychology.

REFERENCE:

Deevey, E. S. The hare and the haruspex: A cautionary tale. *American Scientist*, 1960, **48**, 415–429.

BYSTANDER INTERVENTION IN EMERGENCIES:

DIFFUSION OF RESPONSIBILITY [1]

JOHN M. DARLEY   AND   BIBB LATANÉ

Ss overheard an epileptic seizure. They believed either that they alone heard the emergency, or that 1 or 4 unseen others were also present. As predicted the presence of other bystanders reduced the individual's feelings of personal responsibility and lowered his speed of reporting ($p < .01$). In groups of size 3, males reported no faster than females, and females reported no slower when the 1 other bystander was a male rather than a female. In general, personality and background measures were not predictive of helping. Bystander inaction in real-life emergencies is often explained by "apathy," "alienation," and "anomie." This experiment suggests that the explanation may lie more in the bystander's response to other observers than in his indifference to the victim.

Several years ago, a young woman was stabbed to death in the middle of a street in a residential section of New York City. Although such murders are not entirely routine, the incident received little public attention until several weeks later when the New York Times disclosed another side to the case: at least 38 witnesses had observed the attack—and none had even attempted to intervene. Although the attacker took more than half an hour to kill Kitty Genovese, not one of the 38 people who watched from the safety of their own apartments came out to assist her. Not one even lifted the telephone to call the police (Rosenthal, 1964).

Preachers, professors, and news commentators sought the reasons for such apparently conscienceless and inhumane lack of intervention. Their conclusions ranged from "moral decay," to "dehumanization produced by the urban environment," to "alienation," "anomie," and "existential despair." An analysis of the situation, however, suggests that factors other than apathy and indifference were involved.

A person witnessing an emergency situation, particularly such a frightening and

dangerous one as a stabbing, is in conflict. There are obvious humanitarian norms about helping the victim, but there are also rational and irrational fears about what might happen to a person who does intervene (Milgram & Hollander, 1964). "I didn't want to get involved," is a familiar comment, and behind it lies fears of physical harm, public embarrassment, involvement with police procedures, lost work days and jobs, and other unknown dangers.

In certain circumstances, the norms favoring intervention may be weakened, leading bystanders to resolve the conflict in the direction of nonintervention. One of these circumstances may be the presence of other onlookers. For example, in the case above, each observer, by seeing lights and figures in other apartment house windows, knew that others were also watching. However, there was no way to tell how the other observers were reacting. These two facts provide several reasons why any individual may have delayed or failed to help. The responsibility for helping was diffused among the observers; there was also diffusion of any potential blame for not taking action; and finally, it was possible that somebody, unperceived, had already initiated helping action.

When only one bystander is present in an emergency, if help is to come, it must come from him. Although he may choose to ignore it (out of concern for his personal safety, or desires "not to get involved"), any pres-

[1] This research was supported in part by National Science Foundation Grants GS1238 and GS1239. Susan Darley contributed materially to the design of the experiment and ran the subjects, and she and Thomas Moriarty analyzed the data. Richard Nisbett, Susan Millman, Andrew Gordon, and Norma Neiman helped in preparing the tape recordings.

JOURNAL OF PERSONALITY AND SOCIAL PSYCHOLOGY, 1968, Vol. 8, pp. 377-383.

sure to intervene focuses uniquely on him. When there are several observers present, however, the pressures to intervene do not focus on any one of the observers; instead the responsibility for intervention is shared among all the onlookers and is not unique to any one. As a result, no one helps.

A second possibility is that potential blame may be diffused. However much we may wish to think that an individual's moral behavior is divorced from considerations of personal punishment or reward, there is both theory and evidence to the contrary (Aronfreed, 1964; Miller & Dollard, 1941, Whiting & Child, 1953). It is perfectly reasonable to assume that, under circumstances of group responsibility for a punishable act, the punishment or blame that accrues to any one individual is often slight or nonexistent.

Finally, if others are known to be present, but their behavior cannot be closely observed, any one bystander can assume that one of the other observers is already taking action to end the emergency. Therefore, his own intervention would be only redundant—perhaps harmfully or confusingly so. Thus, given the presence of other onlookers whose behavior cannot be observed, any given bystander can rationalize his own inaction by convincing himself that "somebody else must be doing something."

These considerations lead to the hypothesis that the more bystanders to an emergency, the less likely, or the more slowly, any one bystander will intervene to provide aid. To test this proposition it would be necessary to create a situation in which a realistic "emergency" could plausibly occur. Each subject should also be blocked from communicating with others to prevent his getting information about their behavior during the emergency. Finally, the experimental situation should allow for the assessment of the speed and frequency of the subjects' reaction to the emergency. The experiment reported below attempted to fulfill these conditions.

PROCEDURE

Overview. A college student arrived in the laboratory and was ushered into an individual room from which a communication system would enable him to talk to the other participants. It was explained to him that he was to take part in a discussion about personal problems associated with college life and that the discussion would be held over the intercom system, rather than face-to-face, in order to avoid embarrassment by preserving the anonymity of the subjects. During the course of the discussion, one of the other subjects underwent what appeared to be a very serious nervous seizure similar to epilepsy. During the fit it was impossible for the subject to talk to the other discussants or to find out what, if anything, they were doing about the emergency. The dependent variable was the speed with which the subjects reported the emergency to the experimenter. The major independent variable was the number of people the subject thought to be in the discussion group.

Subjects. Fifty-nine female and thirteen male students in introductory psychology courses at New York University were contacted to take part in an unspecified experiment as part of a class requirement.

Method. Upon arriving for the experiment, the subject found himself in a long corridor with doors opening off it to several small rooms. An experimental assistant met him, took him to one of the rooms, and seated him at a table. After filling out a background information form, the subject was given a pair of headphones with an attached microphone and was told to listen for instructions.

Over the intercom, the experimenter explained that he was interested in learning about the kinds of personal problems faced by normal college students in a high pressure, urban environment. He said that to avoid possible embarrassment about discussing personal problems with strangers several precautions had been taken. First, subjects would remain anonymous, which was why they had been placed in individual rooms rather than face-to-face. (The actual reason for this was to allow tape recorder simulation of the other subjects and the emergency.) Second, since the discussion might be inhibited by the presence of outside listeners, the experimenter would not listen to the initial discussion, but would get the subject's reactions later, by questionnaire. (The real purpose of this was to remove the obviously responsible experimenter from the scene of the emergency.)

The subjects were told that since the experimenter was not present, it was necessary to impose some organization. Each person would talk in turn, presenting his problems to the group. Next, each person in turn would comment on what the others had said, and finally, there would be a free discussion. A mechanical switching device would regulate this discussion sequence and each subject's microphone would be on for about 2 minutes. While any microphone was on, all other microphones would be off. Only one subject, therefore, could be heard over the network at any given time. The subjects were thus led to realize when they later heard the seizure that only the victim's microphone was on and that there was no way of determining what any of the other witnesses were doing, nor of discussing the event and its possible solution with the others. When these instructions had been given, the discussion began.

In the discussion, the future victim spoke first, saying that he found it difficult to get adjusted to New York City and to his studies. Very hesitantly, and with obvious embarrassment, he mentioned that he was prone to seizures, particularly when studying hard or taking exams. The other people, including the real subject, took their turns and discussed similar problems (minus, of course, the proneness to seizures). The naive subject talked last in the series, after the last prerecorded voice was played.[2]

When it was again the victim's turn to talk, he made a few relatively calm comments, and then, growing increasingly louder and incoherent, he continued:

I-er-um-I think I-I need-er-if-if could-er-er-somebody er-er-er-er-er-er-er give me a little-er-give me a little help here because-er-I-er-I'm-er-er-h-h-having a-a-a real problem-er-right now and I-er-if somebody could help me out it would-it would-er-er s-s-sure be-sure be good . . . because-er-there-er-er-a cause I-er-I-uh-I've got a-a one of the-er-sei-----er-er-things coming on and-and-and I could really-er-use some help so if somebody would-er-give me a little h-help-uh-er-er-er-er-er c-could somebody-er-er-help-er-uh-uh-uh (choking sounds). . . . I'm gonna die-er-er-I'm . . . gonna die-er-help-er-er-seizure-er-[chokes, then quiet].

The experimenter began timing the speed of the real subject's response at the beginning of the victim's speech. Informed judges listening to the tape have estimated that the victim's increasingly louder and more disconnected ramblings clearly represented a breakdown about 70 seconds after the signal for the victim's second speech. The victim's speech was abruptly cut off 125 seconds after this signal, which could be interpreted by the subject as indicating that the time allotted for that speaker had elapsed and the switching circuits had switched away from him. Times reported in the results are measured from the start of the fit.

Group size variable. The major independent variable of the study was the number of other people that the subject believed also heard the fit. By the assistant's comments before the experiment, and also by the number of voices heard to speak in the first round of the group discussion, the subject was led to believe that the discussion group was one of three sizes: either a two-person group (consisting of a person who would later have a fit and the real subject), a three-person group (consisting of the victim, the real subject, and one confederate voice), or a six-person group (consisting of the victim, the real subject, and four confederate voices). All the confederates' voices were tape-recorded.

Variations in group composition. Varying the kind as well as the number of bystanders present at an

[2] To test whether the order in which the subjects spoke in the first discussion round significantly affected the subjects' speed of report, the order in which the subjects spoke was varied (in the six-person group). This had no significant or noticeable effect on the speed of the subjects' reports.

emergency should also vary the amount of responsibility felt ·by any single bystander. To test this, several variations of the three-person group were run. In one three-person condition, the taped bystander voice was that of a female, in another a male, and in the third a male who said that he was a premedical student who occasionally worked in the emergency wards at Bellevue hospital.

In the above conditions, the subjects were female college students. In a final condition males drawn from the same introductory psychology subject pool were tested in a three-person female-bystander condition.

Time to help. The major dependent variable was the time elapsed from the start of the victim's fit until the subject left her experimental cubicle. When the subject left her room, she saw the experimental assistant seated at the end of the hall, and invariably went to the assistant. If 6 minutes elapsed without the subject having emerged from her room, the experiment was terminated.

As soon as the subject reported the emergency, or after 6 minutes had elapsed, the experimental assistant disclosed the true nature of the experiment, and dealt with any emotions aroused in the subject. Finally the subject filled out a questionnaire concerning her thoughts and feelings during the emergency, and completed scales of Machiavellianism, anomie, and authoritarianism (Christie, 1964), a social desirability scale (Crowne & Marlowe, 1964), a social responsibility scale (Daniels & Berkowitz, 1964), and reported vital statistics and socioeconomic data.

RESULTS

Plausibility of Manipulation

Judging by the subjects' nervousness when they reported the fit to the experimenter, by their surprise when they discovered that the fit was simulated, and by comments they made during the fit (when they thought their microphones were off), one can conclude that almost all of the subjects perceived the fit as real. There were two exceptions in different experimental conditions, and the data for these subjects were dropped from the analysis.

Effect of Group Size on Helping

The number of bystanders that the subject perceived to be present had a major effect on the likelihood with which she would report the emergency (Table 1). Eighty-five percent of the subjects who thought they alone knew of the victim's plight reported the seizure before the victim was cut off, only 31% of those who thought four other bystanders were present did so.

Every one of the subjects in the two-person groups, but only 62% of the subjects in the six-person groups, ever reported the emergency. The cumulative distributions of response times for groups of different perceived size (Figure 1) indicates that, by any point in time, more subjects from the two-person groups had responded than from the three-person groups, and more from the three-person groups than from the six-person groups.

Ninety-five percent of all the subjects who ever responded did so within the first half of the time available to them. No subject who had not reported within 3 minutes after the fit ever did so. The shape of these distributions suggest that had the experiment been allowed to run for a considerably longer time, few additional subjects would have responded.

Speed of Response

To achieve a more detailed analysis of the results, each subject's time score was trans-

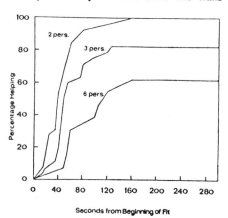

FIG. 1. Cumulative distributions of helping responses.

formed into a "speed" score by taking the reciprocal of the response time in seconds and multiplying by 100. The effect of this transformation was to deemphasize differences between longer time scores, thus reducing the contribution to the results of the arbitrary 6-minute limit on scores. A high speed score indicates a fast response.

An analysis of variance indicates that the effect of group size is highly significant ($p < .01$). Duncan multiple-range tests indicate that all but the two- and three-person groups differ significantly from one another ($p < .05$).

Victim's Likelihood of Being Helped

An individual subject is less likely to respond if he thinks that others are present. But what of the victim? Is the inhibition of the response of each individual strong enough to counteract the fact that with five onlookers there are five times as many people available to help? From the data of this experiment, it is possible mathematically to create hypothetical groups with one, two, or five observers.[3] The calculations indicate that the victim is about equally likely to get help from one bystander as from two. The victim is considerably more likely to have gotten help from one or two observers than from five during the first minute of the fit. For instance, by 45 seconds after the start of the fit, the victim's chances of having been helped by the single bystanders were about 50%, compared to none in the five observer condition. After the first minute, the likelihood of getting help from at least one person is high in all three conditions.

Effect of Group Composition on Helping the Victim

Several variations of the three-person group were run. In one pair of variations, the female subject thought the other bystander was either male or female; in another, she thought the other bystander was a premedical student who worked in an emergency ward at Bellevue hospital. As Table 2 shows, the

[3] The formula for the probability that at least one person will help by a given time is $1 - (1 - P)^n$ where n is the number of observers and P is the probability of a single individual (who thinks he is one of n observers) helping by that time.

TABLE 2

EFFECTS OF GROUP COMPOSITION ON LIKELIHOOD
AND SPEED OF RESPONSE[a]

Group composition	N	% responding by end of fit	Time in sec.	Speed score
Female S, male other	13	62	94	74
Female S, female other	13	62	92	71
Female S, male medic other	5	100	60	77
Male S, female other	13	69	110	68

[a] Three-person group, male victim.

variations in sex and medical competence of the other bystander had no important or detectable affect on speed of response. Subjects responded equally frequently and fast whether the other bystander was female, male, or medically experienced.

Sex of the Subject and Speed of Response

Coping with emergencies is often thought to be the duty of males, especially when females are present, but there was no evidence that this was the case in this study. Male subjects responded to the emergency with almost exactly the same speed as did females (Table 2).

Reasons for Intervention or Nonintervention

After the debriefing at the end of the experiment each subject was given a 15-item checklist and asked to check those thoughts which had "crossed your mind when you heard Subject 1 calling for help." Whatever the condition, each subject checked very few thoughts, and there were no significant differences in number or kind of thoughts in the different experimental groups. The only thoughts checked by more than a few subjects were "I didn't know what to do" (18 out of 65 subjects), "I thought it must be some sort of fake" (20 out of 65), and "I didn't know exactly what was happening" (26 out of 65).

It is possible that subjects were ashamed to report socially undesirable rationalizations, or, since the subjects checked the list *after* the true nature of the experiment had been explained to them, their memories might have been blurred. It is our impression, however, that most subjects checked few reasons because they had few coherent thoughts during the fit.

We asked all subjects whether the presence or absence of other bystanders had entered their minds during the time that they were hearing the fit. Subjects in the three- and six-person groups reported that they were aware that other people were present, but they felt that this made no difference to their own behavior.

Individual Difference Correlates of Speed of Report

The correlations between speed of report and various individual differences on the personality and background measures were obtained by normalizing the distribution of report speeds within each experimental condition and pooling these scores across all conditions ($n = 62-65$). Personality measures showed no important or significant correlations with speed of reporting the emergency. In fact, only one of the 16 individual difference measures, the size of the community in which the subject grew up, correlated ($r = -.26$, $p < .05$) with the speed of helping.

DISCUSSION

Subjects, whether or not they intervened, believed the fit to be genuine and serious. "My God, he's having a fit," many subjects said to themselves (and were overheard via their microphones) at the onset of the fit. Others gasped or simply said "Oh." Several of the male subjects swore. One subject said to herself, "It's just my kind of luck, something has to happen to me!" Several subjects spoke aloud of their confusion about what course of action to take, "Oh God, what should I do?"

When those subjects who intervened stepped out of their rooms, they found the experimental assistant down the hall. With some uncertainty, but without panic, they reported the situation. "Hey, I think Number 1 is very sick. He's having a fit or something." After ostensibly checking on the situation, the experimenter returned to report that "everything is under control." The subjects accepted these assurances with obvious relief.

Subjects who failed to report the emergency showed few signs of the apathy and

65

indifference thought to characterize "unresponsive bystanders." When the experimenter entered her room to terminate the situation, the subject often asked if the victim was "all right." "Is he being taken care of?" "He's all right isn't he?" Many of these subjects showed physical signs of nervousness; they often had trembling hands and sweating palms. If anything, they seemed more emotionally aroused than did the subjects who reported the emergency.

Why, then, didn't they respond? It is our impression that nonintervening subjects had not decided *not* to respond. Rather they were still in a state of indecision and conflict concerning whether to respond or not. The emotional behavior of these nonresponding subjects was a sign of their continuing conflict, a conflict that other subjects resolved by responding.

The fit created a conflict situation of the avoidance-avoidance type. On the one hand, subjects worried about the guilt and shame they would feel if they did not help the person in distress. On the other hand, they were concerned not to make fools of themselves by overreacting, not to ruin the ongoing experiment by leaving their intercom, and not to destroy the anonymous nature of the situation which the experimenter had earlier stressed as important. For subjects in the two-person condition, the obvious distress of the victim and his need for help were so important that their conflict was easily resolved. For the subjects who knew there were other bystanders present, the cost of not helping was reduced and the conflict they were in more acute. Caught between the two negative alternatives of letting the victim continue to suffer or the costs of rushing in to help, the nonresponding bystanders vacillated between them rather than choosing not to respond. This distinction may be academic for the victim, since he got no help in either case, but it is an extremely important one for arriving at an understanding of the causes of bystanders' failures to help.

Although the subjects experienced stress and conflict during the experiment, their general reactions to it were highly positive. On a questionnaire administered after the experimenter had discussed the nature and purpose of the experiment, every single subject found the experiment either "interesting" or "very interesting" and was willing to participate in similar experiments in the future. All subjects felt they understood what the experiment was about and indicated that they thought the deceptions were necessary and justified. All but one felt they were better informed about the nature of psychological research in general.

Male subjects reported the emergency no faster than did females. These results (or lack of them) seem to conflict with the Berkowitz, Klanderman, and Harris (1964) finding that males tend to assume more responsibility and take more initiative than females in giving help to dependent others. Also, females reacted equally fast when the other bystander was another female, a male, or even a person practiced in dealing with medical emergencies. The ineffectiveness of these manipulations of group composition cannot be explained by general insensitivity of the speed measure, since the group-size variable had a marked effect on report speed.

It might be helpful in understanding this lack of difference to distinguish two general classes of intervention in emergency situations: direct and reportorial. Direct intervention (breaking up a fight, extinguishing a fire, swimming out to save a drowner) often requires skill, knowledge, or physical power. It may involve danger. American cultural norms and Berkowitz's results seem to suggest that males are more responsible than females for this kind of direct intervention.

A second way of dealing with an emergency is to report it to someone qualified to handle it, such as the police. For this kind of intervention, there seem to be no norms requiring male action. In the present study, subjects clearly intended to report the emergency rather than take direct action. For such indirect intervention, sex or medical competence does not appear to affect one's qualifications or responsibilities. Anybody, male or female, medically trained or not, can find the experimenter.

In this study, no subject was able to tell how the other subjects reacted to the fit. (Indeed, there were no other subjects actually present.) The effects of group size on speed of helping, therefore, are due simply to the perceived presence of others rather than to the influence of their actions. This means that the experimental situation is unlike emergencies, such as a fire, in which bystanders interact with each other. It is, however, similar to emergencies, such as the Genovese murder, in which spectators knew others were also watching but were prevented by walls between them from communication that might have counteracted the diffusion of responsibility.

The present results create serious difficulties for one class of commonly given explanations for the failure of bystanders to intervene in actual emergencies, those involving apathy or indifference. These explanations generally assert that people who fail to intervene are somehow different in kind from the rest of us, that they are "alienated by industrialization," "dehumanized by urbanization," "depersonalized by living in the cold society," or "psychopaths." These explanations serve a dual function for people who adopt them. First, they explain (if only in a nominal way) the puzzling and frightening problem of why people watch others die. Second, they give individuals reason to deny that they too might fail to help in a similar situation.

The results of this experiment seem to indicate that such personality variables may not be as important as these explanations suggest. Alienation, Machiavellianism, acceptance of social responsibility, need for approval, and authoritarianism are often cited in these explanations. Yet they did not predict the speed or likelihood of help. In sharp contrast, the perceived number of bystanders did. The explanation of bystander "apathy" may lie more in the bystander's response to other observers than in presumed personality deficiencies of "apathetic" individuals. Although this realization may force us to face the guilt-provoking possibility that we too might fail to intervene, it also suggests that individuals are not, of necessity, "non-interveners" because of their personalities. If people understand the situational forces that can make them hesitate to intervene, they may better overcome them.

REFERENCES

Aronfreed, J. The origin of self-criticism. *Psychological Review*, 1964, 71, 193–219.

Berkowitz, L., Klanderman, S., & Harris, R. Effects of experimenter awareness and sex of subject on reactions to dependency relationships. *Sociometry*, 1964, 27, 327–329.

Christie, R. The prevalence of machiavellian orientations. Paper presented at the meeting of the American Psychological Association, Los Angeles, 1964.

Crowne, D., & Marlowe, D. *The approval motive.* New York: Wiley, 1964.

Daniels, L., & Berkowitz, L. Liking and response to dependency relationships. *Human Relations,* 1963, 16, 141–148.

Milgram, S., & Hollander, P. Murder they heard. *Nation,* 1964, 198, 602–604.

Miller, N., & Dollard, J. *Social learning and imitation.* New Haven: Yale University Press, 1941.

Rosenthal, A. M. *Thirty-eight witnesses.* New York: McGraw-Hill, 1964.

Whiting, J. W. M., & Child, I. *Child training and personality.* New Haven: Yale University Press, 1953.

Architecture, Interaction, and Social Control: The Case of a Large-Scale Housing Project

WILLIAM L. YANCEY

While it is clear that social a .d economic factors, particularly the level and stability of income, are major determinants of social and economic life-styles (Kahl, 1957), there is also evidence that the architectural design of the homes in which families live has an effect on the manner in which they live (Festinger, Schacter, & Back, 1950; Gans, 1963; Schorr, 1963; Wilner, Walkley, Pinkerton, & Tayback, 1962). Yet, it cannot be assumed that a particular architectural design will have the same effect, both in its character and significance, on all social groups. The presence or absence of a particular design should have a variant effect on the total social life of a population, depending upon the interdependence of the architecturally related behavior to other dimensions of a group's life-style.

Social life may be influenced by physical factors within the dwelling unit or by spatial relationships between units. The focus of the current study is on factors external to dwelling units and on the social relationships that develop between families. Guttman (1970) warns of the difficulties in locating the boundaries of the physical setting whose social effects we wish to study when we extend housing beyond the physical dwelling. However, restricting investigations to the dwelling alone does not permit the development of guidelines for architecture and facilities that are external to the dwelling unit.

There is considerable research, such as that done by Festinger et al. (1950), Gans (1963), Suttles (1968), and Whyte (1956), which indicates

William L. Yancey received his PhD in sociology from Washington University, St. Louis, in 1967. He is currently an Associate Professor of Sociology and Director of the Urban and Regional Development Center at Vanderbilt University. His major research interests center around cultural and social-economic variations in urban life styles.

This chapter is based in part on research supported by National Institute of Mental Health Grant MH-09189, "Social and Community Problems in Public Housing Areas," and by a grant from the Urban and Regional Development Center, Vanderbilt University. Many of the ideas presented here stem from discussions the author has had with the directors of the Pruitt-Igoe research Alvin Gouldner and Lee Rainwater.

ENVIRONMENT AND THE SOCIAL SCIENCES, edited by Wohlwill and Carson, APA, 1972, pp. 126-136.

that physical proximity of dwellings has an effect on the development of neighboring relationships. At the same time, there is considerable ambiguity in the sociological literature concerning the importance of informal networks among different social classes. On the one hand, there are authors who argue that the frequency of neighboring and sociability is particularly prevalent in upper-middle-class suburbs (Bell & Boat, 1957; Fava, 1957; Whyte, 1965). On the other hand, studies of the urban working lower class have shown rather strong interpersonal networks of neighbors and strong attachment to neighborhoods (Bott, 1957; Fried, 1963; Fried & Gleicher, 1961; Gans, 1962; Suttles, 1968; Young & Willmott, 1957).

Careful reviews of these studies indicate that there is a difference in the character of social relationships found among neighbors in the middle class as compared with those found in the working lower class. While neighboring is found to be frequent in both areas, "the intensity of social interaction tends to decrease as one moves from working class areas to upper income bracket residential suburbs [Herberle, 1960, p. 279]."

Illustrative of this debate are the results of a survey directed by John McCarthy and the author in Nashville and Philadelphia. Using a scale developed by Wallin (1953), they found no relationship between casual neighboring relationships and social status. Measured by education, status shows a weak positive relationship to neighboring, but when measured by income, it shows the opposite relationship. Yet when asked where their close friends lived, lower status respondents were more likely to have friends living nearby than were those of higher status, measured either by education or income.

These results conform to statements by Blum (1964) and Herberle (1960), suggesting that once the distinction is made between casual acquaintances and relatively strong levels of interdependence, lower-class respondents are more closely tied to their neighbors. Within the lower class, friends are more likely to be neighbors. While within the middle class one might be friendly with his neighbors, friendships are more likely to be based on common interests rather than physical proximity (Gans, 1961). Finally, McCarthy and Yancey found that higher status persons are more likely to have friends whose occupations are similar to their own in level of prestige than are members of the working lower class.

There is also considerable literature suggestive of the functions of informal networks for the working lower class. Fried's (1963) research on the depressing effects of urban renewal and relocation, particularly for families who had strong personal ties to the Boston West End, is illustrative. Suttles' (1968) recent research in Chicago's Adams area documents the manner in which the development of neighborhood networks based on physical proximity, age, sex, and ethnicity provided social and moral norms, as well as a means of integration into the larger groups. He writes:

Within each small, localized peer group, continuing face-to-face relations can eventually provide a personalistic order. Once these groups are established, a single personal relation between them can extend the range of such an order. With the acceptance of age grading and territorial usufruct, it becomes possible

69

for slum neighborhoods to work out a moral order that includes most of their residents [p. 8].

A recent study of an all-white slum neighborhood in St. Louis (Wolfe, Lex, & Yancey, 1968) shows the existence of similar informal networks. Of particular interest here, and complementing the work of Suttles (1968), is the finding that the level of personal integration into networks is strongly related to the perception of human dangers in the environment. Persons who were not integrated into such networks were more likely to express concern over allowing their children out of the house, felt that they were vulnerable to strangers entering the neighborhood, felt unsafe on the street at night, and felt that children in the neighborhood were out of control.

There are also some indications that the presence of ecologically local networks is more important to working lower-class urban dwellers than to their middle-class counterparts. Gans (1963) has noted that the move to suburban areas by middle-class families results in part in their having more privacy from neighbors than they had in inner-city apartments. Gans' research suggests that for the middle class the move to suburban areas results in few changes in their life-style that were not intended. He writes, "They are effects not of suburban life, but of the larger cultural milieu in which people form their aspirations [p. 192]."

These results stand in sharp contrast to those reported by Marris (1962) and Young and Willmott (1957). Their studies of the relocation of working lower-class communities by urban renewal suggest that the move to suburbia resulted in significant, and unintended, changes in their life-styles. No longer available in the suburban housing estates were the amenities of the slum—the close proximity to work, to the pub, and to friends and relatives. They changed their way of life and began focusing their energies more sharply on their homes and jointly pursued family life and much less on separate activities by husband and wife participating in sex-segregated peer groups.

In addition to the ethnographic evidence on the relative importance of ecologically local informal networks, there is considerable research indicating that, much to the dismay of urban renewers, working lower-class populations are as satisfied with their neighborhoods as is the middle class (Foote, Abu-Lughod, Foley, & Winni, 1960; Fried, 1963). The recent survey conducted by McCarthy and the author in Nashville and Philadelphia indicated that there was no relationship between social status and neighborhood satisfaction. Over 60% of the respondents were satisfied with their neighborhood, no matter what their social and economic status.

The work of Fried (1963), Gans (1962), and Foote et al. (1960) also indicates that among the working lower class, neighborhood satisfaction is rather closely tied to the presence of informal networks of friends and relatives. Results from the McCarthy and Yancey survey support this proposition. Without social class controls, no relationship was found between the proximity of friends and neighborhood satisfaction. When social class was controlled, neighborhood satisfaction was found to be related to the proximity of friends in the lower socioeconomic group, while no relationship was found in the higher status group.

These survey data suggest that not only are the existence and integration into ecologically informal social networks significant for the working lower class, but the results go slightly beyond the earlier studies, in that they are suggestive of the relative importance of such networks for different social and economic levels. While social and economic factors are the principal variables that determine the life-styles of the poor, they have developed ways of coping with and adapting to poverty, thus making the condition less oppressive. We have argued that among these adaptations is the development of ecologically local informal neighborhood relationships. When these are disrupted, or when a community is designed that makes their development almost impossible, we should expect to see their importance made manifest by other differences that emerge in the life-styles of a particular group. The Pruitt-Igoe Housing Project community is illustrative of one such group.

THE CASE OF PRUITT-IGOE

The Pruitt-Igoe Housing Project consists of 43 11-story buildings near downtown St. Louis, Missouri. The project was opened in 1954, has 2,762 apartments (many of which are currently vacant), and has as tenants a high proportion of female-headed households, on some kind of public assistance. Though originally containing a large population of white families, the project has been all Negro for the past several years. The project community is plagued by petty crimes, vandalism, and much destruction to the physical plant and has a rather widespread reputation as being an extreme example of the pathologies associated with lower-class life (Demerath, 1962; Rainwater, 1966a, 1966b).

In this chapter, it is argued that the architectural design of Pruit-Igoe has had an atomizing effect on the informal social networks frequently found in lower-class neighborhoods. Without the provision of semipublic space and facilities around which such informal networks might develop, families have retreated to the internal structures of their apartments and do not have the social support, protection, and informal social control found in other lower-class neighborhoods.

Pruitt-Igoe represents, in its architectural design, an extreme example of a national housing policy whose single goal is the provision of low-cost housing for low-income families, with little knowledge about or concern for the development of a community and neighborhood. Unlike normal slums, with their cluttered streets and alleys, Pruitt-Igoe provides no semiprivate space and facilities around which neighboring relationships might develop. There is a minimum of what is often considered "wasted space"—space within buildings that is outside of individual family dwelling units. *Architectural Forum* (April 1951), in an early review of the project's design, praised the designers for their individualistic design and the absence of such wasted space between dwelling units.

Walking into the project, one is struck by the mosaic of glass that covers what were grassy areas and playgrounds. The barren dirt, or mud when it rains, is constantly tracked into the apartments. Windows, particularly those on the lower floors, are broken out. The cost of replacing glass in vacant apartments led the Housing Authority to cover many of them with plywood. Streets and parking lots are littered with trash, bottles, and tin cans. Derelict cars provide an attractive source of entertainment for children. Fences around "tot-lots" are torn; swings, sliding boards, and merry-go-rounds are noticeably unpainted, rusted, and broken.

Within the buildings themselves, the neglect is more apparent. Entering the buildings via one of the three stairwells, one is struck with the stale air and the stench of urine, trash, and garbage on the floors. One is also struck by the unfinished construction—the unpainted cinder blocks and cement. Today, these unfinished walls in the stairwells are decorated with colorful graffitti.

The alternative route into the building is the single elevator. The elevators are used as public restrooms, as well as a means of transportation. Even though they are mopped every morning, the smell of urine is noticeable throughout the day. Many are without handrails and are in need of painting; all have the reputation of breaking down between floors.

On the fourth, seventh, and tenth floors are open galleries or halls, the only level public space within the building, one side of which is lined with broken windows and steel grating. Open garbage is often found on the floor next to the incinerator. The laundry rooms, located off the gallery, are sometimes used as lavatories. Residents and officials were observed urinating in them.

The physical danger and deterioration of Pruitt-Igoe is but a reflection of the more pressing human dangers. Residents of Pruitt-Igoe continually expressed concern with being assaulted, beaten, or raped. We were frequently warned of such dangers and were told never to enter buildings alone and to stay out of the elevators, especially after dark. We were told stories of people being cut by bottles thrown from the buildings and were warned never to stand immediately outside of a building. In addition to the physical violence, there was also verbal hostility and shaming and exploitation from children, neighbors, and outsiders (see Rainwater, 1966a).

One of the first things pointed out by the residents of Pruitt-Igoe was the distinction between the "private" space within apartments and the "public" space and facilities. In early interviews, families were asked what they liked about living in the housing project. Almost without exception, what they liked was limited to the physical space and amenities within the family unit. Characteristic of these first interviews is the following exchange.

Interviewer: *How do you like living here in Pruitt-Igoe?*
Respondent: *I like living here better than I liked living on O'Fallon Street [in a private housing slum] where we had a first floor, but did not have heat provided*

in the winter and windows were broken out. We did have an inside toilet, but no modern plumbing—we had no water. I like living here because it's convenient.

Interviewer: What do you mean by convenient?

Respondent: The apartment itself—it's easier to take care of and to clean. Although the paint on these walls holds dirt badly, the Housing Authority does furnish the paint. We don't have a choice of what kind of paint, but I painted the walls. It's real convenient here, especially in the winter time. We always have lots of hot water here in the winter time. It's always so nice and warm here, and I only have one rent to pay. I don't have to pay for gas and electricity and all that. I just pay once. I like that.

I like this 'partment, it's good for the kids. Here we have separate rooms.

Interviewer: Each child has a separate room?

Respondent: No, but this way the children have a bedroom and the parents have a bedroom. It gives them, and us, more freedom.

When the interviewer changed the focus of the interview by asking, "How do you feel about this building?" the character of the interview changed.

Respondent: Well, I don't like being upstairs like this. The problem is that I can't see the kids. They're just too far away. If one of them gets hurt, needs to go to the bathroom, or anything, it's just too far away. And you can't get outside. We don't have any porches.

And there are too many different kids around here. Some of them have parents, some do not. There are just a variety of families. Some have husbands, some not.

If it weren't for the project police the teen-agers would take over. I've got some children that are teen-agers, but I still think they are the most dangerous group.

This pattern of responses repeated itself throughout the research. The results of a survey taken in 1965 are summarized in Table 1. In contrast to Pruitt-Igoe, slum dwellers generally were dissatisfied with their specific dwelling while satisfied with their neighborhood.[1] In Pruitt-Igoe, the familiar

TABLE 1
Satisfaction with Housing and Neighborhood

Item	Percent satisfied	
	Pruitt-Igoe (n = 154)	Adjacent slum (n = 69)
Apartment	78	55
Project living	49	—
Neighborhood	53	74

[1] In more recent years, vandalism and lack of maintenance have resulted in the deterioration of the plumbing and heating of the building. Thus, these results would probably not be found to be as striking today as they were when this study was done in 1965.

73

aspects of slum living, such as fires and burning, freezing and cold, poor plumbing, dangerous electrical wiring, thin walls, and overcrowding of children and parents into single rooms, were somewhat abated. Yet, the amenities of lower-class neighborhoods had apparently been lost.

Complementing the pattern of satisfaction with apartment and neighborhood, and again in sharp contrast to the research reviewed above, informal social networks did not form in the corridors and stairwells of Pruitt-Igoe. Residents of the projects had a similar number of friends as other lower-class populations, yet these friendships bore little or no relationship to the physical proximity of families to each other. Relationships with neighbors ranged from an occasional friendship and helping pattern to (more frequently) open hostility or isolation. As one woman explained when she was asked about troubles in the project:

They are selfish. I've got no friends here. There's none of this door-to-door coffee business of being friends here or anything like that. Down here if you are sick you just go to the hospital. There are no friends to help you. I don't think my neighbors would help me and I wouldn't ask them anyway. I don't have trouble with my neighbors because I never visit them. The rule of the game down here is go for yourself.

CONSEQUENCES OF ATOMIZATION

Suttles (1968) notes that in the Adams area in Chicago conflict between residents results in the reinforcement of small informal groups based on age, sex, or ethnicity. Of particular interest here is his discussion of the sequence through which such groups develop. New residents of the area restrict their children's movement to the areas immediately around or close by their homes. As a result, small, continuous face-to-face associations develop around the immediate proximity of the home. They provide means of controlling children and provide "assurances that relieve their apprehension." Conflict with persons outside these small groups forces the residents to "throw their lot in with a definite group of people [Suttles, 1968, p. 228]."

In a similar manner, mothers in Pruitt-Igoe attempt to keep their children in close proximity to their apartments. Yet, in contrast to the slum, the architectural design of the project is such that as soon as a child leaves an apartment he is out of his mother's sight and direct control. There are no areas within the buildings in which the children can play except the galleries, which cannot be seen from the apartments and which are shared by some 20 families.

Mothers fear the early introduction and socialization of their children into sex and other troubles. They also see the adults in the housing project as being irresponsible, deviant, and beyond control. Yet, attempts to control children who are members of unknown families frequently result in conflict between adults. Thus, one woman reported:

74

I used to watch the kids in this building. In the beginning I tried to discipline them. I'd tell them every time I found them doing something mischievous what was wrong and what was right. But kids don't like that; their parents don't like it. They don't want somebody else to discipline their children. They put the blame on you. Watching children is dangerous.

The conflict is further escalated when one of the two adults calls the police. As one woman explained, after she was told the police had been called because her son had gotten into a fight:

Well, I'se not going to get shook because the police are coming. They always come to this house and tell me how bad my children are. It's too bad the parents had to call the police and could never take the time to come up and talk to me first.

Apparently, without the informal networks, informal social control that might otherwise be based on the small social group is not strong enough to resolve such conflicts. Thus, as a means of resolving what might otherwise have been a relatively small complaint, a more powerful authority, the police, is called upon. This in turn further exacerbates the atomization that exists.

The interviews and observations with families in the housing project contain many references to the police. The survey of the Pruitt-Igoe Housing Project showed that over 90% of the residents of the project indicated that there should be more policemen patrolling the area.

Other features of the architecture, apart from the lack of semipublic space and facilities, have contributed to the fears that characterize the community. The design of the stairwells is such that they represent almost completely uncontrolled space. They are public in the sense that anyone can enter them without being challenged; yet they are private in that no one is likely to be held accountable for his behavior in the stairwell. This lack of accountability is particularly prevalent in the center stairwell, where a small anteroom separates the individual apartments from the stairwell. This room creates a buffer zone between the totally private apartment and the stairwell. Residents fear this stairwell more than the others, and it is said to be used by teen-agers as a relatively private place in which they can engage in sexual intercourse. As one teen-ager explained: "All you have to do is knock out the lights on the landings above and below you. Then when someone comes, if they are not afraid of the dark, they stumble around and you can hear them in time to get out."

The isolation, the lack of accountability for entry into the stairwells, and the fears that are centered around them are related to the lack of informal networks. Given the number of families who have rights to this space, it should not be surprising that strangers can enter it without being challenged. While interviewing people in lower-class neighborhoods, one often encounters persons on the street who question you as to where you are going. After an introduction, such persons often give interviewers instructions as to where a family can be found, when they will return home, or how to get through an alley to their apartment. Later, when such an interviewer returns and introduces himself, he often gets a response such as, "Oh yes, you were here earlier." During the three years of intensive research in Pruitt-Igoe, such an experience never occurred. The presence of outsiders was noticed by the residents, but they were never challenged.

Absent from the architectural design of Pruitt-Igoe is what has sometimes been referred to as wasted space. We choose to call it "defensible space." In lower-class slums, the littered and often trash-filled alleys, streets, and back yards provide the ecological basis around which informal networks of friends and relatives develop. Without such semipublic space and facilities, the development of such networks is retarded; the resulting atomization of the community can be seen in the frequent and escalating conflict between neighbors, fears of and vulnerability to the human dangers in the environment, and, finally, withdrawal to the last line of defense—the single family dwelling unit. The sense of security and control that is found in other lower-class neighborhoods is not present.

DISCUSSION

There are at least two alternative hypotheses that might be used to explain the atomized nature of the Pruitt-Igoe community. The first of these stems from the research and literature on social stratification, which rather clearly show that the level of interpersonal trust is lower in the lower class than in any other segment of the population. Thus, it is argued that Pruitt-Igoe, as representative of the lowest class, is therefore a community of people who cannot trust one another. A comparison of Pruitt-Igoe residents' responses to Likert type items measuring the level of trust indicates that while they are less trustful than are persons of higher status, they are not different from other lower-class populations (see Rainwater & Schwartz, 1965).

Perhaps a more credible hypothesis, one which might be termed the "police state" theory, stems from the public nature of life in public housing. Over 50% of the residents are on some form of welfare assistance. Welfare workers and Housing Authority officials maintain a rather close scrutiny of their clients who might otherwise break one of the many rules governing residency in the project. Under such a "police state," residents of the project may fear that becoming friendly with neighbors will result in their being turned in to the authorities. While neighbors were observed calling the police on one another, no cases are known of anyone being turned over to the Housing Authority or welfare office for an infraction of one of their rules.

Without a study comparing Pruitt-Igoe with another housing project with a similar population, similar reputation, and similar administration by caretakers, it is difficult to adequately judge the effects of architecture per se. In contrast to Pruitt-Igoe, public housing in Baltimore shows that an architectural design providing common space and facilities leads to an increased amount of neighboring, visiting, and mutual aid among persons moving from a slum into a public housing project (Wilner et al., 1962).

Architecture does have an effect on the manner in which the poor cope with poverty. Designers of housing for the poor, rather than viewing the space between dwelling units as something to be avoided or reduced as far as possible, should provide semipublic space and facilities around which smaller identifiable units of residence can organize their sense of "turf." Designers should minimize space that belongs to no one and maximize the informal control over the space required to get from one dwelling to another. If housing must be designed for the ghetto—if we must reconcile ourselves to not being able to change the social forces that produce the world of danger that lower-class people experience—then the designer can make some small contribution by facilitating the constructive adaptations that have emerged as a means of defending against the world of the lower class.

REFERENCES

Bell, W., & Boat, M. Urban neighborhoods and informal social relations. *American Journal of Sociology*, 1957, **62**, 391–398.

Blum, A. F. Social structure, social class and participation in primary relationships. In A. B. Shostak & W. Gomberg (Eds.), *Blue collar world*. Englewood Cliffs, N.J.: Prentice-Hall, 1964.

Bott, E. *Family and social network*. London: Tavistock, 1957.

Demerath, N. J. St. Louis public housing study sets off community development to meet social needs. *Journal of Housing*, 1962, **19**, 472–478.

Fava, S. F. Contrasts in neighboring New York City and a suburban county. In R. L. Warren (Ed.), *Perspective on the American community*. Chicago: Rand-McNally, 1967.

Festinger, L., Schacter, S., & Back, K. *Social pressures in informal groups*. New York: Harper, 1950.

Foote, N. N., Abu-Lughod, J., Foley, M. M., & Winni, L. *Housing choices and housing constraints*. New York: McGraw-Hill, 1960.

Fried, M. Grieving for a lost home. In L. J. Duhl (Ed.), *The urban condition*. New York: Basic Books, 1963.

Fried, M., & Gleicher, P. Some sources of residential satisfaction in an urban slum. *Journal of the American Institute of Planners*, 1961, **27**, 305–315.

Fried, M., & Levin, J. Some social functions of the urban slum. In B. Friedman & R. Morris (Eds.), *Urban planning and social policy*. New York: Basic Books, 1968.

Gans, H. J. Planning and social life: Friendship and neighbor relations in suburban communities. *Journal of the American Institute of Planners*, 1961, **27**, 135–139.

Gans, H. J. *The urban villagers*. New York: Free Press of Glencoe, 1962.

Gans, H. J. Effect of the move from city to suburb. In L. J. Duhl (Ed.), *The urban condition*. New York: Basic Books, 1963.

Guttman, R. A sociologist looks at housing. In D. P. Moynihan (Ed.), *Toward a national urban policy*. New York: Basic Books, 1970.

Herberle, R. The normative element in neighborhood relations. *Pacific Sociological Review*, 1960, 3(1), 3–11.

Kahl, J. *The American class structure*. New York: Rinehart, 1957.

Marris, P. *Family and social change in an African city*. Evanston, Ill.: Northwestern University Press, 1962.

Rainwater, L. Crucible of identity: The Negro lower-class family. *Daedalus*, 1966, **95**, 172–216. (a)

Rainwater, L. Fear and the house-as-haven in the lower class. *Journal of the American Institute of Planners*, 1966, **32**, 23–31. (b)

Rainwater, L., & Schwartz, M. J. Identity, world view, social relations, and family behavior in magazines. Chicago: Social Research Incorporated, 1965. (Mimeo)

Schorr, A. L. *Slums and social insecurity.* Washington, D.C.: United States Government Printing Office, 1963.

Suttles, G. D. *The social order of the slum.* Chicago: University of Chicago Press, 1968.

Wallin, P. A Guttman scale for measuring women's neighboring. *American Journal of Sociology,* 1953, **59**, 243–246.

Whyte, W. H. *The organization man.* Garden City, N.Y.: Doubleday, 1956.

Wilner, D. M., Walkley, R. P., Pinkerton, T. C., & Tayback, M. *The housing environment and family life.* Baltimore: Johns Hopkins University Press, 1962.

Wolfe, A., Lex, B., & Yancey, W. *The Soulard Area: Adaptations by urban white families to poverty.* St. Louis, Mo.: Social Science Institute, Washington University, 1968.

Young, M., & Willmott, P. *Family and kinship in East London.* Glencoe, Ill.: Free Press, 1957.

ENVIRONMENTAL PSYCHOLOGY
AND CROWDING:
THEORETICAL APPROACHES

Psychological Environments
Expanding the Scope of Human Ecology[1]

PAUL M. INSEL

RUDOLF H. MOOS

Like people, environments have unique personalities. Just as it is possible to characterize a person's "personality," environments can be similarly portrayed with a great deal of accuracy and detail. Some people are supportive; likewise, some environments are supportive. Some men feel the need to control others; similarly, some environments are extremely controlling. Order and structure are important to many people; correspondingly, many environments emphasize regularity, system, and order.

Henry Murray (1938) first conceptualized the dual process of personal needs and environmental press. He suggested that individuals have specific needs, the strength of which characterizes "personality." The environment potentially satisfies or frustrates these needs. Murray's model for studying behavior thus consisted of the interaction between personality needs and environmental press. Murray's concept of needs provided a point of entry for the development of a variety of measurement instruments to study personality; however, no parallel development in the objective measurement of environmental press was attempted until much later.

Stern, Stein, and Bloom (1956) expanded Murray's contribution. They demonstrated that behavior could be predicted much better when the setting in which the behavior occurred was clearly defined so as to include the social demands of the situation. Pace and Stern (1958) developed the concept of environmental press further by applying the logic of "perceived climate" to the study of "atmosphere" at universities and colleges. They constructed the College Characteristics Index (CCI) which mea-

sured the global college environment by asking students to act as reporters. Specifically, students were asked to answer true or false to items covering a wide range of topics about their college, such as student–faculty relationship, rules and regulations, classroom methods, facilities, etc. The general logic of this approach suggests that the consensus of students' characterizing their college environment constitutes a measure of environmental climate, and that this environmental climate exerts a directional influence on their behavior.

Thus, one might infer a general principle to the effect that the way one perceives his surroundings or environment influences the way one will behave in that environment. While this principle has a commonsense ring to it, it is not usually applied in a practical way to the routine problems and tasks with which psychologists deal. For example, personality and projective tests are frequently administered and interpreted with the assumption that results will portray permanent and enduring qualities that transcend the environment, providing information that can accurately predict behavior regardless of the setting in which the behavior is likely to take place. This assumption is pervasive in spite of much evidence showing that properties of the environment may account for more of the variance in behavior than measures of trait qualities or even biographic and demographic background data (Douglas, 1964; Mischel, 1968; Wolfe, 1966). For example, Friedlander and Greenberg (1971) studied the job performance and retention of 478 hard-core unemployed workers and found that the sole correlate of their work effectiveness and ability to retain jobs was the extent to which they perceived their work environment to be supportive. Personality and background data were found to be unrelated to work effectiveness and job retention.

[1] The work reported in this article was supported in part by National Institute of Mental Health Grant MH16026, National Institute of Alcohol Abuse and Alcoholism Grant AA00498, and Veterans Administration Research Project MRIS 5817-01.

AMERICAN PSYCHOLOGIST, 1974, Vol. 29, pp. 179-188.

Classifying Human Environments

The concept of environment has historically been somewhat ambiguous and amorphous. Formal and systematic study of environments is rooted in the biological sciences where the term *ecology* is most commonly applied to the natural habitats of animals. *Human ecology* is a more recent term extending to the domain of geographers and sociologists who are interested in the distributions of human populations. The term *social ecology* has evolved mainly from the efforts of psychologists and other behavioral scientists to direct their inquiries toward a more complete view of man interacting with both his physical and social environment (Moos & Insel, 1974).

The seeds of social ecology can be found in both ecology and human ecology. Because ecological phenomena may be considered as existing over the entire range of organisms and at a number of different levels of organization, the field of ecology has become fractionated and specialized.

Human ecology departs from animal and plant ecology in the nature of its regulatory mechanisms. Among the special regulatory mechanisms which operate in a human society are public opinion, punishment, rewards, competition, and supply and demand. Social cooperation is perhaps the most important regulatory mechanism in society, serving to mitigate the destructive and predatory elements found in the ecological evolution of other animal communities. Knowledge about the operation of the regulatory mechanisms which keep human societies in balance with the resources of their milieus is one of the concerns of social ecology.

The emerging discipline of social ecology grows out of this interaction of man with his environment. To this extent it transcends human ecology. It reflects the traditional concerns of ecology both in its emphasis on the measurement of objective physical characteristics of environments (e.g., temperatures, rainfall, air pollution, noise levels; the shapes, sizes, and physical arrangements of buildings) and in its inquiry into the short-term evolutionary and adaptive consequences of these environments. Social ecology, however, expands these concerns by systematically dealing with the social environment and its interaction with the physical milieu. And, unlike ecology and human ecology, social ecology has an explicit value orientation in that it is concerned with promoting maximally effective human functioning. Finally, social ecology touches the main currents of scientific thought in psychiatry, medicine, and epidemiology in its special emphasis on the identification of maladaptive responses and their relationship to environmental variables.

Moos (1973a) suggested six different ways of conceptualizing human environments:

1. *Ecological dimensions.* These include (*a*) meteorological and geographical variables (this view of the environment suggests that society has been shaped by climate, topography, and other geographical features of inhabited regions), and (*b*) physical design variables. Here man's behavior is influenced by architecture and physical constraints which limit or even define the range of activities in which man can be involved.

2. *Dimensions of organization structure.* This view of the environment suggests that behavior is influenced by structural dimensions such as size, staffing ratios, salary levels, span of organizational control, etc.

3. *Personal characteristics of milieu inhabitants.* This view implies that the character of an environment depends on the nature of its members and that the dominant features of an environment depend on the typical characteristics of its members, such as age, sex, socioeconomic status, abilities, group memberships, physique, and other background data.

4. *Behavior settings.* This view of the environment originated with Roger Barker (1968), who emphasized the importance of studying behavior settings as natural phenomena. Behavior settings are conceptualized as ecological units which have both an environmental and a behavioral component.

5. *Functional or reinforcement properties of environments.* This view of the environment suggests that people vary their behavior substantially from one setting to another as a function of the reinforcement consequences for particular behaviors.

6. *Psychosocial characteristics and organizational climate.* This conceptualization encompasses both psychological and social dimensions of the environment in a framework of person–milieu interaction. The approach accommodates both an inside perception of what the environment is like as well as an outside observer's impression, although most of the work to date emphasizes the importance of climate as perceived by participating members of the environment.

Measuring Environments

As suggested earlier, a limited literature exists on the development of systematic approaches to measuring environments. This is partly because "environments" are unwieldy and thus difficult to deal with as objects of investigation. This problem has been partially resolved by such investigators as Barker (1968), who focused on specific environmental units which have both a space and a time locus, and Moos (1969), who focused on subenvironments or subunits in which milieu occupants interact with each other on some regular and familiar basis.

Moos and his associates at the Social Ecology Laboratory at Stanford University have made substantial contributions toward developing an indepth program of characterizing and assessing the psychosocial qualities of environments. They have extensively studied eight different environments and have developed perceived climate scales for each environment: (a) psychiatric wards; (b) community-oriented psychiatric treatment programs; (c) correctional institutions; (d) military basic training companies; (e) university student residences; (f) junior and senior high school classrooms; (g) work environments; (h) social, therapeutic, and decision-making groups.

Underlying Patterns of Differing Environments

Common dimensions have emerged from studies of the eight different kinds of environments. These have been conceptualized by Moos (1974d) in three broad categories: relationship dimensions, personal development or goal orientation dimensions, and system maintenance and change dimensions. These dimensions are similar across the eight environments mentioned although vastly different settings may impose unique variations within the general categories.

RELATIONSHIP DIMENSIONS

Relationship dimensions identify the nature and intensity of personal relationships within the environment. They assess the extent to which individuals are involved in the environment and the extent to which they support and help each other. As can be seen in Table 1, examples of relevant subscales in the eight climate scales are involvement, affiliation, staff support, peer cohesion, and spontaneity.

Personal development dimensions consider the potential or opportunity in the environment for personal growth and the development of self-esteem. The precise nature of personal development dimensions varies somewhat among different environments

and depends mainly on the goals of a particular environment. Examples of relevant subscales are autonomy, practical orientation, competition, and intellectuality.

System maintenance and system change dimensions assess the extent to which the environment is orderly and clear in its expectations, maintains control, and is responsive to change. Examples of the subscales one finds here are order and organization, clarity, control, and innovation. The three "basic" categories can best be seen as they fit into the framework of the four environments shown in Table 1.

The eight climate scales mentioned earlier can be classified into one of four types of environments: (a) treatment environments, (b) total institutions,[2] (c) educational environments, and (d) community environments. Treatment environment measures are the Ward Atmosphere Scale (Moos, 1974d) and the Community-Oriented Programs Environment Scale (Moos, 1974a). Total institutions environment measures are the Correctional Institutions Environment Scale (Moos, 1974b) and the Military Company Environment Inventory (Moos, 1973b). Educational environment measures are the University Residence Environment Scale (Moos & Gerst, 1974) and the Classroom Environment Scale (Moos & Trickett, 1974). Community environment measures include the Work Environment Scale (Insel & Moos, 1972) and the Group Environment Scale (Moos & Humphrey, 1973). A final technique, the Family Environment Scale, is being developed.

To give an example of the similarity of differing environments, let us compare the social environment of a psychiatric ward with the social environment of a factory. On the surface these two environments appear rather remote from each other. They have much in common, however. The instruments used to assess these two settings were the Ward Atmosphere Scale (WAS) and the Work Environment Scale (WES). The relevant relationship dimensions on the WAS are involvement, sup-

---

[2] Goffman (1961) suggested that "total institutions" take over the life processes of persons who live within their physical constraints. They differ from other environments in that they require large groups of unselected members to conduct their lives in a similar fashion and on a fixed schedule. These developing life-styles are purportedly designed to fulfill the aims of the institutions. Total institutions have two distinct groups of inhabitants: staff and inmates. These two groups interact on a restricted, often formally prescribed, basis. Goffman suggested that two different social and cultural worlds develop, which move alongside one another but have minimal contact.

TABLE 1

Similarities of Social Climate Dimensions across Environments

Type of dimension	Treatment environment		Total environment			Educational environment	Community environment	
	Ward Atmosphere Scale	Community-Oriented Programs Environment Scale	Correctional Institutions Environment Scale	Military Company Environment Inventory	University Residence Environment Scale	Classroom Environment Inventory	Work Environment Inventory	Group Environment Inventory
Relationship								
Involvement-affiliation	X	X	X	X	X	X X	X	
Spontaneity-expressiveness	X	X	X					X
Support	X	X	X	X	X	X	X	X X
Cohesiveness				X			X	X
Personal development								
Autonomy-independence (personal status)	X	X	X	X	X		X	X
Practical orientation (task orientation, academic achievement)	X	X	X		X	X	X	X
Personal problem orientation (self-discovery)	X	X	X					X
Anger and aggression	X	X						X
Competition					X	X		
Intellectuality					X			
Traditional social orientation					X			
System maintenance and system change								
Order and organization	X	X	X	X	X	X		X
Clarity	X	X	X	X		X	X	X
Control	X	X	X	X		X	X	X
Physical comfort							X	
Work pressure							X	
Innovation-student influence					X X	X	X	X

port, and spontaneity. Relationship dimensions on the WES are involvement, staff support, and peer cohesion. Program involvement on a psychiatric ward refers to how active and energetic patients are in the day-to-day functioning of the ward. Involvement in a factory setting refers to the extent to which workers are concerned and committed to their jobs. Support on a psychiatric ward indicates the extent to which patients are encouraged to be helpful and supportive toward other patients and how supportive the staff is toward patients. Staff support in a factory indicates the extent to which management is supportive of workers and encourages workers to be supportive of each other. The subscales of involvement and support are roughly equivalent in both settings. Spontaneity, however, is more relevant to a treatment or therapeutic environment in which people are often encouraged to

act openly and to freely express their feelings. This aspect of the climate in a factory setting can be seen more appropriately as part of both the staff support and peer cohesion components. On a psychiatric ward, staff support and peer support are one dimension since they correlate so highly with one another. But in a factory setting they are independent.

As mentioned earlier, some environments possess more than one aspect of the same property. For example, work environments have two distinctly different support elements. One element is called *peer cohesion* and accounts for the social and interpersonal relationships that develop among workers and their tendency to stick together and help each other. The second element, called *staff support*, accounts for the degree of friendship and communication between management and nonmanagement personnel and the extent to which management encourages and helps nonmanagement personnel. These two elements identify a distinction between peer support and supervisor or staff support. In psychiatric and correctional environments, peer support tends to merge with staff support. In fact, it is difficult to find programs where these two support variables are not correlated positively. However, in a work environment, nonmanagement personnel frequently spend a great deal of time together maintaining a separate factor of cohesiveness.

PERSONAL DEVELOPMENT

The second category is personal development. Both settings have two subscales in common, namely, autonomy and practical or task orientation. Autonomy on a psychiatric ward involves how independent and self-sufficient patients are encouraged to be in making their own decisions about their personal affairs. For example, can a patient wear what he wants? Can he leave the ward without permission? In a factory setting, the issues are similar in that they are related to personal growth and independence. For example, are employees encouraged to learn more than one job? Can employees use their own initiative to do things?

The second subscale on a psychiatric ward is practical orientation. This component looks at the extent to which the patient's environment orients him toward preparing himself for release from the hospital. Such things as training for new jobs and setting and working toward goals are considered. In a factory the component of task orientation accounts for the extent to which the environment emphasizes good planning and efficiency and encourages workers to "get the job done."

SYSTEM MAINTENANCE

The third category for comparison is system maintenance, in which there are two identical subscales for both psychiatric ward and factory environments. These subscales are clarity and control. Clarity accounts for the extent to which both patients and workers know what to expect in their daily routines and how explicitly rules and policies are communicated. For example, do patients know when doctors will be on the ward? If a patient's medicine is changed, does a nurse or doctor tell him why? In a factory, do employees know when supervisors will be available? Do employees

know who to see when a problem arises? The second component, control, refers to the extent to which staff or supervisors use measures to keep patients or workers under control. On a psychiatric ward, can patients call nursing staff by their first names? In a factory, can employees be absent from work without an authorized or written explanation?

The foregoing hopefully conveys the similar threads that make up the fabric of remotely related environments. The importance of these threads can be seen more clearly in a situation in which a patient is discharged from a psychiatric ward and gains employment in a factory setting. Perhaps diagnostic work-ups could benefit from this type of "total milieu" approach. For example, instead of administering the MMPI or Rorschach and trying to predict from these tests what the most suitable treatment might be for the patient, the psychologist might ask the patient to respond to the ideal form of the Ward Atmosphere Scale. If the patient indicates his need for more support or more order on the WAS, the psychologist would then be in an advantageous position in recommending a ward that had a climate that emphasized support and order. The same approach might be used in a work setting if the climate of the work environment was known.

The three basic dimensions (relationship, personal development, and system maintenance) identified in treatment environments are also found in total institutions and educational and community environments. However, some environments have a unique component within a particular category which is peculiar to them. For example, work pressure is specifically and solely relevant to work environments where things like time pressure, deadlines, strain, urgency, and speed may dominate the job milieu. Another example, falling within the personal development category, is "traditional social orientation," a subscale on the University Residence Environment Scale (URES). This variable accounts for the emphasis on dating, going to parties, and other traditional heterosexual interactions that one finds in student housing programs.

The eight social climate scales discussed earlier were all developed at the Social Ecology Laboratory at Stanford University. Can relationship, personal development, and system maintenance and system change variables be identified in other organizational climate scales? The results of eight different investigators are utilized and summarized in Table 2.

TABLE 2

Dimensions of Organizational Climate Scales

Scale	Relationship	Personal development	System maintenance and system change
Organizational Climate Index (Stern, 1970)	Closeness, group life	Intellectual climate, personal dignity, achievement standards	Orderliness, impulse control (constraint)
College and University Environment Scale (Pace, 1969)	Community	Awareness, scholarship	Practicality, propriety
Institutional Functioning Inventory (Peterson, 1970)	Institutional esprit	Intellectual-aesthetic, extracurriculum, concern for improvement of society, concern for undergraduate learning concern for advancing knowledge, meeting local needs	Freedom, democratic governance, self-study and planning, concern for innovation, human diversity
Learning Environment Inventory (Walberg, 1969)	Intimacy, friction, cliqueness, apathy, favoritism	Difficulty, speed	Formality, goal direction, democratic, disorganization, diversity
Organizational Climate Description Questionnaire (Halpin & Croft, 1963)	Esprit, intimacy, consideration, disengagement	Thrust, hindrance	Production emphasis, aloofness
Agency Climate Questionnaire (Schneider & Bartlett, 1970)	Managerial support, intraagency conflict, new employee concern	Agent independence	Managerial structure
Climate Questionnaire (Litwin & Stringer, 1968)	Warmth, support, conflict, identity	Responsibility, risk, standards, reward	Structure
Dimensions of Group Processes (Fairweather, 1969)	Group cohesiveness	Group performance	Leadership and role delineation

The basic logic and conceptualization appears to be consistent with the scales of other investigators. For example, the College and University Environment Scale (Pace, 1969) has five subscales: (*a*) *community* describes a friendly, cohesive group-oriented campus and is clearly a relationship dimension; (*b*) *awareness* describes a concern about personal, poetic, and political meaning, self-understanding and reflectiveness and is clearly a personal development dimension; (*c*) *scholar* describes an environment characterized by intellectuality, scholastic discipline, and academic achievement and is also clearly a personal development dimension; (*d*) *propriety* describes an environment that is polite, considerate, mannerly, proper, and conventional and where group standards of decorum are important. To the extent to which this variable emphasizes order and clarity within the environment it belongs in the category of system maintenance; (*e*) *practicality* describes an environment characterized by organization, enterprise, material benefits, and social activities. This is also a system maintenance dimension, since its essential aspect reflects orderly supervision and organization.

The second test reviewed is the Institutional Functioning Inventory (Peterson, Centra, Hartnett, & Linn, 1970). This instrument also lends itself to studying colleges and universities and provides 11 variables judged to be important in American higher education. Institutional esprit is clearly a relationship dimension. The following belong to the dimension of system maintenance and system change: freedom (lack of restraint on academic or personal life), democratic governance (extent of opportunity for participation in decision making), self-study and planning (emphasis on continuous long-range planning for the total institution), concern for innovation (commitment to experimentation with new ideas for educational practice), and human diversity (heterogeneity of faculty and student body in background and attitudes). The emphasis of these variables is on system change, which generally tends to be more strongly prevalent in most university environments than is system maintenance. Finally, the other five variables belong to the personal development dimension, that is, intellectual-aesthetic extracurricular interests (availability of activities and opportunities for intellectual and aesthetic stimulation outside the classroom), concern for improvement of society, concern for undergraduate learning, concern for advancing knowledge, and meeting local needs (emphasis on providing educational and cultural opportunities for adults in the surrounding area).

Table 2 indicates subscales for two other organizational climate scales relevant to educational environments, that is, the Learning Environment Inventory (Walberg, 1969) and the Organizational Climate Description Questionnaire (Halpin & Croft, 1963). The elements identified by these two scales can be conceptualized as falling within the three basic categories.

From results based on both educational and industrial environments, Stern (1970) identified two major types of second-order factor dimensions using the Organizational Climate Index (OCI). He indicated that the OCI factor structure essentially replicates his former scale, the CCI. Stern reported that the OCI has been factored three times. One analysis was based on the responses of teachers in elementary, junior high, and senior high schools; a second on Peace Corps trainees; and a third on technicians employed in three different industrial sites. Six factors were extracted in a first-order analysis and two in a second-order analysis. Stern (1970) summarized his results as follows:

The first of the second-order factors describes a variety of press for facilitating growth and self-enhancement; the other reflects organizational stability and bureaucratic self-maintenance. These tend to confirm the hypothesized distinction drawn earlier between anabolic and catabolic press [p. 68].

Stern did not explicitly make a distinction between relationship and personal development dimensions. He also did not include system change dimensions in his category of control or system maintenance press. On the other hand, two variables which appear to be relationship dimensions were identified by Stern as closeness and group life. Three of Stern's variables appear to reflect personal development. He called these intellectual climate, personal dignity, and achievement standards. Stern's last two system maintenance factors are labeled orderliness and impulse control.

Stern's conceptualization is based on factor solutions and closely coincides with our conceptualization, strongly supporting the notion that there is a limited number of underlying patterns which can characterize a rather large and varied group of social environments.

Two more examples (Table 2) show similar conceptualizations. The Agency Climate Questionnaire (Schneider & Bartlett, 1970) and the Climate Questionnaire (Litwin & Stringer, 1968) were both constructed to assess industrial environments. The ACQ is primarily for insurance agencies and has subscales such as (a) managerial support (managers take an active interest in agents as individuals), (b) managerial structure (managers require that agents adhere strictly to budgets), and (c) agent independence (agents receive an accurate picture of job potential when they are contacted). Some of the Litwin and Stringer dimensions are (a) warmth (the feeling of general good fellowship that prevails in a work group atmosphere), (b) support (the perceived helpfulness of the managers and other employees in the group), (c) identity (the feeling that the employee belongs to the company and is a valuable member of a working team), (d) responsibility (the feeling of being one's own boss and not having to double check all of one's decisions), (e) risk (the sense of riskiness and challenge in the job and in the organization), and (f) structure (the feeling that the employees have about the constraints of the groups in terms of rules and regulations). Both scales are strikingly similar in basic dimensions to those identified by the Social Ecology Laboratory in very different environments.

Finally, an example is provided by an assessment of group processes conducted by Fairweather, Sanders, Cressler, and Maynard (1969) in which they compared a ward-based with a community-based psychiatric treatment program. They found three dimensions which characterized group processes and labeled these dimensions (a) group cohesiveness

(cohesiveness, morale, attraction to group, satisfaction with leader), (*b*) group performance (performance, reward, problem input, information input), (*c*) leadership and role delineation (leadership, role clarity).

One may conclude from the work in this area that relationship, personal development, and system maintenance and system change dimensions must all be accounted for in order for an adequate and reasonably complete picture of the environment to emerge.

Environmental Impact on Individual Functioning

The study and assessment of environments are important because of their relevance to individual functioning. The "climate" of environments in which people function relates to their satisfaction, mood, and self-esteem and to their personal growth. Environments shape adaptive potentials as well as facilitate or inhibit initiatives and coping behavior. For example, environments that place an emphasis on relationship dimensions such as involvement and support usually have high morale (Cumming & Cumming, 1962). It has been demonstrated that psychiatric wards and correctional units that emphasize autonomy and personal problem orientation have patients and residents who like the staff and feel they can develop their abilities and increase their self-confidence (Moos, 1974c).

Social environments also have significant impact on more objective criteria of behavioral outcome. For example, Moos, Shelton, and Petty (1973) related the social environment of psychiatric wards to objective indexes of treatment outcome as assessed by dropout rates (how many patients left the ward before treatment was completed), release rates (how rapidly were patients released from the ward), and community tenure (how long patients were able to stay in the community after release from the hospital). Two independent studies found that patients and staff perceived wards that had high dropout rates to be low in involvement, support, order and organization, and program clarity. Wards with high release rates were perceived as strongly emphasizing practical orientation, but inclined toward "unexpressiveness," whereas wards that kept patients out of the hospital longest were perceived as emphasizing autonomy, a practical orientation, order and organization, and the open expression of feelings, particularly angry feelings.

Similar results can be seen in the environment of military basic training companies. Moos (1973d) found that military company "climate" was related to important indexes of outcome, such as total performance on graded tests at the end of basic training, the AWOL (absent without official leave) rate, and the rate of sick call. Companies which did best on total performance criteria were those that emphasized both peer cohesion and officer support. Companies with excessive sick call lists contained men who felt that the work was repetitious and boring, that there was no opportunity for leadership roles and no orientation to the company, and that they were ridiculed in front of others. Company environments had effects on men's moods. For example, companies with high scores on officer control and low scores on personal status had men who felt more anxious. Companies high on officer control and low on peer cohesion had men who felt more depressed. Companies high on officer control and low on both officer support and clarity had men who felt more hostility. Thus, one finds specific relationships between dimensions of basic training company environments and types of negative effects.

Stressful environments have been shown to have cumulative long-term effects on those who function within them. Caffrey (1969) studied the environments of Benedictine and Trappist monks and found a prevalence of coronary heart disease in those environments characterized as competitive with a sense of time urgency. Sales (1969) suggested in his review that environments with work overload are implicated as precursors of cardiovascular disease.

In an extensive review of the literature, Kiritz and Moos (in press) concluded that the evidence supports the hypothesis that "social environmental factors have pronounced effects on human physiological processes." They suggested that

the social stimuli associated with the relationship dimensions of *support, cohesion* and *affiliation* generally have positive effects—enhancing normal development and reducing recovery time from illness, for example. Goal Orientation and System Change dimensions such as *responsibility, work pressure,* and *change* can increase the likelihood of stress and disease.

Toward an Optimum Environment

What are the criteria by which environment can be judged as favorable? Lewis Mumford (1968) viewed an ideal environment as "seeking continuity, variety, orderly and purposeful growth" as opposed to an environment that "magnifies authoritarian power and minimizes or destroys human initiative, self-direction, and self-government [p. 221]." Mumford suggested that optimum environments are organic and the qualities that make them desirable have to do with people, not "machines."

There are, of course, no clear, well-defined criteria for an ideal environment that can meet everyone's requirements. Inhabitants of specific environments would undoubtedly have different criteria and different goals. The point is, however, that the likelihood of achieving an optimum environment is greatly facilitated when critical decisions about changing the environment are in the hands of the people who function within the environment. For an outsider to impose the kind of order and structure according to his own unique view of "Utopia" would undoubtedly result in strong resistance which can manifest itself in many subtle and disguised ways.

Moos (1974c) has presented a methodology for facilitating social change which is particularly relevant to small environments that have a moderate to high frequency of interactions among milieu members. The approach has four basic components:

1. Everyone involved in the environment is given the opportunity to report his view of how the current environment is functioning on the relevant dimensions discussed earlier. In addition, all participants are asked to convey information about their conceptualizations of an ideal social system. Thus, the goals and general value orientations of the milieu occupants are systematically assessed.

2. Individualized feedback is then given on the results of these assessments. Particular attention is paid to similarities and differences in the perceptions of various important groups within the environment; for example, in a hospital setting: patients versus doctors and nurses; in an industrial setting: workers versus management; in a classroom: students versus teachers. In addition, emphasis is placed on the similarities and differences between the "real" and the "ideal" social environment and the subsequent implications for change.

3. Practical planning of specific methods by which change might occur along specified dimensions is then instituted. This planning is usually done with the help of a social systems change "facilitator" who is experienced in the ways in which different types of social systems can change.

4. The change process itself is assessed by one or more reassessments of the characteristics of the social environment. These results are continuously fed back to the participants providing an ongoing, systematic approach to achieving the kind of environment participants would like to have.

This methodology is linked with concepts of problem-solving, coping, and adaptive behavior. Many theorists have discussed each individual's active need for involvement and for the prediction and control over his own environment (White, 1959). The active propensities of man as scientist of different aspects of stimulation and variety-seeking motivation and of the importance of cognition and information seeking are central to planning effective social change methods. This approach is consistent with these important needs which include actively helping to mold one's social environment in desired directions. Its use may even help some individuals achieve a new competence, that of being able to change and control their own environment.

REFERENCES

BARKER, R. *Ecological psychology.* Stanford: Stanford University Press, 1968.

CAFFREY, B. Behavior patterns and personality characteristics related to prevalence rates of coronary heart disease in American monks. *Journal of Chronic Diseases,* 1969, 22, 93–103.

CUMMING, J., & CUMMING, E. *Ego and milieu.* New York: Atherton Press, 1962.

DOUGLAS, J. W. B. *The home and the school.* London: MacGibbon & Kee, 1964.

FAIRWEATHER, G., SANDERS, D., CRESSLER, D., & MAYNARD, H. *Community life for the mentally ill.* Chicago: Aldine, 1969.

FRIEDLANDER, F., & GREENBERG, S. Effects of job attitudes, training, and organization climate on performance of the hard-core unemployed. *Journal of Applied Psychology,* 1971, 55, 287–295.

GOFFMAN, I. *Asylums.* New York: Doubleday, 1961.

HALPIN, A., & CROFT, D. *The organizational climate of schools.* Chicago: Midwest Administration Center, University of Chicago, 1963.

INSEL, P., & MOOS, R. *The Work Environment Scale.* Palo Alto: Social Ecology Laboratory, Department of Psychiatry, Stanford University, 1972.

KIRITZ, S., & MOOS, R. Physiological effects of social environments. *Psychosomatic Medicine,* 1974, in press.

LITWIN, G. H., & STRINGER, R. A. *Motivation and organizational climate.* Boston: Division of Research, Harvard Business School, 1968.

MISCHEL, W. *Personality and assessment.* New York: Wiley, 1968.

MOOS, R. Sources of variance in responses to questionnaires and in behavior. *Journal of Abnormal Psychology,* 1969, 74, 405–412.

MOOS, R. Conceptualizations of human environments. *American Psychologist,* 1973, 28, 652–665. (a)

MOOS, R. *Military Company Environment Inventory manual.* Palo Alto, Calif.: Social Ecology Laboratory, Department of Psychiatry, Stanford University, 1973. (b)

Moos, R. *Community Oriented Programs Environment Scales manual.* Palo Alto, Calif.: Consulting Psychologists Press, 1974, in press. (a)

Moos, R. *Correctional Institutions Environment Scale manual.* Palo Alto, Calif.: Consulting Psychologists Press, 1974, in press. (b)

Moos, R. *Evaluating treatment environments: A social ecological approach.* New York: Wiley, 1974, in press. (c)

Moos, R. *Ward Atmosphere Scale manual.* Palo Alto, Calif.: Consulting Psychologists Press, 1974, in press. (d)

Moos, R., & GERST, M. *University Residence Environment Scale manual.* Palo Alto, Calif.: Consulting Psychologists Press, 1974, in press.

Moos, R., & HUMPHREY, B. *Group Environment Scale technical report.* Palo Alto, Calif.: Social Ecology Laboratory, Department of Psychiatry, Stanford University, 1973.

Moos, R., & INSEL, P. (Eds.) *Issues in social ecology: Human milieus.* Palo Alto, Calif.: National Press, 1974.

Moos, R., SHELTON, R., & PETTY, C. Perceived ward climate and treatment outcome. *Journal of Abnormal Psychology,* 1973, **82,** 291–298.

Moos, R., & TRICKETT, E. *Classroom Environment Scale Manual.* Palo Alto, Calif.: Consulting Psychologists Press, 1974, in press.

MUMFORD, L. *The urban prospect.* New York: Harcourt Brace Jovanovich, 1968.

MURRAY, H. *Exploration in personality.* New York: Oxford University Press, 1938.

PACE, C. R., & STERN, G. G. An approach to the measurement of psychological characteristics of college environments. *Journal of Educational Psychology,* 1958, **49,** 269–277.

PACE, R. *College and University Environment Scales.* (Tech. manual, 2nd ed.) Princeton, N.J.: Educational Testing Service, 1969.

PETERSON, R., CENTRA, J., HARTNETT, R., & LINN, R. *Institutional Functioning Inventory: Preliminary technical manual.* Princeton, N.J.: Educational Testing Service, 1970.

SALES, S. Organizational role as a risk factor in coronary disease. *Administrative Science Quarterly,* 1968, **14,** 325–336.

SCHNEIDER, B., & BARTLETT, C. Individual differences and organizational climate by the multi-trait, multi-rater matrix. *Personnel Psychology,* 1970, **23,** 493–512.

STERN, G. *People in context: Measuring person–environment congruence in education and industry.* New York: Wiley, 1970.

STERN, G., STEIN, M., & BLOOM, B. *Methods in personality assessment.* Glencoe, Ill.: Free Press, 1956.

WALBERG, H. Social environment as a mediator of classroom learning. *Journal of Educational Psychology,* 1969, **60,** 443–448.

WHITE, R. Motivation reconsidered: The concept of competence. *Psychological Review,* 1959, **66,** 297–333.

WOLFE, R. The measurement of environments. In A. Anastasi (Ed.), *Testing problems in perspective.* Washington, D.C.: American Council on Education, 1966.

Crowding and Human Behavior

STEVEN ZLUTNICK and IRWIN ALTMAN

A social problem receiving a great deal of attention today is that of over-population, or crowding, and its implied deleterious effects on the quality of life, both physical and psychological. Planned parenthood and the increased demand for birth control have become the watchwords of social reform and further indicate the degree to which the general public has embraced the problem. Many fear physiological, as well as psychological, effects of what has often been termed "people pollution." Some have already concluded that the effects are enormous, some are pessimistic of any solution, and others hasten to achieve quick and dramatic solutions.

That the world's numbers are growing at an alarming rate is well documented Ehrlich (1968) points out that from 6000 B.C. to 1650 A.D. the world population had grown to 500 million from 5 million; that is, it had doubled every 1,000 years or so. By 1850 it had reached 1 billion, doubling every 200 years. By 1930 the world population had climbed to 2 billion, requiring only 80 years to double. At the present growth rate, the doubling time appears to be slightly over 35 years.

Although concomitant increases in disease, food shortages, air and water pollution, and a host of assorted environmental-physical effects may often accompany such growth, this chapter focuses on potential *social* and

Steven Zlutnick will receive his PhD in clinical psychology from the University of Utah in 1972. He is currently Director of Training and Evaluation in Postgraduate Education, Department of Psychiatry, University of Utah College of Medicine, and Director of Parent Training for the Garfield Training Center, Salt Lake City, Utah. His research interests currently focus on conditioning and epileptic disorders.

Irwin Altman received his PhD in social psychology from the University of Maryland in 1957. He is currently a Professor and Chairman of the Department of Psychology, University of Utah. His major research interests concern the growth and management of interpersonal relationships with emphasis on environmental and ecological aspects of social bonds.

Preparation of this chapter was supported in part by Grant EG8-70-0202(508) from the Office of Education, United States Department of Health, Education, and Welfare.

ENVIRONMENT AND THE SOCIAL SCIENCES, edited by Wohlwill and Carson, APA, 1972, pp. 44-58.

psychological effects of crowding. Specifically, the following questions are addressed.

1. *What scientific knowledge exists regarding the effects of crowding on human social and psychological functioning?* While many hold strong views about the horrendous effects of overcrowding, including crime, war, riots, mental illness, and a host of other evils, there appears to be some doubt, as described below, as to how confident one can be about such predictions in terms of available scientific evidence.

2. *What does "crowding" mean, and what factors affect its impact?* As with so many other popular terms, crowding has a variety of meanings, depending upon the context. But, as the other chapters in this book indicate, there are several ways to conceptualize the phenomenon of crowding, and all may be useful in some respect. Some writers emphasize physical density or number of people per unit of space, others stress subjective feelings, while others focus on physiological responses.

3. *What are some directions of analysis and alleviation of any negative effects of crowding?* Given several properties of crowding, we will suggest some directions for research and avenues of action and policy to alleviate the possible effects of crowding. Because solutions are partly predicated on one's definition of the problem, it is crucial to link research and action with the conceptual meaning of crowding. For example, if one defines crowding solely as "number of people per unit of space," then one's natural solution to alleviate crowding effects is to reduce the number of people per unit of space. Because we see crowding as more complex than density alone, alternative solutions to the problem become available.

THE STATE OF KNOWLEDGE REGARDING EFFECTS OF CROWDING

To say that relatively little rigorous empirical data exists on the psychological and social effects of crowding on human behavior is a gross understatement. A review the authors conducted of a representative sample of knowledge of crowding effects turned up three types of investigations: (*a*) laboratory-oriented research involving some type of controls; (*b*) correlational studies in natural settings involving use of records, such as crime rates, census data, etc.; and (*c*) popularized speculations and guesses. The last category is the most voluminous; the first is the one least evident in the scientific literature.

Experimental Studies

In a search by the authors of the *Psychological Abstracts* and *Sociological Abstracts* of the past 10 years, only a handful of studies emphasizing the *experimental* analysis of psychological and social effects of crowding on human behavior were found. For example, Hutt and Vaizey (1966) studied autistic, brain-damaged, and normal children between the ages of three and eight. The children were observed in a small group with regard to aggressive behavior (fighting, snatching, or breaking toys), social interactions, and time spent on the outer boundaries of the room as a function of different "social densities," or number of children within the same spatial area. For groups ranging in size from 6 to 12, the data indicated that brain-damaged children increased in aggression as group density increased, while normal subjects became more aggressive only in larger groups. For social encounters, normals showed a decrease in interaction in larger groups; brain-damaged children showed more interaction in medium-sized groups; and autistics showed less interaction in large groups. Furthermore, as density increased, the autistic children spent significantly more time at the boundary of the room, although the effect held generally for all populations.

In a later study, Hutt and McGrew (1967) manipulated "spatial density" by observing the same-sized groups in different-sized areas. Social interaction of nursery school students with one another and with adults increased as density increased (somewhat contrary to the earlier study), as did aggressive behavior.

In the last two years, a few other studies of crowding have appeared, and it is likely that the number will increase geometrically in subsequent years. For example, Freedman, Klevansky, and Ehrlich (1971) reported three experiments on the effects of density on human performance. The subjects were given a variety of intellectual tasks to perform, some simple, some complex, under various conditions of crowding. In all cases, subjects worked alone, in the presence of others, in groups of five to nine, in spaces varying in gross square footage from 35 to 160 square feet. They worked for several hours at a time on several successive days. The results indicated no differences in performance on any task as a function of density conditions. Such experiments are difficult to interpret since the absence of differences may be attributable to a variety of design and methodological conditions; that is, it is difficult to *confirm* the statistical null hypothesis. In a partial report of ongoing work, Freedman (1971) suggested some effects of crowding on cooperation–competition, punitiveness, and liking of others. Males in a more crowded situation appeared to be more competitive, gave more punitive sentences in a mock jury situation when crowded, and reported crowded situations to be more unpleasant. Surprisingly, women tended to exhibit similar behaviors in *less crowded* circumstances.

In another study, Griffitt and Veitch (1971) studied the effects of variation in temperature and group size on attraction responses. Those placed in high-temperature settings and those placed in crowded situations (12–16 person groups with about four square feet per person) rated a stranger less attractive than did those in cool and spacious rooms (ratings were of a hypothetical other person about whom subjects were given questionnaire information). There was no interactive effect of density and temperature variables, and there were some potentially confounding effects of temperature on crowding, since subjects not only rated the crowded conditions as less pleasant but also as warmer.

A recent study by Baxter and Deanovich (1970) examined attributed anxiety responses in a crowded situation. Female subjects were placed in a crowded condition, that is, with a separation between them and an experimenter of only a few inches, versus an uncrowded condition, that is, where the separation was about four feet. They viewed two doll figures in close proximity (doll crowding) or with some separation They were instructed to rate the anxiety felt by the dolls, representing people, under scenarios depicting positive or threatening situations for the dolls. The results indicated some effects of subject crowding, with more anxiety attributed to the doll figures under crowding, but only later in the rating series. Also, the data suggested that these effects held primarily when both the subject and dolls were crowded.

Aside from such studies and related literature on personal space and territorial intrusion, human experimental literature on the effects of crowding is almost nonexistent. While there are studies of confined groups, they typically do not manipulate group size or area of the environment.

Correlational Studies

The majority of empirically based conclusions concerning crowding effects came from studies of relationships between various actuarial measures of population density, for example, people per acre or people per dwelling unit, and an assortment of statistical indicators of social disorganization such as crime, mental illness, and disease rates.

Crime. Schmid (1937, 1960) found high population densities and high crime rates in ghettos and central city areas and a progressive decrease in both as one moved toward suburbs of Minneapolis and Seattle. Many other studies confirmed this relationship in other major cities (Bordua, 1958; Lander, 1954; Lottier, 1935–39; Shaw & McKay, 1942; Sorokin & Zimmerman, 1929; Watts, 1931).

Schmitt (1957) found a high correlation between population density, juvenile delinquency, and adult crime in Honolulu during the years 1948–51, with a large number of juvenile delinquents and adult prisoners from overcrowded neighborhoods having multiunit construction and a large ratio of population to residential land. Juvenile delinquency, for example, occurred at a rate of 15.8 cases per 1,000 in census tracts with under 20 people per net acre, 18.2 cases per 1,000 families in tracts with 20.5 to 59.9 persons per acre, and 25.5 per 1,000 families in tracts with 60.0 or more people per acre. Schmitt (1966) further distinguished between two measures of population density: population per acre (outside residences) and people per dwelling unit (inside residences). In examining the relationship between these two measures of density and social breakdown (e.g., mental illness, tuberculosis, venereal disease, crime, illegitimate births), he found that population per acre correlated with such variables, whereas density per dwelling unit did not.

Mental illness. The correlational data for mental illness as a function of population density parallel that of crime rates. Faris and Dunham (1965) reported a decreasing incidence of mental illness from city centers outward to suburbs in a number of cities. Using an interview approach, Lantz (1953) also found a higher incidence of mental illness in military officers from densely populated areas. Chombart de Lauwe (1959) identified a threshold of psychological crowding between 2 and 2.5 persons per room, which, when exceeded, was associated with a greater incidence of aggressiveness and other antisocial behavior. Other supporting data have been found by Hollingshead and Redlich (1958), Queen (1948), Schroeder (1942), Pollock and Furbush (1921), Malzberg (1940), and Landis and Page (1938). Similar data on suicide have been reported by Cavan (1928), Schmid (1933, 1955), and Sainsbury (1956).

Social interaction. A study of social interaction by Smith, Form, and Stone (1954) revealed a gradual decrease in intimacy, number, and frequency of personal contacts from the periphery of the city to more densely populated city centers. Barker and Gump (1964) reported that students in larger schools were less involved in school activities than those in smaller schools.

In general, it is dangerous to make direct causal linkages between indicators of social disorganization and population density. One need not consider the matter long to realize that many alternative explanations could be invoked to account for much of the density-related data. For example, pure density is not the only variable that distinguishes the center of a city from its suburbs. Economic status, health facilities, physical well-being, and education are but a few factors that might be related to social disorganization of the type reported above. And, obviously, the fact that two variables correlate in no way guarantees causation. Therefore, while these correlational studies are suggestive, no hard conclusions about psychological and social effects of crowding on human behavior can be drawn from them.

Popular Speculations and Hypotheses

In spite of the paucity of conclusive data, there appears to be wide consensus in popularized writings about the evils of crowding. No doubt, much of this derives from the preceding types of data and from animal studies, such as the classic description of the behavioral sink by Calhoun (1962) and the work of Christian and his associates (Christian, 1961; Christian, Flyger, & Davis, 1960) on deer and mice. Also, conclusions about social and psychological effects of crowding may derive from physical science and biological studies of pollution, disease, etc.

To get some idea of the source of many popular hypotheses or "myths" about crowding, the authors undertook a 10-year review of the *Reader's Guide to Periodical Literature* and uncovered a veritable unending source of

94

TABLE 1

Popular Conceptions of the Effects of Crowding/Overpopulation on Human Behavior

A. Physical effects

1. Mass starvation-famine (*U.S. News & World Report*, 1965)
2. Pollution of the environment (*Commonweal*, 1968; *Vital Speeches*, 1968)
3. Slums (*Look*, 1965)
4. Disease (epidemics, etc.) (*Foreign Affairs*, 1965)
5. Physiological breakdowns (malformations, etc., reproductive efficiency, etc.) (*Newsweek*, 1968)

B. Social effects

6. A deterioration of education and service systems (*Senior Scholastic*, 1967)
7. Higher crime rates (*Vital Speeches*, 1968)
8. Riots (*Newsweek*, 1968)
9. War (*Christian Century*, 1966; *Living Wilderness*, 1967; *Science Newsletter*, 1965; *National Review*, 1962)
10. Economic stress (unemployment, poverty, etc.) (*Reader's Digest*, 1965; *Christian Century*, 1962)
11. More controls by "Big Brother" (*National Review*, 1965; *Reader's Digest*, 1965)

C. Interpersonal and psychological effects

12. Mental illness (disorder) (*Reader's Digest*, 1965)
13. An increase in drug addiction and alcoholism (*Vital Speeches*, 1968)
14. Family disorganization (*Vital Speeches*, 1968)
15. A loss of freedom (*Living Wilderness*, 1967)
16. A loss in the quality of life (*Look*, 1965; *National Review*, 1962)
17. An increase or decrease in the amount of interaction (*Newsweek*, 1968)

"expert" opinions on the effects of crowding on human behavior. From some 35 articles, we induced 17 propositions concerning crowding or overpopulation (which shall be used synonymously for this exercise) that are currently being cited in the popular literature. The authors of articles ranged from ecologists to politicians to journalists, and most documented their cases with either no data or the type of data described above. Table 1 presents these propositions, with recent examples of where they were cited.

These hypotheses, propositions, or popular conceptions can be grouped according to three types of effects:

1. *Physical effects:* starvation, pollution, slums, disease, physical malfunctions (the authors' review of the scientific literature did not focus on these effects);

2. *Social effects:* poor education, poor physical and mental health facilities, crime, riots, war; and

3. *Interpersonal and psychological effects:* drug addiction, alcoholism, family disorganization, withdrawal, aggression, decreased quality of life.

The data supporting these propositions are either lacking or typically based on (*a*) animal research, (*b*) correlational data, or (*c*) opinion. Therefore, the authors' conclusion, based on only a preliminary analysis, is that, in spite of the tremendous need for rigorous data regarding this significant social problem, such knowledge does not appear to exist. We just cannot be confident about the effects of crowding on social and psychological behavior in humans. This is a harsh conclusion, but unless massive amounts of empirical research have been missed in the literature review, it appears to be warranted. While the authors may be personally convinced that overpopulation and crowding have serious effects on social and psychological aspects of behavior in humans, there is, as yet, inadequate scientific evidence that is unequivocal, replicable, or carefully designed. More is obviously needed.

What Does Crowding Mean and What Factors Determine Its Presence?

In order to understand the meaning and determinants of crowding, it is important to delineate the numerous ways the concept has been used. The most common approach has been to use density, or number of people per unit of space, as the basis for definition and to attribute crowding effects to density. The authors believe this to be a useful but incomplete strategy. For example, writers like Schmitt (1957, 1966) and Hutt and McGrew (1967) view density as a complex phenomenon and suggest that one must consider such factors as "inside" density, that is, number of people per unit of living space, and "outside" density, that is, number of people in a larger community (e.g., census tract), or social density (number of people per unit of space) and spatial density (amount of space per person). (Also see Carson, 1969, for a discussion of this point from the perspective of planning and design professions.) To illustrate the complexity of the problem, one might consider the distinction between a dormitory with 50 beds versus the same number of people in separate rooms, or conditions that exist in elevators, theaters, and subways where the concentration of people is high versus those in concentration camps, ghettos, and other equally high density areas. While these examples are somewhat contrived, they are intended to illustrate that number of people per unit of space may be too simplistic a conceptualization of crowding. This does not mean that density in this sense is unimportant, only that more may be involved in the phenomenon of crowding. Without considering this possibility, we necessarily limit our focus and perhaps our understanding and ability to alleviate crowding problems.

From the authors' perspective, the concept of crowding involves a multidimensional set of interlocked properties, such as (a) *situational/environmental characteristics* of high density of people per unit of space for long periods of time, in environments where resources are limited; (b) certain *interpersonal events* where persons are unable to adequately control their interactions with others, and/or where the psychological and physiological costs controlling interactions are high; and (c) *personal/subjective events* where there is a network of personal and subjective feelings reflecting an inability to control interpersonal exchange, discrepancies in expectations, and incongruities with past experience.

96

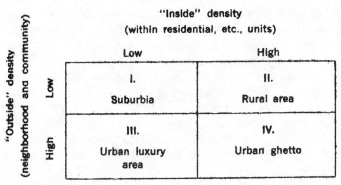

Fig. 1. Density of people as a determinant of crowding.

Following is an analysis of this conceptualization.

1. *The situation or environment as a determinant of crowding.* An extension of Schmitt's (1966) distinction between inside and outside density may be particularly useful at this time. Inside density refers to the number of people per unit of living space within a residence or some other locale, for example, an apartment or a home, whereas outside density refers to the number of people per unit of space in a larger environmental unit within which the inside density unit is embedded, for example, street, neighborhood, census tract, etc. From this two-factor definition, a variety of living situations can be broadly categorized (see Figure 1). Typical suburban living involves a relatively small number of people inside residences and a relatively small number of people outside residences in the immediate community. At the other extreme is the big-city ghetto, which often has a high concentration of people inside as well as outside residences. Rural areas are often characterized by high population densities within a home but with few people immediately outside the home. The East Side luxury areas of New York, on the other hand, have residences with relatively small numbers of people inside but high concentrations in the outside neighborhood and city.

This classification is incomplete, for there are many situations that cannot be incorporated. For example, a full elevator, a packed movie theater, and a busy restaurant involve high concentrations of people inside the setting and, if in a city, would have high outside densities. Yet, most would agree that the long-range psychological effects of such situations are probably inconsequential and that they also differ markedly from ghettos or other high inside–high outside density settings.

To delineate such situations, another dimension of crowding is proposed —*temporal duration.* When one speaks of extreme crowding, reference is implicitly made to *long-term* situations extending over days, months, or even years. Thus, it seems important to employ a *temporal* dimension in describing and studying crowding phenomena.

A third facet of the environment that seems important is the *richness of environmental resources.* Two homes with equivalent space and density can differ enormously in how space is laid out, the interior decor, and the quality of facilities in general. An environment that is relatively bare or poor in resources might be more susceptible to the effects of crowding.

Thus, there appear to be several properties of the environment, which include, but go beyond, density, that seem essential to an understanding of the phenomenon of crowding. Piecing these together, it might be said at this time that extreme crowding might exist when (a) inside and outside densities are high, (b) when people are in such situations for long periods of time, and (c) when the environment is limited in resources.

2. *Interpersonal determinants of crowding.* An old theory of memory loss stated that forgetting occurred because of decay of memory traces over time. The view that time itself is the cause of forgetting is no longer widely accepted, but it is believed that events that occur in time interfere with prior memory. Similarly, physical density, time, and richness of the environment might only function as necessary conditions to produce effects of crowding. One such underlying process of an interpersonal nature concerns *people's ability or inability to control interactions with others.*

Much has been written about personal space, privacy, and territoriality. Central to these concepts is the idea that people establish boundaries around themselves to maintain their psychological integrity, protect their environment, and pace and manage interaction with others. Control of interpersonal interaction is accomplished in a variety of ways, including manipulation of the physical environment, verbal and nonverbal communication, and a variety of intrapersonal factors. Regarding the use of the environment, we open and close doors, arrange furniture in certain ways, establish seating patterns around tables, etc. We also actively use nonverbal communication to control and pace interaction, for example, face toward or away from other people, assume certain body positions and postures, etc. Words are also employed to control interaction by means of content or substance and by paralinguistic variations in inflection, tone, pauses, silences, interruptions, etc. In addition, interpersonal exchange is often managed by autistic processes such as daydreaming, "tuning out" other people, and perhaps even using drugs and alcohol. Thus, a whole spectrum of techniques is used to pace relations with other people. One hypothesis is that when these control mechanisms break down, especially in high-density situations, a condition commonly described as crowding may exist. These notions are implicit in the animal research conducted by Calhoun (1962) and others, who demonstrated breakdowns in social and physiological functioning under conditions of high density.

The cost of controlling interaction may be great in the usual ghetto situation, where both inside and outside density are extremely high, where contact with other people is continuous, where environmental resources are limited, and where the temporal duration of exchange with others is lengthy. This is exactly opposite to the suburban situation and in some sense in between the rural and East Side luxury areas (see Figure 1). In the rural situations, the requirements to control interaction are high inside, that is, with a large family or several families in one home, but they are low outside, due

98

to the remoteness of neighbors. Here the individual can manage interaction by leaving the high-density inside situation and going into the low-density outside situation, that is, he can easily get away from people. Conversely, the big-city luxury situation involves a high amount of outside interaction but low inside interaction, and the individual can control exchange by remaining in the low density situation (i.e., staying at home).

Thus, a central factor that may underlie sheer physical density and other environmental characteristics concerns ability to control interpersonal interaction. To the extent that it is impossible to do so, or because the "price" in physiological and psychological terms is high, we might have the conditions essential for a situation commonly described as crowding.

3. *Psychological factors.* Although difficult to conceptualize precisely, a third facet of crowding must be considered, namely, subjective or personal factors. A number of factors interact here: the notion of an individual's past history in relation to the parameters of crowding (particularly in relation to density), his perceived ability to control interactions involving varying degrees of density, and possible discrepancies in expectations about densities encountered in the environment. It is readily apparent that all of these notions are interrelated and overlap to some extent.

An individual raised in a rural environment in which inside density is high and outside density is low might have a great deal of difficulty adapting to a ghetto type of environment since the outside densities differ remarkably between the two. Likewise, an only child accustomed to relative quiet in his environment might find a room with eight people in it crowded compared with a youth from a family of eight children. Thus, it would appear that one's past experiences with densities will greatly affect his evaluation and perceptions as to what does and does not constitute a crowded environment.

The individual's perceived or real ability to control interactions will also contribute to the occurrence of a crowded situation. A number of factors present themselves at this juncture. A person might literally be placed in a position where it is physically impossible to avoid contact with others, such as an overcrowded prison compound or a ghetto apartment house with larger numbers of people per room. Or it may simply be the case that the individual does not have the social skills necessary to successfully adapt to high-density (or perceived high-density) situations. For example, an introvert might easily feel crowded in a situation that an extrovert finds socially enjoyable. Thus, the subjective experience of being crowded may be an important element in understanding the phenomenon.

A further aspect to be considered under the rubric of psychological factors would be that of an individual's expectations (or predictions) as to what densities will obtain in a given situation. For example, a young man making a social call on a girl he hopes to date might well feel crowded when he discovers that she already has a visitor. Thus, it appears to be the case that psychological factors, in addition to pure situational–environmental and interpersonal factors, are going to greatly influence an individual's conception of crowding.

In summary, we have proposed that the concept of crowding be dealt with at several levels: physical, interpersonal, and psychological. Using all these levels of analysis, we described a number of possible parameters of crowding: (*a*) a high inside and outside density of people per unit of space, (*b*) for long periods of time, (*c*) in an environment of limited resources, (*d*) with little ability to control interaction with others (or a high cost of doing so in terms of physiological and psychological processes), and (*e*) where there is a network of personal and subjective feelings reflecting inability to control interaction, discrepancies in expectations and attitudes, and incongruity with past experience.

It is possible that not all these conditions need obtain in "crowded" situations. Nevertheless, these parameters convey the notion of crowding as (*a*) a multidimensional concept that can be investigated by a number of avenues of research and (*b*) sufficiently complex that remedial actions and policy making to ameliorate negative consequences might then be pursued along several lines simultaneously, rather than in terms of simple unilateral solutions such as density.

A Strategy of Research on Crowding

The most current tactic of research and thinking on crowding asks, either explicitly or implicitly, "What is the effect of crowding on human behavior?" While this is a practical and productive approach, there appear to be other equally promising avenues of research that take into account the view of "crowded man" as a coping, striving, adapting organism who often acts or shapes his environment. Thus, in addition to asking what is the effect of density alone on human behavior, we propose two additional questions: (*a*) How does man successfully adapt to crowding and what psychological and physiological prices does he incur in so doing? and (*b*) What type of long-term etiology or history results in successful or unsuccessful adaptation to crowding? Thus, there are three general avenues to pursue.

1. *Crowding as a determinant of behavior.* Here the focus lies on physical–environmental conditions that give rise to perceptions and expectations of crowding, changes in social interaction, and a variety of dependent measures. Although we have stated previously that this should not be the sole strategy of research on crowding, nevertheless, the amount of research even here is found to be seriously lacking.

2. *Coping and adaptive responses to crowding.* The subtle implications of much thinking and research on crowding are that it invariably has adverse effects. An alternative assumption is that man *will adapt* and ultimately survive and that an attempt should be made to understand the mechanisms underlying his ability to do so and how it might be facilitated.

Thus, the real issue is *how* the organism adapts to his environment, not whether or not he can, and the psychological and physiological costs incurred in successful adaptation. Since many of these costs may be cumulative and result in any of a variety of long-term outcomes, it is probably necessary that we track and correlate various levels and styles of coping with concomitant physiological and psychological processes.

3. *Historical antecedents and responses to crowding.* Different long-term environmental histories may result in unique patterns of responding to crowding. For example, as discussed previously, the person raised in an urban environment probably develops a different set of responses to high-density situations than the rural person. And a child from a large family is not likely to react to a crowded apartment in the same way as an only child. Therefore, possible research questions include: (*a*) How do such response patterns develop? (*b*) What functions do they serve? and (*c*) What historical etiology contributes to different modes of adaptation to crowding?

Methodological strategy. We believe that there is no single ideal methodological approach for studying a phenomenon as complex as that of crowding. While the correlational studies that dominate the field have serious limitations, they do provide potentially important information as part of a total research strategy. However, it is extremely crucial that more effort be devoted to developing a body of knowledge based on rigorous experimental approaches in both laboratory and field naturalistic settings.

Furthermore, the phenomenon of crowding is not the property of any one discipline, and we should be sensitive to the findings, concepts, and methodology of related fields such as biology, physiology, sociology, etc.

To reiterate a position taken earlier, the authors are personally convinced that overpopulation and crowding are potentially disastrous social problems. But the mere fact that an issue is socially relevant does not obviate the necessity to empirically verify conclusions about it.

ACTION PROGRAMS AND POLICY DECISIONS

It should be clear that the state of knowledge regarding the effects of crowding on human behavior is too sparse to permit any firm recommendations regarding ameliorative action. In fact, we do not appear to be in a scientifically defensible position to suggest the nature and magnitude of any effects. The most honest statement is that as yet we just do not know much about the psychological effects of crowding.

In spite of this, we need only see the plight of people in ghettos and underprivileged environments to know, as human beings, that the situation is intolerable and demands immediate, practical solutions. But, as we have tried to demonstrate in this chapter, how one conceives of the problem and its definition and causes will determine the strategy of solution. For example, the popular conception of the negative effects of crowding is seen largely as an issue of "too many people in too little space." With this density theory as "the theory," the natural solution is to reduce the number of people per unit of space and thereby eliminate the problem. This is often accomplished by massive low-cost housing programs that are designed to provide more space

101

per person or per family. While this may be desirable, our conceptualization, if accurate, suggests that there are many other possible solution strategies. For example, if lack of environmental richness is also a factor, then planners and decision makers may also have to pay more attention to the interior quality of apartment design, the quality of the neighborhood environment, and a host of environmental features that relate to functional and cultural characteristics of the population.

Beyond environmental design is the whole issue of control of interpersonal interaction and the possibility of training people to use environments to achieve control over interpersonal events in a smooth and noncostly fashion. Thus, there may be routes to solving the crowding problem in addition to reducing density in the environment. If the framework proposed here is correct, particularly that aspect involving control of interpersonal exchange, it may be possible to train people to become more sensitive to their environments and to learn how to shape and control interaction with others by active use of the environment. Thus, it may be possible to develop new modes of coping with and controlling interaction with others, in spite of high population densities. The solution, in addition to reducing density, may also include teaching and training people to deal more effectively with one another in such dense conditions. While we may not be able to control population growth at zero level or we may not be able to eliminate high-density situations, we may be able to develop new modes of interpersonal interaction that preserve the integrity of the individual and that allow him to cope with multitudes of others in ways that minimize psychological and physiological costs. We are not proposing explicit techniques to do this, but are only suggesting that a broader conceptualization of the problem of crowding than in terms of density alone can have potential implications for both research and action. The validity of the ideas presented here, from both a scientific and pragmatic nature, remains to be determined. But at this stage of knowledge regarding crowding effects on humans, we propose a strategy of research and action that conceives of crowding as a relatively complex phenomenon. This will not only broaden our vistas with regard to acceptable parameters of research, but it will also permit a broader perspective regarding action programs and policy decisions.

REFERENCES

Barker, R. G., & Gump, P. V. *Big school, small school.* Stanford: Stanford University Press, 1964.

Baxter, J. C., & Deanovich, B. S. Anxiety arousing effects of inappropriate crowding. *Journal of Consulting and Clinical Psychology,* 1970, **35,** 174–178.

Bordua, D. Juvenile delinquency and "anomie." *Social Problems,* 1958, **6,** 230–238.

Calhoun, J. B. Population density and social pathology. *Scientific American,* 1962, **206,** 139–148.

Carson, D. Population concentration and human stress. In B. F. Rourke (Ed.), *Explorations in the psychology of stress and anxiety.* Ontario: Longmans Canada Limited, 1969.

Cavan, R. S. *Suicide*. Chicago: University of Chicago Press, 1928.

Chombart de Lauwe, Y. M. J. *Psychopathologie sociale de l'enfant inadapte*. Paris: Centre National de la Recherche Scientifique, 1959.

Christian, J. J. Phenomena associated with population density. *Proceedings of the National Academy of Sciences*, 1961, **47**, 428–449.

Christian, J. J., Flyger, V., & Davis, D. E. Factors in the mass mortality of a herd of sika deer *cervus nippon*. *Chesapeake Science*, 1960, **1**, 79–95.

Ehrlich, P. R. *The population bomb*. New York: Ballantine, 1968.

Faris, R., & Dunham, H. W. *Mental disorders in urban areas*. Chicago: Phoenix Books, 1965. (Orig. published 1939.)

Freedman, J. L. The crowd—Maybe not so madding after all. *Psychology Today*, 1971, **5**, 58–62. (a)

Freedman, J. Population density and human performance and aggressiveness. In A. Damon (Ed.), *Physiological anthropology*. Cambridge: Harvard University Press, 1971. (b)

Freedman, J. L., Klevansky, S., & Ehrlich, P. R. The effect of crowding on human task performance. *Journal of Applied Social Psychology*, 1971, **1**, 7–25.

Griffitt, W., & Veitch, R. Hot and crowded: Influences of population density and temperature on interpersonal affective behavior. *Journal of Personality and Social Psychology*, 1971, **17**, 92–99.

Hollingshead, A. B., & Redlich, F. C. *Social class and mental illness*. New York: Wiley, 1958.

Hutt, C., & McGrew, W. C. Effects of group density upon social behavior in humans. In, Changes in behavior with population density. Symposium presented at the meeting of the Association for the Study of Animal Behavior, Oxford, July 17–20, 1967.

Hutt, C., & Vaizey, M. J. Differential effects of group density on social behavior. *Nature*, 1966, **209**, 1371–1372.

Lander, B. *Toward an understanding of juvenile delinquency*. New York: Columbia University Press, 1954.

Landis, C., & Page, J. D. *Modern society and mental disease*. New York: Farrar & Rinehart, 1938.

Lantz, H. R. Population density and psychiatric diagnosis. *Sociology and Social Research*, 1953, **37**, 322–327.

Lottier, S. Distribution of criminal offenses in metropolitan regions. *Journal of Criminal Law and Criminology*, 1938–39, **29**, 39–45.

Malzberg, B. *Social and biological aspects of mental disease*. Utica, N.Y.: State Hospital Press, 1940.

Pollock, H. M., & Furbush, A. M. Mental disease in 12 states, 1919. *Mental Hygiene*, 1921, **5**, 353–389.

Queen, S. A. The ecological study of mental disorders. *American Sociological Review*, 1948, **5**, 201–209.

Sainsbury, P. *Suicide in London*. New York: Basic Books, 1956.

Schmid, C. Suicide in Minneapolis, Minnesota, 1928–1932. *American Journal of Sociology*, 1933, **39**, 30–49.

Schmid, C. *Social saga of two cities: An ecological and statistical study of the social trends in Minneapolis and St. Paul*. Minneapolis: Minneapolis Council of Social Agencies, 1937.

Schmid, C. Completed and attempted suicides. *American Sociological Review*, 1955, **20**, 273.

Schmid, C. Urban crime areas. *American Sociological Review*, 1960, **25**, 527, 542, 655–678.

Schmitt, R. C. Density, delinquency and crime in Honolulu. *Sociology and Social Research*, 1957, **41**, 274–276.

Schmitt, R. C. Density, health and social disorganization. *Journal of the American Institute of Planners*, 1966, **32**, 38–40.

103

Schroeder, C. W. Mental disorders in cities. *American Journal of Sociology*, 1942, **48**, 40–51.

Shaw, C., & McKay, H. D. *Juvenile delinquency and urban areas.* Chicago: University of Chicago Press, 1942.

Smith, J., Form, W., & Stone, G. Local intimacy in a middle sized city. *American Journal of Sociology*, 1954, **60**, 276–285.

Sorokin, P. A., & Zimmerman, A. T. *Principles of rural–urban sociology.* New York: Holt, 1929.

Watts, R. E. Influence of population density on crime. *Journal of the American Statistical Association*, 1931, **26**, 11–21.

A SOCIAL-PSYCHOLOGICAL MODEL OF HUMAN CROWDING PHENOMENA

Daniel Stokols

Previous research on crowding has generally lacked a theoretical perspective. Moreover, there has been a tendency to view crowding in terms of spatial considerations alone and a failure to distinguish between the physical condition (density) and the psychological experience (crowding). In the present discussion, a heuristic model of human crowding phenomena is proposed which permits an integration of various theoretical perspectives and the derivation of experimental hypotheses. Although the limitation of space remains as the essential ingredient of crowding, the proposed model introduces personal and social variables which have a direct bearing on a person's perception of spatial restriction as well as on his attempts to cope with this constraint. The relation between the dimensions of the model is examined in terms of social-psychological theory. Finally, a program for future research is discussed.

Within the past decade, growing concern for the quality of the physical and social environment has prompted scientists from various academic disciplines to concentrate their research efforts upon contemporary ecological problems. A fundamental assumption underlying ecologically oriented research has been that an understanding of the relationship between organisms and their environment, gained through scientific inquiry, will ultimately provide guidelines for social planning and urban design.

Among the ecological phenomena which have attracted the attention of behavioral scientists are

JOURNAL OF THE AMERICAN INSTITUTE OF PLANNERS, March 1972, pp. 72-83.

those related to spatial limitation and crowding. Problems of spatial restriction represent formidable topics for scientific inquiry due to their high degree of complexity. Like most concomitants of overpopulation and urbanization, such as pollution and scarcity of resources, crowding phenomena are highly interrelated with other societal problems— for example, poverty and racial discrimination. Hence, at the urban level it is difficult to separate the behavioral effects of spatial limitation from those of other variables.

Another source of complexity which hinders a comprehensive understanding of crowding is the variety of levels at which it is manifested throughout society. We can speak of a crowded home, neighborhood, or city. The types of variables which interact with spatial restriction undoubtedly vary from one level to the next. Consequently, the effects of crowding on human behavior are probably different at each level.

Finally, the ambiguity of vocabulary used to describe crowding phenomena has also made it difficult to subject problems of spatial limitation to empirical study. For instance, many writers often use the terms "density" and "crowding" interchangeably rather than distinguishing between the physical condition, density, and the psychological experience, crowding. Such confusion not only impairs the precise specification of independent and dependent variables, but also obstructs the development of a broad theoretical perspective from which to approach crowding phenomena.

In order for crowding to be rendered amenable to scientific inquiry, some of the above-mentioned complexities and ambiguities must be recognized, and an attempt must be made to resolve them. In this article I develop an analysis of human crowding phenomena and propose a conceptual model of crowding situations and their effects on human behavior. First, however, a brief review of previous approaches to the study of crowding is presented.

A consideration of the contributions, as well as the inadequacies, of these approaches provides the foundation on which the proposed framework is developed.

Previous Research on Crowding

There have been four basic lines of behavioral research which relate to the issue of crowding: animal studies, correlational surveys utilizing census tract data, experiments on the human use of space, and experimental studies directly concerned with the effects of crowding on human behavior.

The well-known animal studies of Calhoun (1962, 1966) and his associates (Marsden, 1970) exemplify the first approach. By limiting the amount of space available to a community of Norwegian rats, Calhoun observed a phenomenon known as the "behavioral sink," that is, the simultaneous gathering of several animals at specific points in the community (for example, feeding areas) over long periods of time. Calhoun linked the crowded conditions of the behavioral sink to pathological behaviors exhibited by certain animals in the community: the neglect of maternal duties, hyper- and homosexuality, and the withdrawal of individual animals from social interaction.

An experiment by Christian, Flyger, and Davis (1960) provides further evidence regarding the detrimental effects of crowding upon animal populations. In this study, a herd of deer was confined to a small island and allowed to reproduce. As the number of deer increased, a pronounced decrease in reproductivity was observed.

The correlational studies of Schmitt (1957, 1966), Chombart de Lauwe (1959), Winsborough (1965), and Mitchell (1971), which have relied upon census tract data, are examples of the second type of crowding research. The typical approach of such surveys is to correlate various measures of population density (for example, number of persons per net acre or per dwelling unit) with several indices of social and medical pathology (for example, rates of crime, tuberculosis, and suicide). Usually, the effects of variables, such as income level and education, are controlled through the technique of partial correlation.

The findings of these surveys suggest that population density is generally associated with social disorganization. Winsborough, however, has demonstrated that the positive correlation between density and pathology disappears when certain measures of social status are utilized as control variables. And Schmitt (1963) has observed that in Hong Kong, density per acre is not invariably associated with behavioral anomalies; other factors such as cultural traditions and the nature of residential land use seem to mediate the relationship between population density and human behavior.

The ecological research of Barker (1965, 1968) on behavior settings, and the work of Hall (1959, 1966) and Sommer (1967, 1969) on proxemics (the use of space in everyday behavior) represent the third type of investigation of crowding. Although these studies do not focus directly upon the behavioral effects of crowding, their inquiry into the perception and use of space is certainly germane to a consideration of problems arising from spatial restriction.

Barker, in his naturalistic studies on "undermanned" versus "overmanned" behavior settings, found that students of small schools generally achieved satisfaction by being competent, accepting challenges, and engaging in group activities, while students of large schools derived satisfaction more frequently out of vicarious, rather than direct, participation in group functions. The main implication of Hall's work on proxemics is that people differ in their habits, attitudes, and values concerning the use of space and interpersonal distance, and that differences along these dimensions are largely culture-bound. Finally, the message of Sommer's research regarding "personal space" is that the perception of spatial relations among objects is significantly influenced by the type of activity which generally occurs in a given area.

Experimental investigations directly concerned with the effects of spatial limitation on human behavior reflect the most recent approach to the study of crowding phenomena. Such studies have generally been of two types, those which define crowding in terms of group size and those which manipulate it in terms of room size. The research of Ittelson, Proshansky, and Rivlin (1970), Hutt and Vaizey (1966), and Griffit and Veitch (1971) represent the first type of investigation, while those of Freedman (1970) and Freedman, Klevansky, and Ehrlich (1971) represent the second. Results from the first set of studies indicate that members of larger groups are more aggressive and asocial than those of smaller ones, regardless of whether the setting is a psychiatric ward, a playground, or a psychological experiment. The second set of experiments, however, demonstrates that when group size is kept constant but room size is varied, the task performance of subjects in the small room is no less efficient than that of subjects in the large room. Freedman did observe, though, in the small room condition, that interpersonal relations within female groups were more intimate and friendly than the affective behaviors manifested in male groups.

From the four categories of research outlined above, a preliminary picture of crowding phenomena begins to emerge. The animal studies portray crowding as a stress situation which develops over time. The physical condition of spatial limitation, which places constraints upon certain social activities (for example, allocation of food and sexual behavior), represents the necessary condition for crowding phenomena. As population density increases, spatial constraints become more acute until, finally, they eventuate in social disorganization and physiological pathology. Situations of crowding, then, are characterized both by the element of spatial restriction and by the manifestation of its deleterious effects on organisms over time.

The research on human populations, however, indicates that spatial restriction is not inevitably associated with social maladies. The survey studies, for instance, suggest that in Asian societies cultural traditions serve to offset the detrimental effects of high population density. Experiments concerning the human use of space provide further evidence that cultural norms mediate the perception and adjustment of interpersonal space. Such research also suggests that the type of activity performed in a given area largely determines whether the amount of available space is perceived as adequate or too limited. Finally, the laboratory investigations of human crowding demonstrate that when group size is held constant and the physical consequences of spatial restriction (for example, high temperature, stuffiness, limited movement) are controlled, high density exerts virtually no ill effects on human task performance. The research on human subjects, then, considered in light of the animal studies, indicates that spatial restriction serves as a necessary antecedent of, but not always a sufficient condition for, the arousal of crowding stress.

Although previous empirical approaches provide some insights into the nature of human crowding phenomena, interpretation of the findings from each line of inquiry is rendered difficult by methodological or conceptual inadequacies. For example, the applicability of data from animal research to the analysis of human crowding is limited by problems of ecological validity (Brunswik, 1956) which arise whenever one generalizes from communities of rats to societies of men. The findings of survey studies are plagued by the causal ambiguities of correlational research. The results from experiments on personal space, while interesting, do not relate specifically to the experience of human crowding. And the more direct experimental investigations of human crowding have not been guided by any coherent theoretical perspective.

The lack of a conceptual framework concerning crowding has led to a failure in laboratory studies to distinguish between the different types of variables which mediate the experience of crowding stress, such as spatial, temporal, social, and personal factors. Hence, most investigators have defined crowding in terms of spatial considerations alone. Moreover, there has been little consensus among experimenters regarding the specification of independent and dependent variables. Thus, in some studies the manipulation of density has been accomplished through variations in group size, while in others it has been effected through the use of small and large rooms.

Direct experimental investigation appears to be the most advanced and promising approach to the analysis of human crowding. In order to resolve some of the ambiguities which have previously hindered research, a conceptual framework for the experimental study of human crowding is introduced in the ensuing discussion.

A Conceptual Framework For The Analysis of Human Crowding

An Elementary Definition of Crowding   Before the concept of human crowding can be framed as a psychological research topic, some attempt must be made to define, or describe, this concept. As a preliminary definition, we will assume that a state of crowding exists, and is perceived as such by an individual, when the individual's demand for space exceeds the available supply of such space. A similar conceptualization of crowding has been proposed by Kwan (1967) and by Proshansky,

Ittelson, and Rivlin (1970).

While the above definition is rudimentary, it enables us to draw a crucial distinction between the concepts of *density* and *crowding*. Density denotes a physical condition involving the limitation of space. Crowding, on the other hand, refers to a situation in which the restrictive aspects of limited space are perceived by the individuals exposed to them. The recognition of spatial inadequacy arouses the experience of psychological and physiological stress. Thus, density is a univariate condition of limited space, without motivational overtones, whereas crowding is a multivariate phenomenon, resulting from the interaction of spatial, social, and personal factors, and characterized by the adverse manifestations of stress.

Some Additional Distinctions   In order to delineate, more specifically, the scope of the proposed model, four additional distinctions regarding the conceptualization of crowding are required. First, it is important to differentiate between crowding as a *stressor situation* and the experience of crowding as a *syndrome of stress*. The first concept refers to sources of crowding stress, that is, those variables whose interaction evokes the experience of being crowded. The second concept connotes the experience of crowding itself and its various levels of impact within the individual or group, that is, the manifestations of physiological and psychological stress, or social disorganization. Each of the above meanings is represented as a separate dimension of the proposed model.

Secondly, we can distinguish between *nonsocial* and *social* crowding. In the first case, a person's supply of useable space is restricted at what he perceives to be an inadequate level by purely physical factors. For example, an astronaut may feel crowded because of the cramped quarters of his space capsule, or a person sitting at a table may feel crowded if his desk is overly cluttered with books, papers, and a typewriter. Among the major types of variables affecting an individual's experience of nonsocial crowding are: spatial factors including the amount and arrangement of space, stressor variables such as noise or glare which heighten the salience of physical constraints, and personal characteristics including idiosyncratic skills and traits.

In situations of social crowding, the individual's awareness of spatial restriction is related directly to the presence of other persons, as well as to his relationship to them. The number of people in a given area largely determines the proportion of space available to each person. While situations of nonsocial crowding involve spatial restriction caused by physical variables alone, conditions of social crowding introduce social constraints on available space and imply competition with other persons for scarce resources (for example, space and materiel).

An individual may feel crowded in the midst of strangers, but quite comfortable and secure in the presence of an equal number of friends. The factors which determine one's experience of social crowding include the variables already mentioned in relation to nonsocial crowding, as well as social factors such as group structure and activity variables. The ensuing discussion focuses upon social crowding situations because they involve a greater number of component variables than do nonsocial situations and thereby afford a more complete application of the proposed model of crowding.

A third major distinction can be drawn between situations of *crowding* and those of *undercrowding*. The first situation involves an acute restriction of space, while the latter is characterized by an excessive abundance of space (that is, a situation in which an individual's supply of space greatly exceeds his demand for space; *uncrowded* situations, on the other hand, are those in which there is a balance between an individual's supply of and demand for space). Each type of situation elicits characteristic forms of stress. While crowded persons may feel constrained and infringed upon, undercrowded individuals tend to experience a need for enclosure and affiliation with others. The present discussion is concerned mainly with crowding situations, although the proposed model of crowding can be extended to a consideration of undercrowded conditions.

The fourth and final distinction concerns the levels at which human response to crowding can be considered. Two basic levels of crowding phenomena are distinguishable: the sociological, or *macrocosmic*, level; and the psychological, or *microcosmic*, level. The first represents the level at which most urban designers and environmental behavioral scientists approach crowding. Its main concern is with the effects of large scale urban population density upon societal and cultural integration. The psychological, or microcosmic, level is primarily concerned with the impact of perceived spatial restriction on the individual's behavior. The experience of crowding is viewed as a syndrome of psychological stress, the intensity of which is determined by several independent factors. This article deals primarily with the microcosmic level.

An Equilibrium Model of Human Response to Crowding

Because the individual and the environment are the basic units involved in crowding phenomena, the variables which mediate an individual's perception of and response to crowding can be subsumed under two major categories: qualities of the physical and social environment, and personal attributes of the individual. Qualities of the physical environment include the amount and arrangement of available space, as well as stressors which affect the salience and immediacy of spatial variables (for example, noise, glare, and length of exposure time). Features of the social environment include variables which are introduced by the presence of other persons (for example, status allocation, the division of labor, and group size). Finally, personal attributes of the individual include momentary states of arousal (for example, hunger and sexual arousal), idiosyncratic skills and weaknesses related to effective operation in the environment (for example, intelligence, strength, and agility), and personality characteristics (for example, internal-external locus of control and comparison level).

The present model applies to situations involving spatial restriction in which personality and social factors interact with physical variables to induce psychological or physiological stress in the individual. The experience of such stress provokes behavioral, perceptual, or cognitive responses designed to alleviate physical discomfort or psychological strain. Hence, the model represents a multivariate schema of response to crowding in that it incorporates several distinct sets of input and output variables. Moreover, the relationship between input and output factors is one of equilibrium in the sense that extremes in one type of variable are compensated for through adjustments in other types of variables so as to maintain a state of equilibrium between the individual and the environment.

As illustrated in figure 1, the model consists of four basic dimensions: environmental variables, E; personal attributes, P; intensity and type of stress, S; and adaptive and maladaptive responses to stress, R. There are five major phases of crowding phenomena which are inherent in the model. Their numerical ordering denotes a chronological sequence of events: (1) the interaction between E and P variables which determines their respective salience and immediacy to the individual; (2) the perception of that subset of interactions between E and P variables which induces crowding stress in the individual (that is, psychological and physiological strain); (3) the provocation of tension-reducing responses in the person (these may include cognitive, perceptual, or behavioral adjustments); (4a) the enactment of specific responses aimed at modifying either environmental qualities or (4b) personal attributes (for example, moving to a less crowded area, or adjusting one's perception of the situation so as to render it more tolerable); and (5a) the adaptive or maladaptive consequences of environmental, as well as (5b) personal, adjustments.

In the present framework, a response is adaptive to the extent that it relieves either environmental or personal sources of strain and breaks the cycle

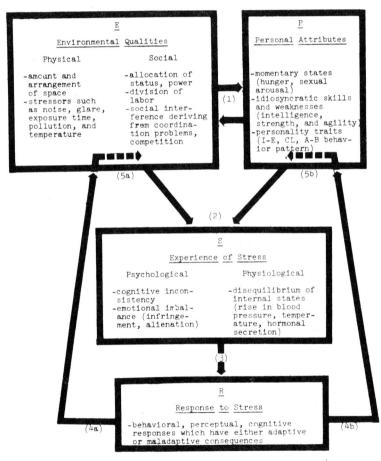

FIGURE 1   *An Equilibrium Model of Human Response to Crowding*

of crowding stress (in figure 1, this is represented by the broken arrows). A response is maladaptive to the degree that it intensifies strain due to environmental and personal factors and thereby perpetuates the cycle of crowding stress (in this case, the arrows of [5a] and [5b] in figure 1 would be solid).

According to the present analysis, all crowding situations involve stress, and the occurrence of this stress cannot be predicted on the basis of spatial considerations alone. Rather, the experience of crowding must be understood as a phenomenon which develops over time, and whose developmental pattern and intensity are determined through a combination of environmental and personal factors. If several people occupy a small room in which there is a relatively small amount of space per person, yet these people feel completely comfortable and unrestricted, then a situation of crowding does not exist. On the other hand, if fewer persons in a larger room feel restricted and infringed upon by each other, then a state of crowding does exist.

Regardless of the specific environmental and personal factors involved, all situations of crowding seem to involve similar manifestations of stress. The basic forms of crowding stress have already been mentioned, namely, psychological and physiological strain. Psychological stress can be characterized as two types: cognitive inconsistency stemming from the realization that one's demand for space exceeds the available supply of such space, and emotional imbalance resulting from feelings of infringement, alienation, and lack of privacy. Physiological stress involves a disequilibrium in one's internal response systems (for example, increased blood pressure, temperature, or adrenalin secretion) and can be triggered by purely spatial variables, as evidenced in the discomfort of feeling cramped. It may also arise through the interaction of spatial variables with social and personality factors. A person with high affiliative needs, for example, who finds himself in a small room with several unfriendly strangers, may experience physiological symptoms of anxiety stemming from feelings of alienation and detachment. Thus, physiological stress is often aroused by psychological strain.

In the present model, the experience of crowding stress provokes tension-reducing responses which occur in order to reduce physical or psychological discomfort. The particular form of one's response to crowding will be a function of the relative intensity of environmental and personal factors and of the degree to which they can be modified. When spatial variables can be readily altered, a person who feels crowded will most likely adopt a behavioral mode of response. For example, an individual can increase his amount of personal space by leaving the crowded situation. In cases where overt behavioral adjustments of spatial variables are limited, perceptual and cognitive modes of reducing crowding stress will be more likely to occur. In such situations, a person may modify his standards of spatial adequacy so as to alleviate the sensation of crowding.

Adaptive responses to crowding are those which reduce the stressful effects of perceived spatial restriction. The reduction of stress is accomplished through the effective adjustment of either physical, social, or personal factors. Maladaptive responses, on the other hand, are those which fail to alleviate the experience of crowding stress. For example, a person's decision to remain at a crowded party with several strangers would be adaptive if it eventually led to pleasant interaction and friendship with other persons. The decision to remain, however, would be maladaptive if the person was unable to strike up a conversation with someone at the party and left feeling alienated and depressed.

The major features of the proposed model of
human crowding have been delineated above;
hypotheses regarding the interaction of its various
components remain to be specified. In the ensuing
discussion, the relationships between the four
dimensions of the model are considered in terms of
social-psychological theory. A set of experimental
hypotheses is derived by examining examples of
situations in which environmental and personal
factors engender the experience of crowding.

ENVIRONMENTAL AND PERSONAL SOURCES
OF CROWDING STRESS

Some of the environmental and personal factors
which yield conditions of crowding are categorized
in figure 1. Because these variables are quite
numerous, only a representative sample will be
discussed. It should be emphasized that the variables included in each box of figure 1 are not
intended to comprise an exhaustive inventory of
the parameters of crowding. Rather, they reflect
the variety of factors, within each of the four
dimensions of the model, which may contribute to
an individual's experience of crowding. Determination of the relative salience and importance of each
factor, across various situations of crowding, is a
task for future research.

Physical Variables   The amount and arrangement of space are probably the most salient
physical dimensions of a crowded situation. The
amount of space available to a person represents a
crucial determinant of his behavioral freedom. As
space becomes scarce, the number of behavioral
alternatives available to an individual decreases.
Although the amount of space sets limits on one's
range of behavioral freedom, the intensity of
spatial restriction can be altered, somewhat,
through various arrangements of the available
space. For example, a small room may be made to

appear larger by surrounding it with mirrored walls or by judiciously arranging furniture. As Michelson (1970) points out, the arrangement of dwelling space in Japan may be one factor which mitigates the adverse effects of high poupulation density there.

In light of the research on crowding, mentioned earlier, spatial limitation appears to be a variable whose latent unpleasant properties are activated only through its interaction with other aspects of the specific situation. The immediacy and salience of reduced space are intensified, for instance, through the operation of physical stress factors such as temperature and noise. Griffit and Veitch (1971) observed that interpersonal affective responses were significantly more negative under conditions of high temperature and high density than under those of comfortable temperature and low density. Also, it is plausible that noise, through its unwelcomed infringement on the individual's personal space, also serves to increase the salience of spatial restriction and thereby intensify the experience of crowding.

Social Factors   The presence of other persons introduces several factors which may heighten the individual's sense of spatial restriction. The type of activity engaged in with others will directly affect the salience of limited space. The impact of activity variables on the experience of crowding is evident at a football game, where thousands of people are packed into a giant stadium. While the game is being played, everyone is completely engrossed in the action, and the limitation of space goes unnoticed or is forgotten. As soon as the game ends, however, the restrictions of spatial limitation are immediately felt. Each person becomes concerned with exiting the stadium as quickly as possible. It is at this point that the individual must coordinate his actions with those of other persons. The necessity of behavioral coordination as a means of limiting social interference and insuring the efficient use of space (for example, avoidance of traffic jams) represents one social factor which may intensify the experience of crowding.

The extent to which an individual perceives himself to be competing with others for scarce resources represents another social variable which heightens the salience of limited space. In the previous example, access to the stadium exits represents a commonly desired resource. The individual's realization that the other fans are competing with him for a direct path to the exits is likely to exacerbate his sensation of spatial restriction. In other situations, competition may concern nonspatial commodities such as power and prestige. In such instances, competitive feelings arouse a tendency to view the presence of others as a threat to the individual's general welfare and an infringement on his privacy. In the context of spatial limitation, these perceptions are likely to promote the experience of crowding and a heightened concern for personal space.

For a group which is characterized by a high degree of organization and clearly defined goals, the susceptibility or immunity of its members to crowding stress can be considered in terms of the two basic aspects of group structure suggested by Homans (1950), the internal and external systems. The first facet of social structure encompasses those factors which promote cohesion and minimize conflict among group members (for example, a well-defined leadership hierarchy, status consensus, and widely held norms). The second system of social structure concerns variables which enable the group to adapt to the demands of its external environment (for example, the division of labor, which facilitates task efficiency).

The internal and external systems operate to maintain social equilibrium. To the extent that these systems are weak, group structure breaks down and its members experience stress. Since limited space can be characterized as an external contingency which threatens the group's equilibrium, the capacity of the internal and external systems to deal effectively with spatial constraints determines whether or not members of the group will experience crowding stress. For example, if the group members are unable to coordinate their activities efficiently, the restrictions of limited space are likely to become salient. Or, if the "correspondence of outcomes" (Thibaut and Kelley, 1959), that is, the commonality of interest, among group members is low, interpersonal relations within the group will tend to be quite competitive. As noted earlier, intragroup competition interferes with the ability of each member to cope with spatial constraints and thereby promotes the experience of crowding.

Personal Factors This set of variables includes momentary states of arousal, idiosyncratic skills, weaknesses, and personality traits which affect an individual's ability to cope with the limitation of space. It is quite plausible that certain personal attributes serve to protect an individual from the ill effects of crowding, while others tend to predispose him to the dissatisfactions and health hazards of crowding situations.

The temporary states of hunger and sexual arousal, for example, may heighten a person's experience of crowding by making salient his competition with others for scarce resources, or by increasing his need for privacy. Under conditions of spatial limitation, then, prolonged hunger and sexual deprivation would intensity an individual's frustration, dissatisfaction, and sense of crowding.

Idiosyncratic skills and weaknesses will also have some bearing upon a person's ability to cope with spatial constraints. An intelligent person, for example, will be more able to find creative solutions to problems of crowding than will an unintelligent one. Similarly, a strong person will be able to exert control over limited resources more readily than will a weak person. And, under conditions of limited space, an agile individual will find it easier to coordinate his actions with those of other people than will a clumsy one. The personal traits of intelligence, strength, and agility, thus, would contribute to the minimization of crowding stress.

The dimension of "internal-external locus of control" (Rotter, 1966) represents a personality characteristic that may be quite relevant to the intensity of the individual's crowding experience. This dimension concerns the degree to which a person perceives the quality of his experiences as being under either personal or environmental control. In situations of crowding, it is plausible that "internal" individuals will be able to perform more efficiently than "external" individuals within the constraints of spatial restriction. This would be especially true if behavioral modes of alleviating crowding stress were available. But if conditions of crowding are prolonged and unrelievable, "internals" may experience more frustration with being confined and unable to exert their usual control over the situation. "Externals," however, perceiving themselves to be generally under environmental control anyway, might experience relatively less dissatisfaction with spatial restriction. In situations such as these, "externals" may be more readily adaptable to crowding stress than "internals."

The concept of "comparison level," as formulated by Thibaut and Kelley (1959), is also relevant to a consideration of personal factors which affect the individual's perception of crowding. Comparison level (CL) is a criterion of outcome acceptability with which an individual evaluates the attractiveness of a situation in terms of what he expects or feels he deserves. Individuals who are generally used to having large amounts of space at their disposal (for example, individuals raised in a rural setting) would be likely to develop a higher CL regarding the amount of space considered to be adequate in any situation than would individuals who have had more experience with spatial limitations (for example, residents of a large city). Hence, the former would be more apt to experience frustration over spatial constraints than the latter. This conceptualization may explain Cassel's (1970) observation that newcomers to a situation of crowding tend to be more vulnerable to its adverse effects than persons who have had previous experience with crowded situations.

Another individual characteristic which may mediate the experience of crowding is the coronary-prone behavior pattern described by Jenkins (1971). This behavioral syndrome is characterized by extremes of competitiveness, impatience, and overinvolvement with work. Individuals who manifest this pattern are referred to as "Type A's," whereas individuals who tend to be patient, easy-going, and relaxed are labelled "Type B's."

In situations of crowding, Type A's should be highly susceptible to the dissatisfactions and bodily imbalances caused by spatial restriction, while Type B's should be relatively resistant to these strains. The characteristics of impatience, competitiveness, and restlessness, embodied in the coronary-prone behavior pattern, would be likely to arouse an accentuated sense of frustration and anxiety under conditions of prolonged and unalterable crowding.

THE EXPERIENCE OF, AND RESPONSE TO, CROWDING STRESS

Psychological Stress   Two manifestations of psychological stress in situations of crowding have been distinguished above, cognitive inconsistency and emotional imbalance. In many instances, the former type of stress precipitates the latter.

Cognitive inconsistency, in the context of crowding phenomena, has been characterized as the recognized disparity between an individual's supply of and demand for space. A person's realization that he is unable to supplement his supply of space evokes an awareness that his range of behavioral freedom is restricted. According to Brehm (1966), such an awareness should provoke "psychological reactance," that is, a motivational state involving feelings of preemption and infringement, and resulting in behavior directed toward the reestablishment of threatened or eliminated freedom. A similar conclusion is reached by Proshansky, Ittelson, and Rivlin (1970), who consider crowding to be a situation involving the restriction of an individual's behavioral choice. They point out that a person's reactance against crowding will be especially intense if his restriction of freedom is due to the presence of other persons who infringe upon his privacy.

In situations of crowding, then, psychological reactance can be viewed as the motivational or emotional consequence of cognitive inconsistency stemming from the recognized discrepancy between one's supply of and demand for space. According to the present model, an individual will alleviate his reactance to crowding through an appropriate adjustment of either environmental variables, personal factors, or both. Furthermore, his adoption of a behavioral, perceptual, or cognitive mode of response will depend upon the relative intensity and flexibility of these factors.

Brehm's reactance theory, Festinger's (1957) dissonance theory, and the cognitive consistency theory of Rosenberg and Abelson (1960) provide a basis for considering some of the manifestations and determinants of the three modes of response to psychological stress under conditions of crowding. According to Brehm, the greater the magnitude of an individual's reactance, the more he will attempt to reestablish his lost or threatened freedom. The magnitude of reactance will depend upon the importance of that freedom to the individual, as well as upon the degree of freedom of behavior eliminated or threatened. Brehm discusses two basic means of reestablishing freedom.

The first involves a direct reestablishment of freedom through the enactment of the forbidden or threatened behavior. When there are restraints against this type of response, the second mode of reestablishing freedom, which involves the symbolic attainment of freedom "by implication," will occur. In this case, the person will engage in behavior similar to that which has been prevented.

An example of direct reestablishment of freedom would be an individual's exit from an overly crowded room. If, however, the person was confined to the crowded area, then he might attempt to reestablish his freedom symbolically, by withdrawing from social interaction. This type of behavior would symbolize, or approximate, the unavailable behavioral option of leaving the room. Through this mode of response, the person would reestablish his autonomy by implication.

The methods of alleviating reactance, discussed by Brehm, represent behavioral modes of inconsistency-resolution. Yet, in certain situations of crowding, the costs of attempting to reestablish one's behavioral freedom, either directly or indirectly, far outweigh the potential advantages of such action. Conditions of crowding may arise from which it is physically impossible to withdraw and within which withdrawal from social interaction would be maladaptive. The members of a jury, for example, may find themselves operating under such conditions, especially if their chamber is cramped and their deliberation prolonged. In such situations, where reactance against spatial restriction cannot be alleviated behaviorally, a perceptual or cognitive mode of stress-resolution must be employed.

The members of the jury might alleviate their reactance by becoming thoroughly engrossed in deliberation so as to minimize the salience of their spatial restriction. By concentrating on the gravity of their decision rather than on the discomforts of their chamber, they are able to alleviate the strain of feeling crowded. This type of reactance-resolution represents a perceptual mode of response to crowding. By focusing upon the task dimensions of the situation, the spatial constraints which cannot be eliminated directly or indirectly become less noticeable and hence less stressful.

The adjustment of cognitive elements so as to render them less discrepant represents an alternative mode of reactance-resolution and is especially adaptive in situations where reestablishment of freedom is either impossible or too costly. The jurors, in our example, realizing that they must remain together until a final verdict is reached, make an implicit decision to give up the freedom of voluntarily leaving the jury chamber. Such a decision should elicit reactance against behavioral restriction to the extent that room space is inadequate and the deliberation prolonged. In terms of Festinger's (1957) dissonance theory, reactance against spatial and temporal stress factors can be characterized as a cognitive element, dissonant with the decision to remain in the situation. Cognitive dissonance, deriving from the discrepancy between the discomforts of crowding and the decision to endure them, can be alleviated, essentially, by increasing the desirability of the chosen alternative (remaining in the jury chamber) and decreasing the desirability of the rejected alternative (leaving the chamber). For example, the jurors may attempt to convince themselves that the case on which they are deliberating is extremely interesting and unique. Participating in jury deliberation would therefore seem enjoyable. Or they may persuade themselves that withdrawal from the jury would represent a dishonorly abdication of civil duty.

According to the cognitive consistency theory of Rosenberg and Abelson (1960), the jurors' attitude toward remaining in the chamber should become more favorable to the extent that their action can be instrumentally linked to positively evaluated objects or values. For example, the decision to remain on the jury may be judged as a good, wise, useful, or moral action if it is associated with the "pursuit of justice" or the attainment of valuable experience. In terms of reactance-resolution, the more favorable the jurors feel about their decision to remain in the chamber, the more tolerable will be their spatial restriction and the less reactance they will feel toward it.

Physiological Stress   It has so far been assumed that the individual will be able, ultimately, to alleviate his psychological reactance against crowding through the utilization of behavioral, perceptual, or cognitive modes of inconsistency resolution. Yet under certain conditions, the person will be unable to cope successfully with psychological stress resulting from involuntary or prolonged exposure to crowding. The maladaptive consequences of inappropriate (or inadequate) response to crowding will be manifested as feelings of frustration, alienation, and impatience, but they become particularly noticeable and potentially dangerous as manifestations of physiological disorders.

Physiological stress arising from reactance against the experience of crowding can be quite detrimental to an individual's health and general well-being. Researchers in the medical and public health professions have continually emphasized the general relationship between stress and physiological maladies (Cannon, 1932; Levine and Scotch, 1970; Selye, 1956). Rene Dubos (1968) reports that "physiological tests have revealed that crowding commonly results in an increased secretion of various hormones which affect the whole human physiology. An adequate hormonal activity is essential for well-being, but any excess has a variety of harmful effects" (p. 153).

Cassel (1970) has also discussed the relationship between hormonal disequilibrium and the incidence of disease. He contends that crowding increases the risk of disease by heightening social and emotional strain, rather than by increasing the opportunity for spread of infection. Cassel proposes that the role of social factors is to increase the susceptibility of the organism to disease through "the activation of inappropriate neuroendocrine arousal mechanisms" (p. 18).

In certain instances, physiological imbalance may have adaptive value for the individual, especially if it continues to provoke responses which finally eventuate in an alleviation of crowding stress. A detailed analysis of human adaptation to physiological stress is provided by Dubos (1965) and Selye (1956). For the purposes of the present discussion, though, it is sufficient to point out that prolonged exposure to the psychological and physiological stresses of crowding can have detrimental consequences for the individual's health.

A SET OF EXPERIMENTAL HYPOTHESES CONCERNING CROWDING

The preceding analysis of human crowding phenomena suggests several hypotheses which can be tested experimentally.

1. The limitation of space will engender an experience of crowding to the extent that it introduces noxious physical effects (for example, rise in temperature, stuffiness) or places constraints on personal or social activities (e.g., the restriction of free movement).

2. Under conditions of spatial limitation:

(a) a noisy situation will be perceived as more crowded than a quiet one;

(b) a cluttered area will appear more crowded than one in which physical objects are neatly arranged;

(c) situations involving social interference (for example, competition) will be perceived as more crowded than those in which such interference is absent;

(d) individuals who perceive their reinforcements, in general, to be internally controlled will feel more crowded as time of exposure to the situation increases, and

(e) persons who are, by nature, aggressive or impatient will experience a stronger sensation of being crowded than individuals who are characteristically easygoing and relaxed.

In order to test the above hypotheses, independent variables representing physical, social, and personal sources of crowding stress can be factorially combined to assess their additive and interactive impact upon the individual. This approach permits an orthogonal manipulation of factors such as the amount and arrangement of space, noise level, or social interference. The quantity of available space per person, for example, can be varied through the use of large and small rooms, as suggested by Freedman (1970). Personality measures may also be included in the design as group composition variables or covariates.

The experimental analysis of human crowding also requires careful specification of dependent measures designed to assess the experience of crowding. Four types of assessments may be employed: subjective reports of discomfort (for example, in terms of feeling "cramped") or of dislike for other people in the group; observational indices of stress in terms of reduced eye contact with others, hostile remarks, or facial expressions; performance criteria relating to task efficiency; and physiological indicators of strain such as increased blood pressure or galvanic skin response.

Although the proposed model is primarily concerned with the psychological aspects of crowding phenomena, the experimental approach outlined here is potentially relevant to macrocosmic levels of crowding. Since urban crowding can be conceptualized as an aggregation of microcosmic crowding phenomena, the understanding of crowding at the psychological level could have broad implications for dealing with sociological manifestations of crowding.

Author's Note: *The preparation of this paper was supported by United States Public Health Service Grant 5-T01 MH 07325. The author wishes to express his appreciation to John Schopler, Marilyn Rall, Bepi Pinner and C. David Jenkins for their comments and suggestions concerning the issues discussed in this paper. Thanks are also due to Nehemia Friedland and Jeannette Stokols for their critical readings of the manuscript; and to Sidney Cohn and Vaida D. Thompson for their comments on an earlier version of the paper.*

REFERENCES

Barker, R. G. (1965) "Explorations in Ecological Psychology," *American Psychologist,* 20(1): 1-14.

Barker, R. G. (1968) *Ecological Psychology* (Stanford: Stanford University Press).

Brehm, J. (1966) *A Theory of Psychological Reactance.* (New York: Academic Press).

Brunswik, E. (1956) *Perception and the Representative Design of Psychological Experiments* (Berkeley: University of California Press).

Calhoun, J. B. (1962) "Population Density and Social Pathology," *Scientific American,* 206 (February): 139-148.

Calhoun, J. B. (1966) "The Role of Space in Animal Sociology," *The Journal of Social Issues,* 22(4): 46-59.

Cannon, W. B. (1932) *The Wisdom of the Body* (New York: W. W. Norton).

Cassel, J. (1970) "Health Consequences of Population Density and Crowding," unpublished manuscript, School of Public Health, University of North Carolina, Chapel Hill.

Chombart de Lauwe, P. (1959) *Famille et Habitation* (Paris: Editions du Centre National de la Recherche Scientific).

Christian, J., Flyger, V., and Davis, D. (1960) "Factors in the Mass Mortality of a Herd of Sika Deer *Cervus nippon,*" *Chesapeake Science,* 1: 79-95.

Dubos, R. (1965) *Man Adapting* (New Haven: Yale University Press).

Dubos, R. (1968) *So Human an Animal* (New York: Scribners).

Festinger, L. (1957) *A Theory of Cognitive Dissonance* (Evanston: Row, Peterson, and Co.).

Freedman, J. (1970) "The Effects of Crowding on Human Behavior," unpublished manuscript, Department of Psychology, Columbia University.

Freedman, J., S. Klevansky, and P. Ehrlich (1971) "The Effect of Crowding on Human Task Performance," *Journal of Applied Social Psychology,* 1: 7-25.

Griffit, W., and R. Veitch (1971) "Hot and Crowded: Influences of Population Density and Temperature on Interpersonal Affective Behavior," *Journal of Personality and Social Psychology,* 17(1): 92-98.

Hall, E. (1959) *The Silent Language* (Greenwich, Conn.: Premier Books).

Hall, E. (1966) *The Hidden Dimension* (Garden City, N.Y.: Doubleday)

Homans, G. (1950) *The Human Group* (New York: Harcourt, Brace, and World).

Hutt, C., and M. Vaizey (1966) "Differential Effects of Group Density on Social Behavior," *Nature,* 209 (26 March): 1371-1372.

Ittelson, W., H. Proshansky, and L. Rivlin (1970) "The Environmental Psychology of the Psychiatric Ward." In H. Proshansky, W. Ittelson, and L. Rivlin (eds.), *Environmental Psychology* (New York: Holt).

Jenkins, C. D. (1971) "Psychologic and Social Precursors of Coronary Disease," *New England Journal of Medicine,* 284 (4 February): 244-255; (11 February): 307-317.

Kwan, W. T. (1967) "Overcrowding as a Form of Environmental Stress—a Preliminary Inquiry," departmental paper, Department of City and Regional Planning, University of North Carolina, Chapel Hill.

Levine, S., and N. Scotch (1970) *Social Stress* (Chicago: Aldine Publishing Co.).

Marsden, H. (1970) "Crowding and Animal Behavior," paper presented at American Psychological Association 1970 annual convention.

Michelson, W. H. (1970) *Man and his Urban Environment: A Sociological Approach* (Reading, Mass.: Addison-Wesley).

Mitchell, R. (1971) "Some Social Implications of High Density Housing," *American Sociological Review,* 36 (February): 18-29.

Proshansky, H., W. Ittelson, and L. Rivlin (1970) "Freedom of Choice and Behavior in a Physical Setting." Pp. 173-182 in H. Proshansky, W. Ittelson, and L. Rivlin (eds.), *Environmental Psychology* (New York: Holt, Rinehart, and Winston).

Rosenberg, M., and R. Abelson (1960) "An Analysis of Cognitive Balancing." Pp. 112-163 in C. Hovland and M. Rosenberg (eds.), *Attitude Organization and Change* (New Haven: Yale University Press).

Rotter, J. B. (1966) "Generalized Expectancies of Internal versus External Control of Reinforcement," *Psychological Monographs,* 80 (1, Whole No. 609).

Schmitt, R. S. (1957) "Density, Delinquency and Crime in Honolulu," *Sociology and Social Research,* 41 (March-April): 274-276.

Schmitt, R. C. (1963) "Implications of Density in Hong Kong," *Journal of the American Institute of Planners,* 29 (3): 210-217.

Schmitt, R. C. (1966) "Density, Health, and Social Disorganization," *Journal of the American Institute of Planners,* 32(1): 38-40.

Selye, H. (1956) *The Stress of Life* (New York: McGraw-Hill).

Sommer, R. (1969) *Personal Space—the Behavioral Basis of Design* (Englewood Cliffs, N.J.: Prentice Hall).

Thibaut, J., and H. H. Kelley (1959) *The Social Psychology of Groups* (New York: Wiley).

Winsborough, H. (1965) "The Social Consequences of High Population Density," *Law and Contemporary Problems,* 30(1): 120-126.

IMPORTANT ISSUES IN RESEARCHING
THE EFFECTS OF CROWDING ON HUMANS

Chalsa Loo*

The purpose of this article is to discuss several important yet rarely considered factors involved in researching the effects of crowding and density on humans. These factors pose problems for research and define future research needs. Differences in defining the concepts of crowding and density and differences in structuring a crowded condition are the factors given greatest attention.

One of the most current and crucial problems facing humanity is that of overpopulation. Much has been said about the ill effects of overcrowding; ecologists have pointed to similarities between the results of crowding in animals and the violence and child-beatings in the slums arising from the tensions of a high density condition. While animal research can provide valuable leads for research on humans, some skepticism must be exercised in accepting analogies from mice to men without first researching the effects of crowding on humans themselves.

One framework in which to understand the problems that arise as a result of overpopulation is that of supply and demand such that the population of the world can be no greater than that number which can provide itself with a minimum subsistence from the world's resources. The demand for resources increases with an increase in population, but the supply is frequently finite and cannot match the demand. Resources tend to either dwindle or remain constant, and, even with technological advances in increasing the food supply, the advance is not great enough to match the increase in population. Our society is already experiencing the strains of overcrowding in the schools, on the freeways, in environmental deterioration, and in employment difficulties. Attacking the social problem is an enormous task calling on the talents and concerns of specialists in all areas—psychologists, urban designers, sociologists, economists, biologists, physicians, and public policy makers.

Since crowding seems to be a natural consequence of excessive popula-

* Chalsa Loo received her B.A. in psychology from the University of California at Berkeley and then received her M.A. and Ph.D. (1971) at the Ohio State University in Clinical and Developmental Psychology. Her research interests have spanned the areas of social, clinical, and developmental but her most immediate research interest lies in the area of crowding and human behavior. Presently she is pursuing research and psychotherapeutic activities in the Department of Psychiatry and is conducting a seminar on Crowding and Behavior in the Department of Psychology at Stanford University.

REPRESENTATIVE RESEARCH IN SOCIAL PSYCHOLOGY, 1973, Vol. 4, pp. 219-226.

tion growth, urgent questions are being asked of behavioral scientists about the effects of crowding on human behavior. For the behavioral scientist there are two crucial issues. The first issue is based on the assumption that conditions of overpopulation presently exist and will become increasingly exacerbated with time. This issue involves answering questions having to do with the effects that crowding has on humans, such as: Does high density harm people? Does it damage family life? Does it adversely affect a child's social and mental development? What are the behavioral and emotional consequences of crowding on adults and children? Will humans adapt to a crowded environmental condition; if so, how, and if not, what non-adaptive behavior will result?

The second issue relates to and is dependent on the first. Once the specific effects resulting from overcrowding are understood, the behavioral scientist can then focus on effective preventive or preparatory measures of various kinds, should they prove to be needed.

Methods of Studying the Effects of Crowding

Bivariate analyses using census tract data have positively correlated density with pathology such as crime, mental illness or physical illness. These correlational studies have yielded incomplete information, however, because variables associated with crowding have not been controlled. One cannot properly point to Calcutta or the slums of America and deduce that the problems are a direct, inevitable result of overcrowding. We are dealing with a complex interaction of associated phenomena such as low income, inadequate food, lack of education, social prejudice, etc.

Studies using multivariate analyses, where the effects of confounding variables such as income and ethnicity are controlled, provide more accurate information than correlational studies which ignore partial correlation. Winsborough's study (1965), for instance, found that the positive correlation between density and pathology disappeared when certain measures of social status were controlled.

Studying children in a naturalistic setting has been another method of examining the effects of density on behavior. Whiting (1970) found that aggression among Kenyan children increased when the number of children in a group was beyond six. Murphy (1937), Markey (1935), and Jersild and Markey (1935) observed children in free play and suggested that conflicts are more numerous where play space is more restricted. The greatest weakness of some of these studies is that relevant variables had not been controlled. For example, age and age range may have confounded Murphy's results since the group in the smaller play space had a narrower age range. Murphy suggests that this may have resulted in a larger number of conflicts since children closer in age would compete over the same toys and since the larger age range in the group in the larger play space may have stimulated "big-brother" behaviors, which would reduce the number of conflicts. While Jersild and Markey found that the group with the larger play space had fewer fights, they also found that this group had a higher IQ and more imaginative play.

134

While correlational studies, naturalistic observations, and animal studies can provide leads to how humans are affected by crowded conditions, the most highly controlled approach requires experimental studies directly concerned with the effects of crowding on human behavior. Experimental investigation of this type has been the most recent approach to the study of crowding: the number of such studies is few, and the results are not always consistent. Since extensive experimental research on human crowding is lacking, no one has yet hypothesized the factors accounting for inconsistent results. The present author believes that a careful scrutiny of the different ways of defining crowding and structuring a crowded condition must be made. It is very likely that inconsistent results might be explained by the fact that various investigators have defined crowding differently and have structured the crowded situation differently.

Differences in Defining the Concepts of Crowding and Density

Differences exist among researchers on how to define the concept of crowding. Crowding has been defined to exist when the individual's demand for space exceeds the available supply of such space (c.f., Proshansky, Ittelson, and Rivlin, 1970; Stokols, 1972). Esser (1971) prefers to define crowding as a mental state in which stimuli are experienced as inappropriate and stressful. Thus, crowding will occur when stimuli come in too fast or when the central nervous system functions inadequately. While Esser feels that a high density condition can cause stimulus overload, he believes that an individual can experience mental crowding even when others are not around. Desor (1972), on the other hand, defines crowding as "receiving excessive stimulation from social sources," indicating the necessity of other people to define density and crowding.

Stokols (1972) differentiates between the concepts of crowding and density. He defines density as a physical condition involving the limitations of space, and defines crowding as an experiential state where the individual perceives a spatial restriction and experiences psychological and physiological stress. Defining density and crowding in this manner, it is apparent that the two variables are not mutually exclusive, for crowding can be experienced in some, but not all high density conditions. A researcher may compare, for example, two density conditions, a low-density condition with n subjects and a high-density condition with $n + 2$ subjects. If, however, there is no experienced stress for the subjects in the high density condition because there is still enough space for individual needs, then the researcher cannot properly deduce that crowding has no effect. What he may be studying are two density conditions, neither of which represents a crowded condition.

Important distinctions need to be made in defining the concept of density. Density is defined as the interaction between number of individuals and amount of space. Too many researchers, however, present conclusions stated as "a high density condition was not correlated with . . ." and fail to distinguish between spatial and social density.

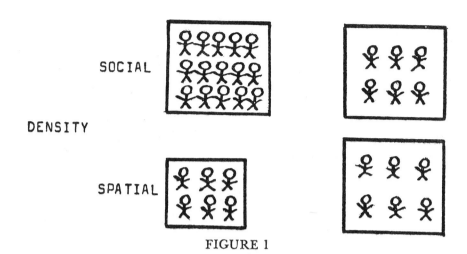

FIGURE 1

Spatial density research compares the behavior of groups of the same number in spaces of differing sizes while social density research compares the behavior of groups of differing numbers in the same sized space.

Research comparing the effects of spatial and social density is noticeably lacking. P. McGrew (1971) found a trend towards less physical contact between children in a high social density as compared to a high spatial density and Loo (1972) hypothesized important differences between social and spatial density. To test whether differences do exist, one would need to compare the two conditions while keeping the area per person equal in the high density conditions and in the low density conditions. We can then ask the question, "Does increasing the density by *reducing* available space have the same effect as *increasing* the numbers of individuals in the same given space?" When the space is reduced the individuals can be the same persons in both high and low spatial density conditions; but when the number of individuals is increased in the high social density condition new people must be added. The introduction of new people may confound the results by raising the question, "What are the effects of intruders into an already existing social system?" rather than answering, "What are the differences in behavior between having more individuals versus fewer individuals in the same amount of space?" Methodologically these two questions can be distinguished by whether individuals are used as their own controls (in which case the investigator would be studying the effects of intrusion when people are added to the high social density condition) or whether totally different individuals are used for each density condition (in which case the investigator would be studying the effects of social density in its "pure" form). Besides comparing the effects of social and spatial density, it behooves researchers to compare spatial density due to intrusion with spatial density without intrusion.

It is quite likely that discrepant results among studies on density may be due to the different effects of social and spatial density. For example, Hutt and Vaizey (1966) and Loo (1972) both studied the effects of a high and low density on preschool children. Hutt and Vaizey found aggression to be positively correlated with high density while Loo found aggression to be negatively correlated with high density. At first glance, the two studies appear to contradict each other until the reader finds that the former was a study of social density while the latter was a study of spatial density. Differences in results may also be attributable to different methods of studying density, different area/child allotments or differences in the total number of children in the group.

Differences in Structuring a Crowded Condition

Researching the effects of crowding and density on humans is not only complicated by differences in defining these concepts but by differences in structuring a crowded condition. What many researchers fail to recognize is that the experience of crowding is largely influenced by the degree of structure imposed on the members of the group by the experimeter. The experimenter imposes two types of structure on his subjects: (a) an architectural structure and (b) an activities structure. Taking these two factors into consideration, it is not coincidental that there have been more significant results in studies on the effects of density on children than there have been in studies on adults. In comparing the studies of density on adults such as that of Freedman, Klevansky, and Ehrlich (1971) and that of Stokols, Rall, Pinner, and Schopler (1972) with those on children there are three important differences; the first is the degree of structure of the environment, the second is the degree of structure of the activities imposed on the individuals, and the third is the age of the individuals being studied. These three factors may account for the fewer significant results in the studies of density on adults than those on children.

Desor's study (1972) demonstrated that crowding is much more than merely a matter of space and that decreasing the density of people is by no means the only method of alleviating crowding. Desor found that holding room area constant while varying architectural features alters the feeling of crowdedness. The architectural features which reduced the feeling of crowdedness were adding fewer doors, adding a bisecting partition, and making the area more rectangular rather than square in shape.

Studies on children have used few if any fixed structures (such as chairs or desks), and the toys provided are usually portable. Studies on adults, however, have generally used highly structured architectures by providing a chair or desk-chair for each individual. Providing such an architectural structure provides each member with a secure territory of his own. The experimenter has clearly delineated the personal boundaries.

He has also prevented ambiguity over territorial space which would normally exist had no chairs or desks been introduced or had there been fewer chairs provided than there were people. Unless an individual's demand for space exceeds the territory provided for him by the condition, a sense of crowdedness will not be experienced. Environmental structures which create territorial havens for individuals greatly reduce the possibility that a state of crowdedness will be experienced.

It is assumed that ambiguity of territoriality due to fewer environmental structures is greatest in the conditions used in the studies on children and that this would create greater conflict, competitiveness, anxiety, and uncertainty in individuals exposed to this condition. Adults exposed to a highly structured environment are likely to feel less anxiety and fewer feelings of crowdedness since their territory has been marked for them. Freedman, Klevansky, and Ehrlich (1971) structured their high density condition so as to reduce even further the noxious factors associated with crowding such as lack of air, physical discomfort, restriction on movement, high temperatures, odors, etc. Such restrictions make it very difficult to find significant results and it can be argued that unless some of these factors are included, one is not studying density or crowding as it is normally experienced.

The degree of crowdedness experienced is also determined by the activities of the participants. Desor studied four different situations holding room area constant and found that there was a significant difference in the number of people that could occupy the spaces without feeling overcrowded. Adults are likely to experience less anxiety since the activities during the observation time have been determined by the experimenter. This is especially true with the studies that have examined the effects of density on the task performance of adults, where subjects are instructed to take various paper and pencil tests individually or participate in highly structured tasks as a group.

Children, on the other hand, have largely been observed under unstructured free play situations, where each child has the freedom to participate or not participate with others and to structure his activities according to his own wishes. The freedom of such structurelessness creates an emotional difference; it is expected that mobility, excitability, and the general emotional level of the participants would be higher in a condition where activities are highly unstructured.

The third variable differentiating adult studies from child studies is an obvious one, age. Although obvious there have been no research studies that have compared the effects of density or crowding on various ages of humans.

Individual Differences

The effects of density and crowding will vary depending upon the individual. Henry David Thoreau once said, "I would rather have a pumpkin all to myself than be crowded on a velvet cushion." While many may feel akin to Thoreau in their desire for uncrowded conditions, there may be those who prefer "velvet" conditions to that of a "pumpkin patch" over and above their concern for more space. What the relevant personal variables are that make the difference have not been explored to any depth or detail. Some research suggests that each individual has a "body-buffer" zone, that is, a personal space surrounding him which when violated by the intrusion of another will lead to tense and uncomfortable feelings. Some of the most promising variables to be explored would be temperament and emotional predispositions, activity level, degree of impulsivity, etc.

Dependent Variables

The effects of density and crowding appear to differ depending upon which dependent variables the investigator is examining. A survey of the literature strongly suggests that a high density condition has a far greater effect on social and affective behaviors than it does on task performance. Unfortunately, there are no studies of the effects of density on the task performance of children to compare with those on adults. Since Loo (1972) did find a trend towards greater numbers of interruptions in the high density situation, it is possible that the effects of increasing density on children's task performance may be greater than on the task performance of adults.

Summary

The intent of this article was to highlight the different factors that need to be considered in dealing with the area of density and crowding. The effects of density are not simple; unraveling and differentiating these variables poses a formidable task for future research. Investigators need to recognize the differences that presently exist in defining density and crowding. They need to understand how the architecture and activities that are structured into the conditions may significantly affect their results. Crowded conditions may affect different people differently and the personal characteristics which determine these differences need to be explored. Understanding the relationship between man and his environment is an extremely complex task but the social relevance of the problems of overpopulation and overcrowding makes further research ultimately necessary.

REFERENCES

Choldin, H. Population density and social relations. Paper presented at meetings of Population Association of America, Toronto, 1972.

Desor, J. A. Toward a psychological theory of crowding. *Journal of Personality and Social Psychology*, 1972, *21*, 79-83.

Esser, A. The psychopathology of crowding in institutions for the mentally ill and retarded. Paper presented at the 5th World Congress of Psychiatry, Mexico City, 1971.

Freedman, J., Klevansky, S., & Ehrlich, P. The effect of crowding on human task performance. *Journal of Applied Social Psychology*, 1971, *1*, 7-25.

Hutt, C., and M. Vaizey. Differential effects of group density on social behavior. *Nature*, 1966, *209*, 1371-1372.

Jersild, A. T., & Markey, F. V. Conflicts between preschool children. *Child Development Monographs*, 1935, No. 21.

Loo, C. The effects of spatial density on the social behavior of children. *Journal of Applied Social Psychology*, 1972, 2, 372-381.

Markey, F. V. Imaginative behavior of preschool children. *Child Development Monograph*, 1935, No. 18.

McGrew, P. L. Social and spatial density effects on spacing behavior in preschool children. *Journal of Child Psychology and Psychiatry*, 1970, *11*, 197-205.

Murphy, L. B. *Social behavior and child personality.* New York: Columbia University Press, 1937.

Proshansky, H., W. Ittelson, & L. Rivlin. Freedom of choice and behavior in a physical setting. pp. 173-182 in H. Proshansky, W. Ittelson, and L. Rivlin (eds.), *Environmental Psychology.* New York: Holt, Rinehart, and Winston, 1970.

Stokols, D. A social-psychological model of human crowding phenomena. *Journal of the American Institute of Planners*, 1972, *38*, 72-83.

Stokols, D., M. Rall, B. Pinner, & J. Schopler. Physical, social, and personal determinants of the perception of crowding. *Environment and Behavior*, in press.

Whiting, B. B. The effect of urbanization on the behavior of children. Mimeographed report, Jan. 1970.

Winsborough, H. The social consequences of high population density. *Law and Contemporary Problems*, 1965, *30* (1), 120-126.

A Social-Spatial Model of Crowding Stress [1]

Chalsa M. Loo

University of California at Santa Cruz

Normalcy and Pathology of Environmental Psychology

Principles have been formulated to explain the relationship between human beings and their environment. Wohlwill (1970), for example, posits three principles:(1) all behavior occurs in some environmental context, (2) the environment imposes constraints on the range of behaviors permissible in it, and (3) people develop forms of adaptation to environmental conditions. Wohlwill's principles end on a positive note. There is the implication in his third principle that human beings do adapt and cope regardless of the constraints placed uponthem by the environment. Wohlwill's statement assumes a normal relationship between human beings and their environment. Yet, the relationship is not always normal. Conditions exist where the environmental constraints are neither coped with nor controlled well by individuals. Environmental conditions can, at some times and for some people, create dysfunctional states of stress and anxiety, where adaptation becomes difficult if not impossible. A pathological condition may even result.

This paper is an attempt to suggest a theoretical model for conceptualizing of the normal and abnormal relationship between human beings and their environment with regards to crowding. In so doing, I am positing a construct of normalcy and pathology of environmental psychology. Normalcy and abnormalcy are dependent upon the psychological state of the person in relationship to his/her environment. The environment shall be defined in terms of its social and spatial dimensions. Several researchers of crowding have suggested that crowding and density be conceptualized in terms of a social and a spatial dimension for purposes of conceptual clarity and definitive terms (McGrew, 1970; Loo, 1973).

The following principles underlie this discussion of normalcy and pathology of crowding: (1) all persons have spatial and social needs, (2) these needs are individually and situationally variable; that is, the spatial and social needs vary depending upon the individual and the situation, (3) all behavior occurs in some environmental context having both social and spatial components, (4) the environment imposes constraints on the range of behaviors permissible in

---

[1] Presented at the Symposium entitled "Theoretical developments pertaining to personal space and human crowding" at the Western Psychological Association Convention, San Francisco, April 1974.

it, (5) the environment has an emotional and psychological
effect on individuals based on the degree to which the environment frustrates or accommodates the social and spatial
needs of the individual, (6) under normal conditions individuals develop forms of adaptation to their environment; they
cope with or change their environment in a functional manner,
and (7) under abnormal conditions, individuals fail to cope
with their environment; the constraints of the environment
dysfunctionally affect persons psychologically, resulting
in anxiety and stress.

Crowding Stress

Social needs can vary from a desire to be alone to a
desire to be among large crowds--it can vary from a desire
for privacy (to oneself or with a selected other person) to
a desire for public exposure. Spatial needs can vary from
a desire for closed space to a desire for vast space.   In
terms of crowding, the types of stress that are environ-
mentally linked can be categorized into three types: social
crowding stress, spatial crowding stress, and intrapsychic
crowding stress. Social crowding stress refers to a situation where anxiety is experienced because the degree of presence or absence of others fails to meet individual needs.
Spatial crowding stress refers to a situation where anxiety
is experienced because the amount of physical space surrounding the individual fails to meet individual needs.   Intrapsychic crowding stress refers to a situation where anxiety
is experienced becuase of an overload of stimulus input
representing more than what can be adequately coped with by
the individual. These three categories are not mutually
exclusive; they can overlap and exist simultaneously, and
it is assumed that intrapsychic crowding can exist when
there is either spatial or social crowding.

A social-spatial model of crowding stress integrates
three factors: (1) social and spatial dimensions, (2)the
states of crowded, uncrowded, and undercrowded, as discussed by Stokols (1972),and (3) phobias that are representative of the social-spatial dimension and the states of
crowdedness dimension. A phobia is defined as a persistant
and excessive fear attached to an object or situation which
objectively is not a significant source of danger. Phobias
are diagnostic labels for a syndrome of neurosis typified
by anxiety and fear which the individual realizes are irrational but from which he cannot free himself. All people
experience minor fears and stresses but in phobic reactions
such fears are intense and interfere with everyday activities. One can conceive of phobias as a severe and as an
object- or situation-specific form of stress. Normally, the
individual affects his/her environment and the environment
has an effect on the individual. With phobias, the strength
of the environment vastly outweighs the effect that the individual has on his/her environment.

The states of crowdedness (crowded, uncrowded, and undercrowded) represent states on a continuum; each continuum is
subsumed under a social and a spatial spectrum. In terms of
social crowding stress, normalcy (no stress) is represented

in the socially uncrowded condition. The number of people
meets the individual's social needs, be this no other people
or many other people. Stress is experienced in the socially
crowded and socially undercrowded condition but differs in
quality. In the socially crowded condition stress is due
to the presence of too many people, representing more than
that desired or more than can be adequately coped with. The
phobia related to this condition is ochlophobia, a fear of
crowds. Anthropophobia (a fear of people) or xenophobia
(a fear of strangers) can also be subsumed under this condition. In the socially undercrowded condition, stress is due
to having too few people present. There is a need for affiliation with others and social contact. The phobia related
to this condition is monophobia, a fear of being alone.

	SOCIAL CROWDING		
STATE:	Socially Crowded	Socially Uncrowded	Socially Undercrowded
STRESS:	Too Many People	No Stress	Too Few People
PATHOLOGY:	Ochlophobia	Normalcy	Monophobia

In terms of spatial crowding stresses, normalcy (no
stress) is represented in the spatially uncrowded condition.
The amount of physical space meets the psychological and
task needs of the individual. Stress is experienced in the
spatially crowded and spatially undercrowded conditions,
differing in quality. In the spatially crowded condition,
stress is due to too little space available for individual
comfort. Space is restricted and a need for more space
exists. Claustrophobia is the phobia representing an exaggeration of the stress of spatial crowding. Persons who
are claustrophobic are fearful of closed places; they may
fear being in closets or may go to great lengths to avoid
entering a small room or passageway even when it is essential for them to do so.
In the spatially undercrowded condition, stress is due
to an excessive abundance of space. There is a need for
enclosure and psychological safety created by environmental
boundaries. Agoraphobia (fear of open spaces) is the phobia
related to the exaggeration of this condition. Several
writers have noted that the condition of agoraphobia is
worse when there is no boundary to a large open visual
field. Minor visual features of the environment affect the
intensity of the agoraphobia. The wider and higher the
space walked into, the greater the fear. The phobia dimin-
ishes as soon as a boundary is imposed, be this a hedge,
fence, trees, undulation of the ground or simply an umbrella
held above the head of the agoraphobic (Clevenger, 1890;
Weiss, 1964). Agoraphobia also applies to the fear of
leaving the home. Some writers hypothesize that separation
anxiety is a common complication of agoraphobia, such that
fear of open spaces symbolizes fear of leaving home, mother,
and security. One of the most common fears expressed by

agoraphobics is that they will go mad and lose control
(Marks, 1969). They may have strong unconscious feelings
(sexual or aggressive) urging for release but fear an inability to control such urges in an environment which is
so vast and open as to not provide external constraints or
controls for them. In the literature, agoraphobia is sometimes defined as a fear of open spaces and at other times
represents fears of shopping, crowds, traveling, closed
spaces, and being left alone, as well (Marks, 1969). Such
all inclusiveness seems to complicate and confuse the model
of crowding stresses, so I am here defining agoraphobia in
its most specific form. The broader definition of agoraphobia used by Marks might well be replaced by "non-specific
insecurity fears" (Snaith, 1968).

SPATIAL CROWDING

STATE:	Spatially Crowded	Spatially Uncrowded	Spatially Undercrowded
STRESS:	Too Little Space	No Stress	Too Much Space
PATHOLOGY:	Claustrophobia	Normalcy	Agoraphobia

Crowding stresses can also be due to a compounding of
social and spatial crowding, where stress can be alleviated
by either a reduction in numbers of people in by an increase
in space. The example of the Brattle Theatre breakdown of
social norms (Milgram, 1969) is an illustration of this.
Two lines of waiting patrons for the theatre occupying a
small area of space led to a breakdown in the normal procedure of "first come, first served". The chaos was avoided
by the management's alteration in increasing the amount of
space available; the chaos was also nonexistent when the
waiting lines contained fewer patrons.

This model of conceptualizing of manners of responding
to environmental constraints is an attempt to integrate
clinical and social psychological phenomena related to the
relationship between human beings and their environment in
terms of crowding. It emphasizes the noncoping reponses to
social and spatial dimensions of crowding. It is assumed that
individuals function most securely and happily when they
have a sense of control over their environment and where
their environment provides them with the greatest latitude
and flexibility of behaviors and conditions. When these conditions do not exist, individuals will experience some
stressful reactions. The degree of severity of the stress
shall be greatly determined by individual experiences and
individual vulnerabilities.

References

Clevenger, S. Heart disease in insanity and a case of pan-
    phobia. Alienist and Neurologist, 1890, Vll, 535-543.
Loo, C. Important issues in researching the effects of crowding
    on humans. Representative Research in Social Psychology, 4:1,
    Jan, 1973.

Marks, I. Fears and Phobias. New York, London: Academic Press, 1969.

McGrew, P. Social and spatial density effects on spacing be-havior in preschool children. Journal of Child Psychology and Psychiatry, 1970, 11, 197-205.

Milgram, S. and Toch, H. Collective behavior: crowds and social movements, in the Handbook of Social Psychology, Lindzey, G. and Aronson, E. (Eds.) Addison-Wesley Pub-lishing Co., 1969.

Snaith, R. A clinical investigation of phobias, British Journal of Psychiatry, 1968, 114, 673-697.

Stokols, D. A social-psychological model of human crowding phenomena. Journal of the American Institute of Planners, 1972, 38, 72-83.

Weiss, E. Agoraphobia in the Light of Ego Psychology. Lond-don: Grune and Stratton, 1964.

Wohlwill, J. The emerging discipline of environmental psych-ology. American Psychologist, 25, 1970, 303-312.

The Environmental Crisis In Human Dignity

Harold M. Proshansky

The environmental crisis in human dignity lies not just in the overuse, the misuse, and the decay of physical settings, but far more significantly in how we conceive of the individual in relation to any such setting. In the design and organization of physical settings, the human properties of the individual are ignored, oversimplified, or implicitly assumed, because of the influence of such socioenvironmental values as scientific-technological progress, urbanism, pseudoprogress (novelty and change), and the value placed on an ever increasing acceleration of technological change. Spaces and places are improperly designed not only in physical terms; designs overlook human needs for privacy, territoriality, freedom of choice, etc., and the conceiving of the individual as a simple "machine man." Unintended consequences are often ignored and no attempt is made to evaluate just how well the setting actually works. The danger is that the person will adjust and at the price of a continuing erosion of the. properties that make him distinctively human. It is imperative that as behavioral scientists turn to the systematic study of man/environment problems they recognize the need to maintain the contextual reality and integrity of any such problem as it evolves, develops, and becomes modified in the time framework of a complex society.

All of you will recall I am sure the period in the late 1960s and early 70s when many citizens and special interest groups in American society became acutely aware of an impending crisis related to man's physical environment. What was a way of life in the urban setting was rapidly becoming a way of death. Air pollution, contamination of waterways, overcrowding, the blight of the ghetto, the use of insecticides, the clamor and congestion of planes, trains, and automobiles, and any number of other "physical indicators" provided clear and unmistakable signs of this crisis. What could be clearer and more unmistakable than the sharp increase in the number of deaths from lung and heart maladies that occurred in Pittsburgh and also in London because of brief periods of persistent and intense air pollution.

THE JOURNAL OF SOCIAL ISSUES, 1973, Vol. 29, No. 4, pp. 1-20.

I argued even at that time, as I do now, that not one but *two* environmental crises confront us. What moved citizens, scientists, and administrators alike to be concerned and to take action in the late 1960s was the fact that the man-made environment could injure, hurt, and eventually destroy large numbers of individuals. Thus at the root of this environmental crisis was the value of *human life*. The loss of human life is tragic, more so when the events and conditions responsible for it are subject to control by the members of a society. But there is more to life than just living it. In the midst of the new environmentalist movement, there was to some degree the recognition of this other kind of crisis, namely, the *crisis in human dignity*.

As yet this other crisis has not stirred modern society to take any significant action. The dictionary tells us that "dignity" means the quality or state of being esteemed or worthy. If the value of human life strives to keep each and every person alive and physically well, then it must be said that the value of human dignity seeks to build on this base. *Its objective is to maintain and enhance all of the "human" qualitites that distinquish human beings from lower organisms.* The individual's capacity to think, plan, create, have aesthetic experiences, make choices, avoid pain, relate to others in complex ways, and to experience a sense of self apart from others are all involved in achieving and defining this dignity. A built environment that subverts, interferes with, or prevents the use of these qualities or capacities indeed threatens human dignity.

In certain respects the environmental movement continues to say something about the crisis in human dignity. The view is vigorously taken that physical settings should not only be safe, but also provide experiences that satisfy and uplift the human spirit. In the context of unending noise, the accumulation of garbage, the decay and overcrowded conditions of the ghetto, the kaleidoscope of neon-lighted gin mill districts, and the human degradation of an urban skidrow, the ambience of urban life in America hardly expresses or reflects that measure of the person we call "human." And outside the urban setting—on the highway so to speak—the monotony of gas stations, billboards, shopping centers, trailer camps, and hamburger stands merely confirms the very restricted, vacuous, and undifferentiated nature of our built environment.

The environmental crisis in human dignity, as I conceive it, is far more subtle and therefore far more extensive than what the environmentalists in the late 1960s and even now believe

147

it to be. A great deal more is involved than the blight of the ghetto, the noise of the city, the monotonous ugliness of the landscape, or the appalling inadequacy of some public high-rise housing projects. *The crisis lies not just in the overuse, the misuse, and the decay of both the immediate and broader physical environment, but rather in how we conceive of the individual in relation to any existing setting including the newest ones and those still on the drawing board.* This is true regardless of whether the setting is an apartment, family home, school room, business office, playground, subway car, college dorm, bathroom, government building, neighborhood setting, and so on.

The fundamental problem lies not simply in what happens to a physical setting—how we use it, modify it, or take care of it—but in the assumptions we make about human beings when we design a setting for given groups of persons involved in specified activities for particular human purposes. I think my friend and colleague Bill Ittelson stated the problem brilliantly when he asked, "If we cleaned up all our cities and eliminated all those aspects that threaten human life and human dignity, would this still be enough?" Neither of us believe so, because there is far more to the individual's relationship to his physical setting than just whether it is safe, meets obvious needs, and is immediately satisfying by being free from disturbing and unpleasant sensory experiences.

The major portion of the discussion that follows will consider the person as a biological, psychological, and social being in relation to the physical settings that circumscribe his existence. The threats to human dignity rooted in the failure to consider man in these terms are many and varied, and so we shall do no more than consider those that in our judgment represent fundamental human problems.

The "environmental crisis" itself, however, cannot be understood simply by considering the nature of the existing threats to human dignity that characterize contemporary physical settings. The origin and nature of these threats both in the present and for the future can only be understood in the light of the contemporary all-embracing *socioenvironmental* values that prevail, and the consequences these values have in inexorably determining the nature of our physical world. By a socioenvironmental value, I mean a broad, pervasive, and deeply rooted general standard for determining and evaluating the relationships between the members of a society and their physical environment. Said far more simply, socioenvironmental values dictate what a society should do to and with its physical environment, and what in turn it can expect this environment to do to and for it.

SOCIOENVIRONMENTAL VALUES

If the emergence of the urban setting in the 19th century made possible still greater advances in science and technology, then the latter in their turn, relentlessly transformed the nature of the city from one decade to the next, and indeed continue to do so. It's not merely the spread of urbanism that must concern us, but the changing nature of that urbanism. As an end in itself, it is continually nourished by the socioenvironmental value, *scientific and technological progress*. It is not just that man must conquer and have mastery over his physical environment, he must relentlessly continue this mastery and control, in fact increase it by modifying and overcoming each built environment that he creates. As my colleague Arthur Schlesinger has stated it, "Science makes, dissolves, rebuilds and extends our environment every day [1973, p.5]." The inexorability of scientific and technological progress is rooted in the egocentric view that there is no end to man's ability to master his environment and transform it to meet any and all new conceptions of life he may evolve or exigencies he may confront.

The ideology of modern capitalism views the person not only as separate and distinct from his physical setting but also as being continually challenged by this environment. In order to meet this challenge, the physical environment has to be conquered, mastered, and controlled by the continuing efforts of modern science and technology in relation to those individuals who are best suited to organize, direct, and administer the production, distribution, and consumption of economic goods and services. I do not believe it would be an exaggeration to say that in this context the physical environment is to be manipulated, exploited, and used exclusively to serve man. There seemed to be no reason why he has to serve it, except in the sense of not killing the goose that lays the golden eggs.

The socioeconomic ideology of a complex society structures and restructures the existence and experience of the members of that society; it not only changes over time, but in the process it spawns still other consistent but more specific and contemporary values. Thus I draw your attention to *urbanism* as a second socioenvironmental value. Originally evolved in the development of an industrialized economy, the city provided the geographical, human, and material integration necessary to sustain this kind of economy. Today it is abundantly clear that it is no longer a way of life, it is the way of life. The evidence is clear that larger and larger numbers of people are being concentrated in smaller and smaller geographical areas. Projections made in 1950 of the growth of urbanism over the next 50 years have already been borne out by what has happened in the last twenty years. What we are talking about is increasing numbers of people living, working, recreating, being ill, learning, dying, and doing many other things in settings characterized by multiple dwellings, large institutional settings (e.g., schools, hospitals), mass transportation, functionally and socially differentiated areas, commercial and industrialized enterprises, and so on. Urbanism as a socioenvironmental value can be described as a value with a vengeance. Its influence is pervasive and inexorable.

But there is a third socioenvironmental value that is often confused with scientific and technological progress in mastering the individual's environment. Following World War II, in conjunction with unparalleled economic growth and development, the persistent and pervasive need for *change and novelty* came of age. Often confused with progress it would be better to speak of the consequences of this need as pseudoprogress, for in fact change and novelty do not represent genuine technological advances or significant refinements of man's mastery of his environment. In part this value rests on the untenable assumption that what is different or even looks different is progress or improvement. Some may disagree, but in my judgment it is hard to make a case for technological improvements or advances in human life in the name of electric toothbrushes and shoeshine kits, remote-control home TV sets, gas-lit barbecue pits, disposable clothes, electric pencil sharpeners; and certainly no case at all for the annual change in car models, for clothes styles, equipment design, food packaging, patent medicine remedies, and so on.

Of course there is far less exertion involved in sharpening ten pencils with an electric pencil sharpener than by hand, or in staying in one's car and opening the garage doors electronically, than in having to get out of the car and do it. But making more and more of the individual's life relatively effortless raises the thorny question of what is optimum convenience for the human condition. A clear distinction must be made between the socioenvironmental value of scientific and technological progress and the value of applying this progress in every and any way to achieve novelty, change, and/or convenience in our lives. If we consider the socioenvironmental values I have discussed—increasing urbanism characterized by continuing scientific progress and the pursuit of novelty and change for their own sake—then there is a fourth value that is inherent in the other three but most clearly rooted in the value of scientific progress. I am talking about the value of *rate of change*. It is subtle, pervasive, and in most respects awesome if not frightening. Thus scientific-technological progress is not simply a matter of a continuing mastery over a succession of built environments, but rather of a mastery at faster and faster rates of change. For modern societies time is the enemy: "The planet has changed more in the last hundred years than in the one thousand years preceding [Schlesinger, 1973]." It was Whitehead who told us almost fifty years ago that, "The greatest invention of the nineteenth century was the invention of the method of invention [1925]."

I learned a great deal from Schlesinger's essay, but its greatest impact was that it confronted me directly with what I already knew but never thought about. The time lag between the discovery of the electric motor and its application was 65 years, 1821 to 1886; for radio broadcasting the delay was 35 years, 1887 to 1922; radar only required five years between discovery and application, the atomic bomb only seven years, the transistor only three years, and most recently the solar battery only two years. What could be more compelling about the ever increasing pace of rate of change than the fact that, as Schlesinger points out, "It would have been quite possible for someone who watched the Wright brothers fly for a few seconds in the air at Kitty Hawk in 1903 to have watched Apollo 11 land men on the moon in 1969 [1973, p.4]."

THREATS TO HUMAN DIGNITY

The individual is not only a biological entity but a physical entity as well. It is often necessary to remind students and colleagues alike that like any other object a person has the common physical characteristics of size, weight, depth, and volume, and also that he or she walks, lies, sits, runs, and uses his or her body in a variety of still other ways. The built environment of the urban setting threatens and abuses its inhabitants as physical and biological entities in many ways, some very obvious and others far less so. Let me comment briefly on the obvious ones. Obvious or not, abuse of the individual as a biological and physical entity renders the person's particularly human characteristics something less than they should be and thereby devalues his or her dignity as a human being.

For some groups of individuals the devaluation of human dignity is actually a way of life: for example, those who live in the urban ghettos of the world or on an Indian reservation, those who are incarcerated in mental hospitals and high security prisons, or those who because of age and/or infirmity must cope with an alien physical world, e.g., the blind person, the paraplegic. But these particular groups were not the concern of the environmentalist movement. The environmentalist sounded the alarm of a crisis in the urban environment which would in time touch not some of us but all of us.

What was at issue was the quality of life itself, with particular emphasis placed on the urban setting. Given the individual as a biological and physical organism, and apart from noxious factors in the environment that actually threatened human life, there was and is much in the urban way of life that casts doubt about the value of the person as an experiencing and thinking organism: random and unending noise coupled with dirt and decaying or abandoned homes; overcrowded streets, buildings, stores, and means of transportation; institutional settings such as hospitals, schools, factories, and office buildings in which overcrowding, improper ventilation, and inappropriately used designed space all tended to nullify their social and human purposes; and finally those modern mechanical and electronic facilities of the built environment that rankle, annoy, and exasperate an already tense and frustrated average citizen because they break down with increasing frequency, e.g., commuter trains and electric power.

Clearly all of this can be taken as evidence of at least the beginning of a crisis in human dignity, particularly when, if viewed over time, these problems seem to be intensifying and also spreading to cities which are far less than major metropolitan centers. What also seems to crystallize the crucial issue of the quality of urban life is the realization that some of these frustrations and stresses have existed for a long time and will continue to occur unless significant changes are made. The issue is far more than, for example, what are the effects of a round-trip subway ride in which the passenger is very much crowded in with others, and in addition must stand for say an hour during the trip to and from his other job or place of business. It can be argued, and it has, that these are temporary inconveniences, irksome but not critical: The person feels some discomfort but it is transient. What must be considered, however, environmentalists have argued, is that some individuals—indeed many—have to use the subway in this way forty to fifty years of their lives. What the cumulative effects of these experiences are over time will probably never be known, but one thing is clear and certain, the price is surely a loss of human dignity.

No one can deny that the urban life experiences described above—particularly if they spread and intensify—represent a crisis in human dignity. The crisis, however, goes well beyond these urban stresses, and its roots are far deeper than the failure to provide, maintain, and enhance space, facilities, and services in the urban settings.

The critical fact is that even the most desirable features of the built environment, whether we refer to apartments, school-rooms, commercial offices, hospital wards, playgrounds, family homes, and a variety of other physical settings, necessarily violate human dignity if for no other reason than that they are designed and maintained without regard for those properties of the person that make him a unique higher-order organism.

The quality of the physical environment in effect depends on more than the neat-clean-orderly trio of values. To be a human environment—as we have already suggested—it must reflect a concern with the person as a human being. Let me document this statement in a rather trite fashion. Kira's (1966) systematic study of the bathroom revealed that even in so basic a matter as the physical design and dimensions of the sink, bathtub, and toilet bowl there are "dysfunctions" insofar as what is required by the physical properties of the human body when it is making use of these facilities. The existing designs of sinks and shower stalls, in effect, require postures and movements that are alien to the requirements imposed by the structure of the human body.

Of course, you may ask does it matter; or what are the consequences of these dysfunctions in the design of bathroom facilities? Unfortunately, my answer has to be that we don't know, and we are not likely to because such problems are not studied systematically. Indeed, outside of Kira's study I suspect no one ever conceived of the design of bathroom facilities as a problem for the human frame. One way or another there seems to be an "average person" model with a set of assumed biological and physical characteristics which is used to design the built environment of the individual. We are talking about mundane matters, but it is just these matters that constitute the day to day experience of all of us: where, how, and when we engage in eating, sleeping, listening, reading, working, thinking, walking, recuperating, learning, socializing, and other activities. Involved are particular places, objects, equipment, and facilities, and if we can't design the facilities of a bathroom properly, I dread to think about the rest of the built environment.

It can be argued that everything seems to work, including bathroom facilities. In the operational sense they do work because what is *not* apparently functional for the individual as a biological and physical organism is changed until it is functional. But if Kira's study is any indication, what may be necessary is not always sufficient. Unless we concern ourselves with the individual in all his or her complexity as a biological and physical organism, what seems to work may indeed be more harmful than the obvious inappropriate designs we discard. There is a parallel here to the subway rider we referred to earlier. Nothing may seem to happen, but over a period of years dysfunctions in the design of bathroom facilities may indeed have serious physical and physiological consequences for the user. There is, however, a more basic question than what are the consequences of the dysfunctions in our built environment: Why should there be any dysfunctions at all, at least as to what fits and doesn't fit the human body given the advanced technology of our times?

As a psychologist, of course, I am far more interested in the person as a psychological and social being. Facilities which are alien to the human body, both physically and biologically, and that as a result have negative consequences over time for the person—whether eventual pain or chronic disease—do of course have negative psychological consequences as well. But let us return to the physical impact of the urban setting which we described earlier in terms of crowding, dirt, excessive noise, a breakdown in services, and what for many large cities can only be described as the tension, vibration, and volume of a frenzied daily life. The psychological consequences are known to all of us in terms of such reactions as tension, anxiety, fear, irritability, persistent fatigue, and still other states, all of which are generally subsumed under the heading of urban stress. It is only recently that direct attention has been given to the nature and consequences of this state both in the immediate behavior and experience of the person and over time.

Many dimensions can and indeed have been employed in the attempt to describe the quality of the physical environment, although no systematic effort leading to a meaningful conceptualized scheme has yet been realized. Certainly one general dimension that is necessary—subsuming more specific types—concerns the extent to which a physical setting either facilitates or frustrates human behavior and experience. Such facilitation or frustration, however, must be conceived of in terms that go well beyond the stress produced by the impact of the excessive physical stimulation that a person experiences in an urban setting.

Human Privacy

This brings us to the crux of the matter of the crisis in human dignity. Although scarcely considered by behavioral scientists, there are significant human needs whose origins and satisfactions are inherently related to the nature of physical settings and which are generally being ignored in the design and use of such settings. Let me begin with a compelling example.

It is only within the last five years that behavioral scientists have shown any focused interest in human privacy. It is true that a few political scientists, such as Westin (1967), have systematically considered the problem in the light of the growing invasion of the individual's privacy inherent in an ever increasing urban existence defined by numerous overlapping bureaucratic structures. If one thinks of the nature of electronic bugging equipment and the almost normative character of surreptitious invasions of privacy in so many walks of life, then indeed this alone constitutes a crisis in human dignity. The Watergate affair boggles the mind not just because of the political level at which it occurred or because of the arrogance of those involved; it expresses in both direct and dramatic terms the essence of the crisis in human dignity.

However, there has been far more concern with human privacy as a moral and legal right than as an empirical and theoretical construct for understanding human behavior and experience. All of this despite the fact that its reality and basic significance for many forms of human activity, psychological process, and social relationships have never been in dispute. Only recently my colleagues Maxine Wolfe and Robert Laufer have initiated a study of the development of privacy in American children as a function of chronological age, which they hope in time to enlarge to cross-national in scope. Perhaps of greater importance is the fact that with the cooperation of doctoral students and other faculty members in a year long seminar, Wolfe, Laufer, and I have been able to develop a set of theoretical dimensions for the analysis of psychological and social problems in human privacy, which is not a single phenomenon but an array of interrelated phenomena, or as we said elsewhere, "It is not one

155

thing but many things [Laufer, Proshansky, & Wolfe, 1973]."

Among the significant dimensions of privacy are *self-ego, interaction,* and *life cycle.* Privacy is both the expression and embodiment of the self and ego. The development of self in the child requires that he or she exper.ence aloneness and develop the ability to function in the context of aloneness; secondly, for the adult as well as the child, privacy in various forms can be seen as a way of enhancing and protecting the self.

Privacy also has an *interaction* dimension, since it presupposes the existence of others, the possibility of interaction with them, and the desire to minimize or control this interaction. In order for the person to function effectively over time, there must be a reasonable balance between interaction and privacy. More is involved in privacy than just escape from the demands created by the presence of others; it also functions as an opportunity to rehearse those aspects of behavior which are required by particular roles and social interaction situations. Also let us not forget that privacy is a necessary aspect of various intimate relationships involving two or more persons. Groups as well as individuals require privacy.

There is also a *life-cycle* dimension to privacy. As a phenomenon in human behavior it is by no means static. It must be viewed within a time framework, since the properties of the human life cycle itself are not static. The periods of time devoted to specific activities (i.e., child bearing and child raising) will vary as a function of a changing technology, changing sociocultural patterns, and the historical environment. Indeed, an analysis of the changing nature of privacy in human behavior and experience may be diagnostic of the shifting character of the properties of the life cycle of the members of a society. What must be emphasized, however, is that throughout the life cycle privacy needs and related behaviors change at the same time that there is change in the physical settings in which the individual is expected to function as a member of society: the home, nursery school, playground, elementary school, college dorm, work setting, and still others. Each of these environments and many more which I have not mentioned place the individual in a new and quite different context, and, as such, the opportunities, needs, and behavior patterns for privacy will differ accordingly.

The three dimensions of human privacy I have just discussed should give you some idea of the complexity of this phenomenon. Yet our analysis produced six other equally complex dimensions and I believe the task is by no means complete. If, as we believe, human privacy is fundamental to the psychological development, well-being, and functioning of the individual, then the design of the built environment for human behavior and experience is a crucial issue. Yet not only do we know little about human privacy, but at best its influence on how we design and use space in a variety of situational contexts is based on a number of very primitive if not erroneous assumptions about human needs for privacy.

The crisis in human dignity will grow as urbanism grows and we concentrate larger and larger numbers of people in smaller and smaller areas. What is involved is not simply the lack of privacy engendered by overcrowding in apartments, the ghetto, school, hospitals, business offices, and the like. Even for modern physical settings, new designs and organizations of space combined with new and cheaper forms of building material cause havoc for human privacy. Thus, as some of you already know by experience, in the newest homes, offices, schools, and other settings, visual privacy counts but not auditory privacy. Furthermore, the now common open-office space "pretends" the separation and privacy of clerical, secretarial, and other office workers by employing furniture, plants, and other forms of boundary markers that are neither sound proof or visual proof. It is likely that many secretaries and junior executives will believe and therefore act like they are being observed. However, even if they don't think they are being observed, their belief that they *can be observed* will undoubtedly lead to the same kind of self-conscious behavior. And what about privacy within the home itself—aside from overcrowding—if the walls are thin, the doors have no locks, and the separations between eating, cooking, and socializing spaces are nothing more than partial walls or railings serving as boundary markers? All of this, placed in a broader context in which various telecommunication devices such as television cameras increasingly keep most of us under surveillance in department stores and banks, means that indeed the problem of human privacy is a basic social issue in its own right.

Human Territoriality

Like privacy, *human territoriality* has only recently come to the attention of behavioral scientists. Although found in fairly well defined form among various lower animal groups, its roots in man are undoubtedly social and environmental rather than genetic. There can be little question of this if we keep in mind how individuals in complex democratic societies are socialized with respect to material goods, property, individual success, and the expression of those three values in economic power. But territoriality, defined roughly as the individual's desire to identify, lay claim to, and indeed subsequently control some space (or object) or area, also has considerable significance for the development of self-identity. What is internalized by the child in this process is not only who and what he is, but where he belongs and what is his to exclusively control and own in contrast to what others exclusively control and own. I have discussed *place identity* in other contexts and the significance of territoriality in the development and maintenance of this aspect of self-identity is self-evident.

Is the satisfaction of human territoriality also being eroded in the design and use of built environments? In one sense alone the answer to this question must be yes, if we accept the view that the increasing lack of human privacy means that the individual has somewhat less control over his or her spaces and places. Of course the increasing concentration of individuals in smaller and smaller geographical areas undoubtedly means less and less territory for each person. A desk in an open-office space where a particular "office" is defined by the arrangement of files and other furniture signifies somewhat less in terms of territoriality than the same desk in a comparably sized private office. But beyond such contextual factors, the fact is that space is at a premium; with overcrowding in homes, neighborhoods, hospitals, dormitories, offices, schools, and so on, the sharing of space has become a way of life. I recall that some years back I was sharing a university office with three other colleagues, but never did I ever think that the time would come when three faculty members in an office would share the same desk.

In most settings we don't actually own the space or place that is known "to belong" to each of us. It is assigned to us by virtue of the role we play and the position we have in a given social setting. Of course up to a point such an assignment gives us all the rights and privileges of territoriality as long as we retain the relevant position or role. But I wonder what we do, for example, to the development of the professional identity of our graduate students and young faculty when we except them to be creative, do research, and work with other students while providing very little space and facilities they can claim as their own in this sense. It seems to me that we ought to invert the hierarchy. Those still in their formative professional years require and should have a greater claim to "their space" than those of us who are older and more established. Similarly it seems ludicrous to me to expect good elementary school teaching from teachers in urban settings who at best can lay claim only to a desk or a locker in their schools. Good teaching depends on a secure professional identity, which in return requires a place for the teacher to think, write, and plan in a setting that not only makes these activities possible and under his or her control but also reflects in its design the teacher's crucial role in the educational process. The school principal is an administrator, whereas it is the teacher who carries the direct responsibility of educating. Shouldn't the schoolroom teacher be given similar consideration when it comes to space? I am certain that the question I am raising applies to other professional work settings as well.

Finally, I would like to suggest to you that threats to human privacy and territoriality can also be conceptualized in terms of the individual's need to maximize *freedom of choice*. Clearly, this concept is also useful in considering crowding in any physical setting, for in fact the actual presence of too many others or the belief that there are too many others may limit the person's freedom of choice. Indeed it may well be that the number of persons in a physical setting is experienced by an individual as crowding when it results in the perhaps less than conscious realization that his freedom of choice is reduced by the presence of others, or even of one other person. In privacy he can satisfy whatever needs he has on his own terms; privacy affords him the opportunity in both thought and action to attempt any and all alternatives and to make his choice accordingly. The significance of territoriality in maximizing freedom of choice lies in the fact that given "my space," the person controls the available alternatives and the means to these alternatives and thus can achieve privacy and satisfy other relevant needs. Invasion of his or her territory cuts down freedom of choice. Doxiadis (1968), the architect and city planner, sees the person's freedom of choice as an essential determinant in the planning and organization of cities: "We must learn how to plan and build our cities in such a way as to give all of us the maximum choices. . . . we must study the type of structure that eliminates the smallest number of alternatives [p. 22]." Whether the individual's freedom of choice represents a decision to use the least crowded among a variety of routes, to read in his bedroom rather than the living room, or to formulate any of many other decisions he faces each day, broadening the available possibilities open to him can only enhance his dignity and human qualities, making him less an automaton and more a fulfilled individual.

Social Processes

What about the individual as a *social* being in relation to his physical world? The complex organization we call a community or a society is inherently rooted in the social interactions and the social relationships of its members. It clearly follows that if the present design and operation of urban settings create problems in the person's needs for privacy and territoriality, then they must also thwart and interfere with the desired or needed human relationships and social interactions. Furthermore, they may also provoke and bring about other kinds of relationships and interactions that are clearly not needed or desired. Crowding in transportation, urban housing, schools, hospitals, and many other settings has the potential for creating negative relationships between and among individuals.

Think, however, of all the other possibilities for antagonistic and hostile interactions: poorly designed proximal relationships between spatial areas in which the activities of one person (or persons) interfere with the activities of another (e.g., "She plays the damn piano all day long"); or a particular functional area (e.g., a classroom, a doctor's examining room) whose design interferes with rather than enhances the relationships and activities involving two or more people. Even a setting in which two people cannot see or hear each other well because of poor illumination or persistent and disturbing noise has the potential for interfering with the social interaction process and therefore with the achievement of the common goals of the participants involved in this process. As we all know, it is just that much harder to respond and relate to others when each participant has to compensate for an inadequate physical setting by straining to see or hear or by overcoming bodily discomforts because of temperature variation, uncomfortable furniture, or poor ventilation. Finally, it must be evident that the design and use of household space for families engaged in a plethora of interpersonal activities must also add to or detract from the dignity of those involved. For a married couple to argue and to know that although they are in their bedroom they can still be heard by their children and their neighbors is a case in point. And for a mother with young children, I suspect that her day-to-day relationships with her children may be less than desirable if the design and use of household space makes it difficult for her to know where they are and to get to them when they need her, or which makes them highly dependent on her because getting around the house is difficult for them.

The problems I have noted for you represent only a small number of examples in a vast no-man's-land concerning the influence of the design and use of physical settings on social interaction and social process. And in this respect the problem should be stated positively rather than negatively. Given the defined relationships between persons in an array of interpersonal and institutional settings, what should the structure and content of physical settings be that will enhance and maximize their required role behaviors, the processing of particular activities, and their extended and continuing relationships with each other? Yet, even as I state the problem in this way, urbanism involving technological progress continues at an accelerated rate of change. I mention this so as to alert you to an as yet untouched major problem in human social relationships. Increasingly there are indications that in many aspects of day-to-day life persons rely on telecommunication rather than face-to-face communication. Whether it is the telephone, the walkie-talkie, television, the two-way radio, or similar devices, the nature and process of social interaction undoubtedly involves qualitative differences compared to what happens in face-to-face discussions. Of course, how different will depend on the nature and length of the interaction, its purposes, the people involved, and other factors.

UNDERSTANDING THE CRISIS IN HUMAN DIGNITY

There can be little question that many aspects of the crisis in human dignity relative to the urban setting are rooted in other major social ills of our time: poverty, political corruption, economic exploitation, crime and violence, exploitation and deprivation of minority groups, and still others. The stress of urban life goes well beyond the question of how good the planning of a physical setting was and whether it is being used properly. On the other hand, it should be evident from the previous analysis that even so-called planned and good physical settings—all other things being equal—also represent a part of this crisis, although on a more subtle and less obvious basis. However, whether the threats to human dignity involve such stresses of urban life as crowding, noise, and decaying physical settings or the more subtle factors

I have described, there are a common set of attitudes or values that seem to prevail among all groups concerning the person's relationship to the built environment.

First the assumption is made that, insofar as designing, constructing, and using physical settings goes, there is little that needs to be known about people beyond just plain common sense. Inferences are made about the behavior and experience of the person—if they are made at all—which at best seem to attribute to him the quality of a "machine person," and incidentally not a very complex machine. The value orientation of modern technology is pragmatic rather than humanistic. What works is good, and something works if it can be seen to work by producing its *intended effects*. The individual, as I have said, is viewed in a mechanistically simple fashion as an object with given functions. And if he or she can be observed to do better in these functions without immediately observable difficulties, then still another person-environment problem has been solved.

But there is a more insidious generally held attitude or belief about individuals in relation to their physical setting. Indeed this view holds whether we are talking about the person who rides an overcrowded, poorly ventilated subway train for most of his or her life or a secretary who must work amidst forty others in an otherwise beautiful open-office area. Not only is it assumed that individuals in time will *adapt*, but it is also assumed that if they fail to complain or manifest other overt signs of difficulty, then the designed environment has not had any negative effects on the growth and continued existence of the person.

None of this I should emphasize really represents a cynical attitude toward the individual in relationship to his or her physical setting. The assumptions about people—"adaptable" and "simple machines"—go hand in hand with the socioenvironmental values we discussed earlier. Crucial in this respect is the reverent reliance on advances in modern technology as a basis for creating "new and better" urban settings. And the person is by no means ignored—except that, as we already indicated, his humanness is reduced to the simplest terms and his adaptability measured accordingly. It was René Dubos (1965) who pointed out that human adaptability makes it possible for the person to accommodate himself to conditions which threaten to destroy the values which are characteristically human.

It is for these reasons that we continue to encounter two—and I must use these words—"very incredible" features in the continued building and rebuilding of the physical environment. First, the technological innovator at the design, creation, and management levels is concerned almost exclusively with expected effects and almost not at all with *unintended consequences*. Regardless of the physical setting or purpose for it—planning, designing, and creating a new and better highway, hospital, breakfast cereal, TV set, community school, telephone, playground, housing complex, theater, ad infinitum—the focus is on "solving the problem," which means the realization of explicitly stated objectives or ends.

The fact that the built environment has unintended as well as intended consequences strikes a familiar note if we think of modern medicine and its use of natural and synthetic drugs and antibiotics in combating illness and disease. The concept of side effects in evaluating modern medical treatment is no less applicable to the built environment, particularly if we rely more and more on technology in living our everyday lives. But the difficulty with the "side effects" concept is that it assumes a concern not just with unintended consequences but also with the question of what is happening over extended periods of time. It means designing, organizing, and actually using physical settings in a far more delayed time framework.

But this brings me to the second, no less incredible, feature of the design and use of physical space and its contents: whether it involves the intended or unintended effects, once the built environment has been established and is a reality, no attempt is made to evaluate just how well it works. The evaluation of the person's physical settings as a basis for cumulating knowledge about the desired if not the unintended consequences between means and ends is the rare exception rather than the rule. I made this statement a decade ago and not much has changed since then in this respect.

What is quite worrisome is that we take the built environment for granted. And besides—and this is the point made by Dubos—the danger is not that we will be unable to adjust to our new environment, rather that we may adjust too well. The accelerated rate of change referred to earlier establishes the validity of just this point. How adaptable mankind is to the new technology is revealed by the fact that processes which once took generations are now assimilated into our culture within a few years, although at a price. We speak proudly of "conquering" nature; yet this conquest quite apart of what it has done to nature itself imposes an unprecedented burden on the individual, both in the magnitude of change and its continually increasing rate of acceleration. It is as if a storm were brewing from which we can find no refuge. Modern technology has assumed a life of its own; the very process of change seems at times to have gotten out of hand, so that our industrial society no longer reflects our true needs.

This brings us to the end of the discussion. I don't know whether or not I have convinced you that, relative to the built environment, there is an impending if not already existing crisis in human dignity. But it doesn't matter whether or not you now believe the problem exists in crisis proportions. What is important is that all of us become aware of the fact that man's urban setting both specifically and generally is becoming the major social issue of our times. And that as socially conscious behavioral scientists we have a responsibility to carry out research and take action in an area of human behavior and experience that is still virgin territory. But, as in the case of other social issues, we have a further responsibility and that is to "become involved." By this I mean to seek to establish contact with all those who initate, define, and control our physical settings. Of course we have no answers, but we do have questions and a set of conceptual tools for raising these questions, which at least will sensitize these practitioners of physical settings to become aware of the full range of properties of the person that underlie his sense of personal worth or human dignity.

For those of us long concerned with social issues there is a real challenge in our research efforts with respect to the built environment. The laboratory paradigm for the study of complex human behavior will not be adequate, if it works at all. Understanding the person's behavior and experience in relation to the physical world will require a methodology and indeed a conception of scientific study which maintain the reality and integrity of these phenomena. In this development of a new approach, appropriate concepts and relevant data gathering techniques will have to evolve, responsive to the complexity of man-environment relationships that can only be understood in the context of an ever changing structure of human interactions and social processes. Without this change in our research paradigm, whatever investigations we do are likely to approximate the "fantasy world" that more than a few behavioral scientists created in their attempt to study and define, in terms of "scientifically controlled" experimental studies either in or out of the setting of the laboratory, other complex human phenomena and social issues.

REFERENCES

Dubos, R. *Man adapting.* New Haven: Yale University Press, 1965.
Doxiadis, C. A. Man and the space around him. *Saturday Review*, 1968 (Dec. 14), 21–23.

Kira, A. *The bathroom: Criteria for design.* Ithaca, N.Y.: Center for Housing and Environmental Studies, Cornell University, 1966.

Laufer, R. S., Proshansky, H. M., & Wolfe, M. Some analytic dimensions of privacy. Paper presented at the meeting of the American Psychological Association, Montreal, August 1973.

Schlesinger, A., Jr. The modern consciousness and the winged chariot. Address presented at the 10th Anniversary Convocation, The Graduate School, City University of New York, May 1973.

Westin, A. F. *Privacy and freedom.* New York: Atheneum, 1967.

Whitehead, A. N. *Science and the modern world.* New York: Macmillan, 1925.

CROWDING: EXPERIMENTAL AND
ANTHROPOLOGICAL APPROACHES

Differential Effects of Group Density on Social Behaviour

Corinne Hutt
M. Jane Vaizey

In a study of the social behaviour of different groups of children, one of the aspects selected for specific investigation was the effect of group density. In view of the findings from animal studies, it was hypothesized that increasing group density would have adverse effects on the nature and frequency of social encounters, and that these effects would differ according to the personality of the subject. Furthermore, if earlier hypotheses regarding the physiological activation of autistic[1,2] and brain-damaged[3] children are correct, these two groups of children might be expected to manifest, in exaggerated form, the reactions of introverted or relatively inhibited individuals and extraverted individuals, respectively, in the normal population.

The subjects of this study were fifteen children who were in- or day-patients in the hospital: five were autistic[4], five had unequivocal evidence of fairly gross brain-damage, and five were 'normal' (that is, two normal siblings of patients and three who had recovered from minor behaviour disturbance and were about to be discharged). The last-mentioned three children did not differ significantly on any of the measures from the two who were not patients, and there seemed no *a priori* reason for not grouping all five together as 'normals'. All subjects were between the ages of 3 and 8 years, and the groups were matched for age.

The situation used for the observations was a 27 ft. × 17·5 ft. playroom where the children customarily assembled for 'free play'. Three group sizes were used: (i) small ($n \leqslant 6$); (ii) medium ($n = 7-11$); (iii) large ($n \geqslant 12$). Other children in the hospital formed the rest of the group (only two or three of the subjects were present at any one session). Groups and densities were arranged in a 3×3 Latin-square design, four replicates of this design then being used. An observation period per subject was 15 min and for each subject under each condition the mean of three observation periods was obtained. Observations were recorded on: (*a*) check-lists (1 entry per 10 sec); (*b*) magnetic tape; (*c*) 8-mm ciné film. Two adults, usually nurses, were always present; in the larger groups three adults were often present.

The relative proportions of time spent in aggressive or destructive behaviour (that is, fighting, snatching or breaking toys, etc.) by the three groups of subjects under the different conditions are given in Table 1.

NATURE, March 26, 1966, pp. 1371-1372.

Table 2 shows the amounts of time that were spent in social encounters with other children or adults, and which did not involve any show of aggression.

With increasing density certain children appeared to seek the safety of the boundary (that is, within 3 ft. of the periphery of the room) more frequently (Table 3).

Table 1. MEAN PERCENTAGE TIME ($\pm S.D.$) SPENT IN AGGRESSIVE/DESTRUCTIVE BEHAVIOUR

	Small	Medium	Large
Normal	$3\cdot0\pm1\cdot7$	$4\cdot6\pm2\cdot4$	$16\cdot1\pm5\cdot2$
Brain-damaged	$2\cdot7\pm2\cdot8$	$19\cdot0\pm8\cdot2$	$28\cdot0\pm11\cdot2$
Autist	$2\cdot5\pm3\cdot7$	$1\cdot9\pm2\cdot8$	$2\cdot1\pm3\cdot4$

Table 2. MEAN PERCENTAGE TIME ($\pm S.D.$) SPENT IN SOCIAL INTERACTIONS

	Small	Medium	Large
Normal	$63\cdot0\pm17\cdot3$	$49\cdot3\pm16\cdot2$	$39\cdot1\pm11\cdot0$
Brain-damaged	$23\cdot0\pm4\cdot0$	$43\cdot0\pm15\cdot6$	$31\cdot0\pm14\cdot7$
Autist	$15\cdot0\pm5\cdot3$	$6\cdot5\pm6\cdot7$	$14\cdot2\pm11\cdot8$

Table 3. MEAN PERCENTAGE TIME ($\pm S.D.$) SPENT ON THE BOUNDARY

	Small	Medium	Large
Normal	$15\cdot0\pm6\cdot6$	$13\cdot1\pm4\cdot2$	$10\cdot3\pm5\cdot5$
Brain-damaged	$24\cdot6\pm3\cdot6$	$8\cdot7\pm4\cdot7$	$16\cdot0\pm4\cdot9$
Autist	$21\cdot5\pm7\cdot7$	$30\cdot0\pm9\cdot0$	$55\cdot2\pm6\cdot8$

Analyses of variance were carried out on the data, the appropriate error term in these cases being the 'within cells' variance, since $n > 1$. Subsequently Scheffe's test for multiple comparisons of means was applied.

For aggressive/destructive behaviour, both the main effects between groups and between densities were significant ($F = 6\cdot8$, d.f. 2/36, $P < 0\cdot01$, and $F = 8\cdot3$, d.f. 2/36, $P < 0\cdot01$, respectively), as well as the groups × densities interaction ($F = 4\cdot2$, d.f. 4/36, $P < 0\cdot01$). The brain-damaged subjects became more aggressive with increasing group-density, whereas the normal subjects only became significantly more aggressive in the large group. The autists showed negligible aggression.

For social encounters, there was a significant main effect between groups ($F = 22\cdot3$, d.f. 2/36, $P < 0\cdot01$), and a significant interaction between groups and densities ($F = 2\cdot8$, d.f. 4/36, $P < 0\cdot05$). The normals showed progressively and significantly less social interaction with increasing group-size. The brain-damaged subjects showed significantly more interaction in the medium group, and the autists significantly less.

For time spent on the boundary, both the main effects between groups and between densities were significant ($F = 55\cdot8$, d.f. 2/36, $P < 0\cdot001$, and $F = 5\cdot4$, d.f. 2/36, $P < 0\cdot01$, respectively), as well as the groups × density interaction ($F = 7\cdot9$, d.f. 4/36, $P < 0\cdot001$). As density increased, the autists spent significantly more time on the boundary.

The finding that aggressive/destructive behaviour increased in both normal and brain-damaged subjects under high densities is in agreement with other animal work: Clarke[5] found that voles in a high-density population had more numerous scars from fighting and were in poorer health than animals living in a less dense population; Chitty[6] has suggested that intraspecific strife at high population densities severely limits the number of voles, that "populations change their nature as a result of crowding, and that a change in the condition of the individuals may be reflected in the vitality of their descendants"[7]; Calhoun[8] has described the emergence of a 'behavioural sink' as well as the sexual and social deviations manifested by Norway rats reared under high-density conditions. In fact the behavioural deviations of these rats ranged from 'phrenetic' activity to 'pathological withdrawal', and it is of interest that the brain-damaged and autistic subjects tended to show predominantly these extreme reactions respectively. In a large group two brain-damaged subjects were seen to bite other children, a behaviour not manifested by any other children.

The autists, indeed, showed behaviour characteristic of physiologically highly-activated organisms: they manifested little aggression, and with increasing density retreated more and more to the periphery of the room and often would be found sitting facing the wall. Their social interactions in the large group consisted almost entirely of approaches to the adults—to escape from the general 'mêlée', it seemed.

It is remarkable that despite the greater opportunity for social interaction with the larger groups, the normal subjects in fact showed less. These subjects were apparently endeavouring to minimize their social encounters, and this is an important point in view of Calhoun's finding that the frequency and 'velocity' of social encounters in rats were markedly increased at high densities, and of Leyhausen's[9] implied suggestion that humans living in high-density conditions might show 'crowd-addiction'.

Many writers and authorities, extrapolating from the infra-primate studies, are at present warning of the social dangers of human crowding[9-12]. There is, however, a regrettable lack of empirical evidence from studies of humans in different group densities. The findings of this preliminary study would suggest that the effects of crowding are complex, and that the nature or personality of the individuals involved in the interaction is a critical variable; furthermore, it is likely that in the human species, too, certain density-dependent regulatory mechanisms are capable of operating.

A fuller analysis of the behavioural changes with different group densities is in preparation. We are grateful to the Smith, Kline and French Foundation and the British Epilepsy Association for provision of film and equipment, and to the Nuffield Foundation for financial support.

[1] Hutt, C., Hutt, S. J., Lee, D., and Ounsted, C., *Nature*, 204, 908 (1964).
[2] Hutt, C., and Hutt, S. J., *Anim. Behav.*, 13, 1 (1965).
[3] Hutt, S. J., and Hutt, C., *Epilepsia*, 5, 334 (1964).
[4] Kanner, L., *J. Paediat.*, 25, 211 (1948).
[5] Clarke, J. R., *Proc. Roy. Soc.*, B, 144, 68 (1955).
[6] Chitty, D., *Phil. Trans. Roy. Soc.*, B, 236, 505 (1952).
[7] Chitty, D., in *The Numbers of Man and Animals*, edit. by Cragg, J. B., and Pirie, N. W. (Edinburgh, 1955).
[8] Calhoun, J. B., *Sci. Amer.*, 206, 139 (1962).
[9] Leyhausen, P., *Discovery*, 26, 9, 27 (1965).
[10] Spitz, R., *J. Amer. Psychoanal. Assoc.*, 12, 752 (1964).
[11] Leyhausen, P., *Symp. Zool. Soc. Lond.*, 14, 249 (1965).
[12] Russell, W. M. S., paper to Brit. Assoc. Adv. Science (1965).

The Effects of Spatial Density on the Social Behavior of Children[1]

CHALSA M. LOO

The behavioral effects of high and low spatial density on normal children of ages 4 and 5 were examined. Sixty Ss were observed in groups of six in a free-play situation under both density conditions. Results showed that there was significantly less aggression and less social interaction in the high-density condition than in the low-density condition. There was a significant Density X Sex effect on aggression and signficant main effects of sex on aggression, nurturance, number of interruptions, and number of children interacted with. Several complexities in researching and explaining the effects of density on behaviors are discussed.

The intent of this study was to analyze the effects of spatial density (low and high) on several social behaviors of 4- and 5-year-olds in an experimental setting. Spatial density is distinguished from social density by the fact that the former involves observing same-sized groups in spaces of differing sizes while the latter involves groups of differing numbers in the same-sized space (W. C. McGrew, 1970). The social behaviors that were examined were aggression, dominance, nurturance, number of interruptions, social interactions (number of children interacted with, solitary play, onlooker, and group involvement), resistance, and submission.

Since crowding seems to be a natural outcome of population growth, many ecologists have issued grave predictions about the devastating effects that human

[1]This research was partially supported by an N.I.H. General Research Grant FR 5409 through The Ohio State University College of Medicine, by The Ohio State University Department of Psychology, and by a Dissertation Fellowship through The Ohio State University. Appreciation is due to the Department of Child Psychiatry for the use of their facilities.

JOURNAL OF APPLIED SOCIAL PSYCHOLOGY, 1972, Vol. 2, pp. 372-381.

crowding will produce. The empirical evidence used by most ecologists is based on animal research. The most notable research on the effects of crowding on animals has been done by Calhoun (1962), who found among other effects, a decline in maternal care and increased social withdrawal among rats or mice in a high density situation. While animal research can provide valuable leads for research on humans, some skepticism must be exercised in accepting analogies from mice to men without researching the effects of population density on humans themselves.

Several psychologists have discussed the need for answers to questions about the effects of high population density on human behavior (Barker, 1969; Winkle, 1970; Wohlwill, 1966). Yet few psychologists have shown an interest in researching population problems, and our understanding of how density affects human interactions is limited.

Much of the research on the effects of crowding on humans is characterized by a lack of experimental controls and, consequently, ambiguous results. For example, Jersild and Markey (1935) and Murphy (1937) found that there were more conflicts among preschoolers in a small (versus large) playground, but their research did not control for age; in fact, they speculated that the larger age range of the low-density group probably encouraged more nurturant interactions.

Experimental studies have the advantage of controlling crucial variables. Freedman, Klevansky, and Ehrlich (1971) studied the effects of density on learning and performance tasks of adults and found no significant effects of density on performance. Such results were probably due to the fact that Ss were not permitted to interfere or interact with each other physically and could not move around in the available space. The authors concluded that crowding effects would more likely be found in social interactions than on individual task performances.

There are two notable experimental studies of density on children. The first is Hutt and Vaizey's study (1966) on the effects of social density, in which normal children were found to be more aggressive and less social in high-density conditions. While their results demonstrated that social density is positively correlated with aggression and negatively correlated with social interaction, the effects of spatial density were not explored.

The second study on children was that of P. L. McGrew (1970), who made the important distinction between social and spatial density and found that differences in social density were more potent in eliciting adjustments in spacing behavior than spatial-density differences. She also found a trend toward less physical contact at a higher social density.

The present experiment was designed to study the effects of spatial density on several social behaviors, some of which were suggested by the research of Elder and Bowerman (1963), Douglas (1964), and Sommer (1969). While these investigators have not studied experimentally the effects of density per se, their work had relevance to the question of how reducing space affects human

172

behavior. Sommer (1969) observed that there are instances where crowded conditions lead to an inhibition of man's aggression for purposes of survival. He also contended that the clearest dominance orders are found in closed communities with restricted movement and limited space. Similarly, Elder and Bowerman (1963) found that the authoritarianism of either parent increased as the family size increased. Douglas (1964) found that infant care and management were less adequate in larger families, and Minuchin (1967) conjectured that overcrowded conditions in large families would lead to a lack of privacy and less-individualized responses from others.

Accordingly, the present investigator predicted that there would be a significant effect of density on aggression, dominance, number of interruptions, resistance, submission, nurturance, number of children interacted with, solitary play, and group involvement.

METHOD

Experimental Design

A repeated measures design was used in which Ss served as their own controls by undergoing both density conditions. This design was chosen because individual differences between Ss and differences between groups of Ss appeared great in the pretest sessions. The order effects of administration of low- and high-density conditions were controlled by counterbalancing in order to prevent order effects from being confounded with treatment effects.

Apparatus

The setting for this research was a room which measured 15' x 20' minus two insets (30" x 19" and 45" x 48") making a total area of 265.1 square feet. Portable wooden walls, painted and designed to match the walls of the room, were built, which when erected would reduce the room area to about one-third of its original area or 90 square feet. The portable walls measured 7½' x 12'. The original room was used for the low-density condition and the portable walls were installed for the high-density condition. The room was equipped with a one-way mirror and microphones hanging from the ceiling, permitting the Ss to be seen and heard in the adjoining room.

A wide variety of attractive toys was provided. The wall decorations and toys were identical for both density conditions and were located in a constant location at the beginning of every session.

Subjects

Ss were 60 normal, middle-class children 4 and 5 years of age; 30 were male and 30 were female. There were 10 groups; each group was comprised of three girls and three boys. In order to hasten natural interactions, all Ss in each group were from the same classroom. Each group came for two sessions; each session lasted 48 minutes and consisted of free play in an adult-free situation.

The low-density condition, in which six Ss occupy an area of 265.1 square feet, allowed 44.2 square feet per person. The high-density condition, in which six Ss occupy an area of 90 square feet, allowed 15 square feet per person.

Raters and Reliability

There were six observational raters, three male and three female. Reliability of ratings on all variables was calculated using the intraclass correlation formula (Ebel, 1951) for the last 2 days of training. The reliability coefficients were: aggression, $r = .58$; dominance, $r = .74$; nurturance, $r = .60$; number of interruptions, $r = .50$; number of children interacted with, $r = .56$; solitary play, $r = .91$; onlooker, $r = .71$; group involvement, $r = .87$; resistance, $r = .80$; and submission, $r = .60$. Continuous ratings were more susceptible to rater differences than items rated on a specified time basis. While there were rating differences among the raters, the score for a S on any variable was a sum of all raters' ratings, each S being rated an equal amount of time by each rater. Thus, any rater biases would be equally distributed among Ss.

Procedure

Ss were picked up at their school and driven to the experimental setting. An identification tag was attached to each S. Ss were instructed that the playroom was theirs and they could play with anything in the room. They were told that they would be playing in the playroom for about an hour and that the E would be next door. In the adjoining room, raters began rating on the devised form.

Definitions of Social Variables

A social interaction was defined as a condition in which the child showed that he was aware of the presence of another (or others), as in playing with, talking with, observing; i.e., a condition in which the child behaved with regard to another (others) and the other(s) had a direct effect on the child.

Aggressive behavior was defined as physically attacking another person or toy, being destructive with toys or equipment, aiming to inflict pain, discomfort, embarrassment, or frustration; being cruel, annoying, mean, criticizing; making another person suffer; being assertive in any hostile or threatening manner.

Dominance was defined as aiming to boss, control, lead, direct, prohibit, discipline, pass judgment, give decisions, lay down principles; aiming to be imposing, assertive, authoritative, powerful; trying to command attention; "Do this" or "Don't do that" said in a commanding voice, with an implied "Because I say so"; ordering others to do something.

174

Interruptions were defined as distractions or behavior by others that disrupts the activity of the child. Observers were instructed to (*a*) watch for a change in the child's attention caused by another's activity, noise, or imposition, and (*b*) watch for a temporary or permanent shift in attention as evidenced in eye and head movements. The child must be engaged in an activity in order for him to be distracted from it and have it interrupted.

Nurturant behavior was defined as initiating help or benefit; actively giving to or protecting another; being nice, forgiving, indulgent, kind, sympathetic.

Resistance was defined as being unyielding to dominance, aggression, appeal, or action of any kind that exerts social pressure; defending oneself physically or verbally; withholding compliance, actively ignoring demands or requests; refusing; being stubborn.

Submission was defined as giving in to dominance, aggression, appeal, or action of any kind that exerts social pressure; letting another have his way in order to ease the pressure on himself. Typical behavior: relinquishing toys to a child who demands or requests them; obeying another's directions; "taking" criticism.

The degree of social involvement was subdivided into three categories representing degrees of social interaction. These three variables were: solitary play (meaning no social involvement, *S* showed interest in his own activity, or indifference or avoidance of others), onlooker (meaning that the *S* looked at the activity of others without being an active member or target of others) and group involvement (meaning that the *S* was a functioning member of a group, either a leader or one who took directions from others).

RESULTS

Density and Sex Differences

The means and standard deviations of all variables for male, female, and all *S*s and for low, high, and both densities are presented in Table 1. A three-factor analysis of variance with one repeated measure (density) was performed on all the data for all variables. The three factors were density, sex, and group. Group means were analyzed instead of individual *S* scores since *S*s within each group were assumed to be interdependent.

There were significantly fewer aggressive acts in the high-density condition than in the low-density condition ($F = 5.8$, $df = 1/9$, $p < .05$), and boys displayed significantly more aggressive acts than did girls ($F = 17.8$, $p < .005$). There was a significant Density X Sex effect ($F = 10.8$, $p < .01$). To analyze the interaction between density and sex, a paired *t* test was performed to test for significant differences between mean ratings of aggression in the low- and high-density conditions for males and females separately. While aggression in girls did not significantly differ between densities, aggression in boys was

TABLE 1

MEANS AND STANDARD DEVIATIONS OF ALL VARIABLES FOR MALES
FEMALES, AND FOR BOTH DENSITY CONDITIONS

Variable	Sex	Low		High		Total	
		Mean	SD	Mean	SD	Mean	SD
No. children	F	21.60	4.65	20.33	4.05	20.97	4.403
Interacted with	M	23.80	3.20	21.53	2.90	22.67	3.26
	All Ss	22.70	4.18	20.93	3.59		
No. interrup-	F	35.30	9.64	39.36	6.83	37.33	8.60
tions	M	29.13	4.97	33.33	8.41	31.23	7.22
	All Ss	32.22	8.33	36.35	8.30		
Dominance	F	10.46	8.51	14.90	12.53	12.68	10.94
	M	15.63	10.96	14.93	7.09	15.28	9.23
	All Ss	13.05	10.23	14.92	10.26		
Aggression	F	5.76	5.51	5.26	4.01	5.52	4.83
	M	20.23	14.22	12.20	9.34	16.20	12.69
	All Ss	13.00	13.07	8.73	8.07		
Resistance	F	6.90	4.34	6.53	3.26	6.72	3.84
	M	7.50	3.99	7.63	3.62	7.57	3.81
	All Ss	7.20	4.21	7.08	3.52		
Submission	F	9.73	5.03	8.90	4.77	9.32	4.92
	M	9.50	5.02	9.40	4.56	9.45	4.80
	All Ss	9.62	5.07	9.15	4.72		
Nurturance	F	7.26	4.32	7.66	4.86	7.47	4.60
	M	4.30	4.21	4.13	2.91	4.21	3.62
	All Ss	5.78	4.55	5.90	4.41		
Solitary play	F	12.53	8.16	14.50	6.61	13.52	7.49
	M	11.16	7.19	14.00	6.72	12.58	7.10
	All Ss	11.85	7.79	14.25	6.72		
Onlooker	F	9.76	6.60	9.66	4.84	9.72	5.79
	M	7.86	4.27	8.50	5.27	8.18	4.81
	All Ss	8.82	5.69	9.08	5.14		
Group	F	25.13	10.20	23.70	8.63	24.42	9.47
	M	28.76	9.27	24.96	7.22	26.87	8.53
	All Ss	26.95	10.00	24.33	8.05		

Note.—N = 30 for each sex

significantly higher in the low-density condition than in the high-density condition ($t = 3.68, p < .001$).

Ss interacted with significantly fewer children in the high-density condition than in the low-density condition ($F = 7.3, p < .05$). Similarly there was a trend toward less time spent in group involvement and more time spent in solitary play in the high-density than the low-density condition and a Density X Group effect. Boys interacted with significantly more children than did girls ($F = 6.9, p < .05$).

TABLE 2

TASK OF ANALYSIS OF VARIANCES FOR AGGRESSION, NUMBER OF
CHILDREN INTERACTED WITH, NUMBER OF
INTERRUPTIONS, AND NURTURANCE

Source	df	Aggression		No. of children interacted		No. of interruptions		Nurturance	
		MS	F	MS	F	MS	F	MS	F
D	1	546.1	5.7*	93.6	7.3*	512.5	2.9	.4	0.0
S	1	3434.7	17.8***	86.7	6.9*	1116.3	13.7**	316.9	11.6**
DS	1	425.6	10.8**	7.5	2.7	-176.5	4.6	2.4	.2

*p < .05
**p < .01
***p < .005

Girls were interrupted to a significantly greater degree than were boys ($F = 13.7, p < .01$) and there was a trend toward greater frequency of interruptions in the high-density condition than in the low-density condition. Girls were significantly more nurturant than boys ($F = 11.6, p < .01$), but there was no significant main effect for density on nurturance.

While there was no significant main effect for dominance, there was a trend toward a Density X Sex interaction. Dominance in boys did not significantly differ between densities, but dominance in girls decreased in the low-density condition and increased in the high-density condition ($t = 2.67, p < .025$).

There was no significant main effect of density on onlooker, nurturance, resistance, or submission, and no significant main effect of sex on number of children interacted with, solitary play, onlooker, group involvement, dominance, resistance, or submission. There was no significant main effect for group on any of the variables.

Session Differences

An analysis of the differences between the first and second sessions was done for the two density conditions using an unpaired *t* test. For the low-density condition, there were no significant session differences for any of the variables; for the high-density condition there was significantly more group play and less solitary play among the *S*s who underwent the high-density condition following the low-density condition than among the *S*s who first underwent the high-density condition ($t = 4.09, p < .001$ and $t = 2.70, p < .01$, respectively). Thus, the density differences were greater in the first session than in the second session for the last two variables.

Discussion

The present study demonstrated that the amount of space provided for a child has a significant influence on his behavior and on the quality of his social relationships with others around him. Contrary to what might have been feared, children were considerably less aggressive in spatially crowded conditions. Furthermore, children isolated themselves by interacting with fewer other children when in a spatially crowded condition. Thus a spatially crowded condition seemed to create physical and psychological restraints on children, as demonstrated by fewer social behaviors. Social isolation may serve to reduce the social pressures and encroaching stimulation.

The finding that boys were significantly more aggressive than girls was not surprising. What was surprising, however, was the finding that there was significantly less aggression among boys in the high-density condition than in the low-density condition. The effect of spatial density on aggression may differ from that of social density. In a condition where space remains constant while people increase, the new members may be perceived as the cause for discomfort. On the other hand, when number of people remain constant while space decreases, members do not see each other as causes of their discomfort; rather they may perceive that they are all pawns to something greater than themselves, their physical environment. In such a condition, it is postulated that aggression between members would be significantly less. The validity of such a postulate must await further research comparing the effects of spatial and social density.

In this study, it appeared that aggression was encouraged by aggressive toys, by spatial conditions that allow enough room to attack and retreat, and by a high excitation level. The high-density condition made gross motor activity difficult or else uncomfortable. It is quite possible, then, that a restriction on movement discouraged the use of certain aggressive toys. We may be witnessing evidence that children adapt their play to the physical requirements of their environment.

Since aggression and solitary play were negatively correlated, further study is needed to determine whether a high density affects one of these variables, which in turn affects the other and if so, which of the two variables is more directly affected by high density.

The finding that Ss interacted with significantly fewer children and spent more time in solitary play (versus group play) in the high-density condition is consistent with the findings of Calhoun (1962) and Hutt and Vaizey (1966) and with the trend found by P. L. McGrew (1970). As Sommer (1969) stated, segregation may serve to reduce conflict and to protect oneself from spatial intrusions. Playing in solitude may be the child's way of increasing psychological distance from others when physical distance is limited. A personal distance or "body-buffer" zone may be operating in such an explanation. The present finding of active isolation of children in a high-density condition is consistent with the greater "alienation" and "impersonality" descriptive of the manner in which persons respond to others in large metropolitan cities.

Crowded conditions may reduce the level of excitement that normally exists when children play with each other, resulting in apathy or inhibited play. Assuming that interaction with other children is conducive to maturity of social behavior, crowdedness over a long timespan may retard the development of mature social behavior in children. This may be particularly true if crowded conditions persist through the ages when large group play normally develops.

The trend found in this study suggested that crowded conditions cause more interruptions of children's activities and that girls, who interact with fewer children, are more likely to be interrupted than boys. Over a long period of time, frequent interruptions may interfere with concentration and thus hinder a child's sense of mastery, resulting in frustration or apathy.

There are several unresolved research questions raised by the present study. The effects of density are not simple; they are complicated by many factors such as duration of the stimulation, number of Ss in each group, area per child, experimental versus naturalistic conditions, spatial versus social density, characteristics of the sample, the equipment and activities within, and the degrees of density studied.

A further distinction must be made between experimental and naturalistic settings. It may be adaptive for animals to be aggressive under crowded conditions in their natural habitat, but not for humans to be aggressive in a crowded experimental setting. Aggression and competition among animals result in more food and space for the stronger. In an experimental setting, however, there are no long-run consequences to be anticipated due to its short-term nature. The consequences of aggression among children in an experimental setting are quite unlike those experienced by animals.

An important consideration of the present findings on aggression is the short-term nature of the study. Aggression, if inhibited, may not remain so over a longer period of time. Aversive stimulation such as crowding may produce negative effects that build up over time; on the other hand, humans may adapt to a restricting environment over time and negative effects may decrease. One hypothesis is that adaptation to stress requires an inhibition of aggression. This hypothesis assumes that a high-density condition is stressful and that aggression is a natural initial outcome of stressful human conditions. Another hypothesis is that crowded conditions alter behavior, irrespective of stress, and whether aggression increases or decreases will depend on the activities allowed or engaged in by the members and the expected and actual duration of the condition.

Further research needs to be directed toward studying the effects of various densities, rather than just two. By examining two densities, it is not known whether the effects of density on social interactions are linear or curvilinear. The high-density condition in the present study represented a crowdedness more extreme than any of the densities in other studies on children.

An understanding of these unresolved questions and complicating factors will lead to a more comprehensive conceptual framework from which to study population density and the relationship between man and his environment.

REFERENCES

Barker, R. G. Wanted an eco-behavioral science. In E. P. Williams & D. L. Rausch (Eds.), *Naturalistic viewpoints in psychological research*. New York: Holt, Rinehart & Winston, 1969.

Calhoun, J. B. Population density and social pathology. *Scientific American*, 1962, **206**, 139–148.

Douglas, J. W. B. *The home and the school: A study of ability and attainment in the primary school*. London: MacGibbon & Key, 1964.

Ebel, R. L. Estimation of the reliability of ratings. *Psychometrika*, 1951, **16**, 407–424.

Elder, G. H., Jr., & Bowerman, C. E. Family structure and child-rearing patterns: The effects of family size and sex composition. *American Sociological Review*, 1963, **28**, 891–905.

Freedman, J. L., Klevansky, S., & Ehrlich, P. R. The effect of crowding on human task performance. *Journal of Applied Social Psychology*, 1971, **1**, 7–25.

Hall, E. T. *The hidden dimension*. New York: Doubleday, 1966.

Hutt, C., & Vaizey, M. J. Differential effects of group density on social behavior. *Nature*, 1966, **209**, 1371–1372.

Jersild, A. T., & Markey, F. V. Conflicts between preschool children. *Child Development Monographs*, 1935, No. 21.

McGrew, P. L. Social and spatial density effects on spacing behavior in preschool children. *Journal of Child Psychology and Psychiatry*, 1970, **11**, 197–205.

McGrew, W. C. An ethological study of social behavior in preschool children. Unpublished doctoral thesis, University of Oxford, 1970.

Minuchin, S., Montalvo, B., Guerney, B. G., Rosman, B. L., & Schumer, F. *Families of the slums*. New York: Basic Books, 1967.

Murphy, L. B. *Social behavior and child personality*. New York: Columbia University Press, 1937.

Sommer, R. *Personal space: The behavioral basis of design*. New York: Prentice-Hall, 1969.

Winkle, G. H. The nervous affair between behavior scientists and designers. *Psychology Today*, 1970, **3**, 31–35.

Wohlwill, J. F. The physical environment, a problem for a psychology of stimulation. *Journal of Social Issues*, 1966, **22**, 29–38.

HOT AND CROWDED:

INFLUENCES OF POPULATION DENSITY AND TEMPERATURE ON INTERPERSONAL AFFECTIVE BEHAVIOR [1]

WILLIAM GRIFFITT [2] AND RUSSELL VEITCH

During exposure to conditions of high population density and high temperature, human interpersonal affective behavior as indicated by measures of liking or disliking another person was found to be more negative than during exposure to comfortable temperatures and low population density. Additional affective variables were also negatively influenced by temperature and density manipulations. The results parallel those in the animal literature reflecting deterioration of "social relations" under conditions of overcrowding and high temperature. The findings are discussed in the context of current population trends and other environmental conditions.

Environmental conditions (usually referred to as "stressors" when abnormal or extreme) are known to influence a wide variety of performance, intellectual, and physiological behaviors (Glass, Singer, & Friedman, 1969; Terris & Rahhal, 1969; Wilkinson, 1969). Investigations of the influence of environmental conditions such as temperature, noise, lack of sleep, vibration, etc., have typically involved such response variables as vigilance, pursuit tracking, and serial learning (Wilkinson, 1969). The importance of determining the nature of environmental influences on intellectual and performance behaviors such as those mentioned is, of course, obvious. The design of optimal man-machine systems and work environments is greatly facilitated through systematic investigations of the interactions among environmental factors and task variables.

In light of growing concern over environmental influences on nonperformance and nonintellectual behaviors (United States Riot Commission, 1968), systematic knowledge concerning the role of environmental conditions with respect to social behavior will as-

sume crucial importance as variables such as noise level and population density reach the status of stressors in years to come. Examination of current and recent literature (Griffitt, 1970), however, reveals an apparent dearth of systematic studies of environmental influences on human social, affective, and emotional behaviors.

The ambient temperature of the environment is one such variable which has received limited examination with respect to its influence on human social behavior. Anecdotally, it is commonly observed that social behaviors in very hot and humid situations are quite different in affective tone from those behaviors in "comfortable" and even cold environments. Interpersonal responses are detectably more negative when one is "hot and uncomfortable" than when one is located in a more comfortable situation. Such observations have been sufficiently compelling to lead some investigators to examine experimentally the effects of ambient temperature on "social behaviors" in nonhuman species. For example, utilizing mice, Greenberg (1969) examined the incidence of aggressive assaults as influenced by genetic strain, population density, and ambient temperature. The frequency of aggressive incidents was found to increase with temperature until at very high temperatures (approximately 95 degrees Fahrenheit) all motor activity (including assaults) declined sharply. Others (Guhl, 1962) have examined similar behaviors in chickens and other nonhuman animals.

[1] This research was supported in part by Grant MH 16351-02 from the National Institute of Mental Health. The authors would like to thank Frederick H. Rohles and Nancy Calentine for their assistance in conducting the experiment. Gratitude is also expressed to Kenneth Kemp for his assistance in analyzing the data.

[2] Requests for reprints should be sent to William Griffitt, Department of Psychology, Anderson Hall, Kansas State University, Manhattan, Kansas 66502.

JOURNAL OF PERSONALITY AND SOCIAL PSYCHOLOGY, 1971, Vol. 17, pp. 92-98.

With few exceptions, information concerning human social responses under conditions of high temperature has been obtained primarily through nonsystematic observations and correlations. For example, in studies concerned with the effects of exposure to high temperatures on physiological, intellectual, and physical functioning, Rohles (1967) observed "continual arguing, needling, agitating, jibing, fist-fighting, threatening, and even an attempted knifing [p. 59]." Further, an analysis of ghetto riots by the United States Riot Commission (1968) revealed that "In most instances, the temperature during the day on which the violence first erupted was quite high [p. 123]." It was reported that in 9 of 18 disorders, the temperature has reached 90 degrees or more during the day, while in 8 cases the temperature preceding the violence had been in the 80s. The above observations are sufficiently in accord with everyday experience to suggest that many interpersonal and social-affective behaviors are negatively influenced by conditions of high temperature.

The results of a recent investigation (Griffitt, 1970) lend support to the later proposition. Subjects were exposed to one of two conditions of ambient effective temperature and asked to respond with respect to attraction to strangers who either expressed agreement or disagreement on various attitudinal issues with the subjects' own views. Attraction responses were found to be significantly more negative under the "hot" condition (effective temperature = 90.6 degrees Fahrenheit) than under the "normal" condition (effective temperature = 67.5 degrees Fahrenheit). Further, subjective reports of the positiveness of affective feelings were positively related to attraction responses but negatively related to effective temperature. It was suggested that a broad class of social-affective behaviors (e.g., attraction, aggression, evaluative activities, etc.) would be negatively influenced by environmental conditions to the extent that such conditions elicit negative affective feelings.

The spatial relationships among people have been cited by many individuals (e.g., Hall, 1966; Little, 1965; Sommer, 1967) as potential sources of positive or negative affective experience. In light of recent and predicted population increase trends, the effects of "crowding" or high population density on social behaviors are of particular interest. Indeed, the United States Riot Commission (1968) referred to the "crowded ghetto living conditions, worsened by summer heat [p. 325]" as a basic factor involved in civil disorders. The physiological and behavioral effects of overcrowding in animals have been described by Christian (1963) and Calhoun (1962), who coined the term "behavioral sink" to describe the gross distortions of behavior which take place when animals are reared in extremely crowded situations. Seriously disrupted functions included courting, nest building, sex behaviors, social organization, and physiological functions.

If, as everyday experience frequently suggests, conditions of overcrowding tend to elicit feelings of discomfort or other negative affective responses, one would expect that interpersonal affective responses would tend to be generally more negative under conditions of high "population density" than under less crowded conditions. As part of the study mentioned earlier, Greenberg (1969) varied the density of mice in enclosed areas and observed the frequency of aggressive assaults. Within at least one genetic strain, frequency of assaults was found to be positively related to population density. These findings are similar to those reported earlier by Thiessen (1966).

The present experiment was designed to examine the effects of effective temperature and population density on social-affective behaviors in humans. It was hypothesized that interpersonal attraction responses and subjective evaluations of affective feelings are more negative under conditions of high effective temperature than under conditions of normal effective temperature, and more negative under conditions of high population density than in low-density conditions. The predictions were derived from an affective model of interpersonal evaluative behavior (Clore & Byrne, in press) and from findings of an earlier investigation (Griffitt, 1970). The use of attitudinal agreement and disagreement in the present investigation as a reliable technique of eliciting differential attraction responses has as its foundation the extensive work of Byrne

(1969) and his associates, demonstrating the positive relationship between the proportion of attitudes expressed by a stranger which are similar to those of a subject and the subject's attraction toward the stranger.

METHOD

Design

As in a previous study (Griffitt, 1970), subjects responded with respect to attraction to an anonymous same-sex stranger on the basis of inspection of the stranger's responses to a 24-item attitude scale. The stranger's attitudes were in agreement with those of the subjects on either .25 or .75 of the issues. The two levels of proportion of similarity were combined factorially with two levels of effective temperature (normal and hot) and two levels of population density (low and high).

Subjects

Subjects were 121 male and female students in introductory psychology at Kansas State University who had been pretested on the 24-item attitude questionnaire. Each was randomly assigned to one of the eight experimental conditions. Each subject reported to the Kansas State University Environmental Research Institute to take part in an experiment described as an investigation of "judgmental processes under altered environmental conditions." To reduce variability in response to the effective temperature conditions, each subject was dressed in cotton bermuda shorts and a cotton shirt or blouse. Males and females participated in separate groups.

Procedure

Upon reporting to the environmental laboratory, subjects entered and were seated in a Sherer-Gillet standard environmental chamber, which is 7 feet wide by 9 feet long with a ceiling height of 9 feet. For half of the subjects, the effective temperature of the room was maintained at an average of 73.4 degrees Fahrenheit (normal). The other half of the subjects participated with the effective temperature maintained at an average of 93.5 degrees Fahrenheit (hot). Effective temperature is an index which combines into a single value the effect of dry-bulb temperature and relative humidity on the sensation of warmth or cold felt by the human body.[3] Subjects in the hot

---

[3] The effective temperature of 93.5 degrees Fahrenheit represents a dry-bulb temperature of 109 degrees Fahrenheit and relative humidity of 46%. Effective temperatures in the hot condition ranged from a low of 91.4 degrees Fahrenheit (107 degrees Fahrenheit dry bulb–43% relative humidity) to 96.7 degrees Fahrenheit (114 degrees Fahrenheit dry bulb–46% relative humidity). The 73.4 degrees Fahrenheit effective temperature represents a dry bulb of 74 degrees Fahrenheit and relative humidity of 93%. The effective temperature range in the normal condi-

condition were exposed to an effective temperature which was well beyond that of 84.6 degrees Fahrenheit, which, according to previous work (Rohles, 1969), is the highest effective temperature rated as comfortable by test subjects. The effective temperature in the normal condition approximates the effective temperature most often rated comfortable by test subjects (Nevins, Rohles, Springer, & Feyerherm, 1966).

Across the two proportion conditions and two effective temperature conditions, two levels of population density were created by running subjects in either large or small groups. In the low-density condition, subjects were run in groups ranging in size from 3 to 5, while high-density subjects were run in groups ranging in size from 12 to 16. With the experimenter added in each case, the available space per person in the low-density group averaged 12.73 square feet, while in the high-density condition, the available space averaged 4.06 square feet per person. Subjects were seated in folding chairs arranged in rows such that face-to-face orientations were minimized, with only those subjects seated side by side able to achieve eye contact. In the low-density condition, excess chairs were removed from the chamber.

During the first 45 minutes of each experimental session, the subjects performed a series of paper-and-pencil tasks. Each subject responded to a 64-item Repression-Sensitization (R-S) scale (Byrne & Griffitt, 1969), a series of six semantic-differential rating scales designed to assess feelings on the dimensions comfortable–uncomfortable, bad–good, high–low, sad–happy, pleasant–unpleasant, and negative–positive. In addition, each subject responded on the dimension hot–cold to assess sensations of warmth. Following the ratings of feelings, subjects performed a symbol-cancellation task designed as a time filler, followed by responding to a short form of the Nowlis (1965) Mood Adjective Check List (MACL).

After completing the MACL, subjects were told that the next phase of the experiment involved making judgments about an anonymous stranger, based on inspection of the stranger's responses to the 24-item attitude questionnaire. Half of the subjects in each effective temperature condition examined the responses of a stranger who agreed with them on .25 of the issues, and the other half received a scale which agreed with them on .75 of the issues. The attitude scales were, of course, bogus ones prepared by the experimenter by the "unique stranger" method (Griffitt & Byrne, 1970) to agree with the subject on either .25 or .75 of the issues. After examining the attitude questionnaire, subjects were asked to rate the stranger on the Interpersonal Judgment Scale (IJS). The IJS is a six-item, 7-point rating scale dealing with the stranger's intelligence, knowledge of current events, morality, adjustment, subject's probable liking of the stranger, and his de-

---

tion was 71.5 degrees Fahrenheit (72 degrees Fahrenheit dry bulb–93% relative humidity) to 76.5 degrees Fahrenheit (77 degrees Fahrenheit dry bulb–95% relative humidity).

183

sirability as a work partner. Ratings on the latter two items are summed to yield the dependent measure of attraction ranging from 2 to 14, with a split-half reliability of .85 (Byrne & Nelson, 1965).

Following the attitude-attraction task, subjects again completed the ratings of feelings, the rating of warmth, and responded to other semantic-differential questionnaires regarding the experimental room, instructions, and experimenter. The purpose of the experiment was then explained, and subjects were allowed to leave.

RESULTS

Temperature

The effects of the effective temperature manipulation on affective experience were examined by scoring the semantic-differential dimensions of feelings from 1 (negative) to 7 (positive) and summing (possible range = 6–42) to yield an overall measure of positiveness of feelings for the first (F_1) and the second (F_2) assessments. In addition, ratings on the hot–cold dimension were scored from 1 (cold) to 7 (hot) to yield two measures of temperature sensation (T_1 and T_2). The

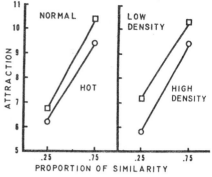

FIG. 1. Mean attraction responses as a function of effective temperature (normal = 73.4 degrees, hot = 93.5 degrees), proportion of similar attitudes (left panel), population density (low = 12.73 square feet per person, high = 4.06 square feet per person), and proportion of similar attitudes (right panel).

means of these scores, as well as the analysis of variance results across the two effective temperature conditions, are shown in Table 1. It is clear that the effective temperature manipulation was successful in achieving the desired effects. As in the previous investigation, the temperature sensation and feelings variables were substantially related, as indicated by the correlations between $F_1 - T_1$ ($r = -.55$, $p < .001$) and $F_2 - T_2$ ($r = -.63$, $p < .001$).

The influence of effective temperature on mean attraction responses to agreeing and disagreeing strangers is depicted in the left panel of Figure 1. Analysis of variance indicated that as predicted, attraction responses tended to be more negative under the hot than under the normal condition ($F = 3.17$, $df = 1/113$, $p < .07$). Mean values of the additional response variables which were significantly influenced by the effective temperature manipulation are shown in Table 1.

Population Density

Mean F_1, F_2, T_1, and T_2 values across the two density conditions are shown in Table 2. It is apparent that reports of affective experience are generally more negative in the high- than in the low-density condition. Additionally, even though the actual mean effective temperatures across density conditions were

TABLE 1

MEAN RATINGS OF FEELINGS (F_1 AND F_2), TEMPERATURE SENSATION (T_1 AND T_2), MOOD, AND OTHER STIMULI ACROSS EFFECTIVE TEMPERATURE CONDITIONS

Variable	Normal (73.4°)	Hot (93.5°)	$p <$
F_1	31.92	23.44	.001
F_2	29.46	19.42	.001
T_1	3.99	6.60	.001
T_2	4.25	6.78	.001
Mood			
Aggression	3.72	4.45	.05
Surgency	5.93	4.75	.01
Elation	5.69	4.16	.001
Concentration	9.12	6.66	.001
Fatigue	5.52	7.06	.01
Social affection	6.69	5.67	.01
Sadness	3.91	4.73	.05
Vigor	6.50	4.51	.001
Room			
Pleasant–unpleasant	4.06	2.84	.001
Comfortable–uncomfortable	3.97	1.90	.001
Experiment			
Pleasant–unpleasant	5.33	2.54	.001
Interesting–uninteresting	5.99	5.56	.07

Note.—Ratings of the room and experiment were made on bipolar semantic-differential scales from 7 (positive) to 1 (negative).

TABLE 2

MEAN RATINGS OF FEELINGS (F_1 AND F_2), TEM-
PERATURE SENSATION (T_1 AND T_2), MOOD,
AND OTHER STIMULI ACROSS
DENSITY CONDITIONS

| Variable | Density | | $p <$ |
	Low	High	
F_1	28.67	26.68	.10
F_2	26.25	22.62	.01
T_1	5.04	5.55	.001
T_2	5.20	5.82	.001
Mood			
Surgency	5.82	4.86	.05
Elation	5.20	4.64	.07
Concentration	8.25	7.53	.10
Fatigue	5.79	6.79	.05
Social affection	6.54	5.82	.07
Vigor	6.15	4.86	.01
Room			
Good–bad	5.01	4.15	.01
Attractive–unattractive	3.32	2.75	.05
Adequate–inadequate	5.78	4.47	.001
Pleasant–unpleasant	3.83	3.06	.01
Well arranged–poorly arranged	5.24	4.21	.001
Comfortable–uncomfortable	3.65	2.22	.001
Experiment			
Pleasant–unpleasant	4.37	3.50	.002
Worthy–unworthy	5.82	5.04	.003
Interesting–uninteresting	6.02	5.53	.04

Note.—Ratings of the room and experiment were made on bipolar semantic-differential scales from 7 (positive) to 1 (negative).

identical, subjects rated themselves as warmer in the high-density than in the low-density condition.

The right panel of Figure 1 illustrates the significantly negative ($F = 6.99$, $df = 1/113$, $p < .01$) influence of population density on attraction responses to agreeing and disagreeing strangers. Further evidence of the negative effect of population density on affective responses is shown in Table 2, which presents the mean values of those response variables significantly influenced by the density manipulation.

Attitude Similarity

Finally, as in numerous previous investigations (Byrne, 1969), attraction responses across all temperature and density conditions evoked by agreeing strangers were significantly more positive than those evoked by disagreers

($F = 62.14$, $df = 1/113$, $p < .001$). None of the interaction F ratios approached significance.

Interrelations among Response Variables

In previous writings (Clore & Byrne, in press; Griffitt, 1970; Griffitt & Guay, 1969), it has been suggested that personal-affective experiences mediate the expression of interpersonal or social-affective behaviors such as evaluations, approach-avoidance, aggression, and attraction. Additionally, it is felt that evaluations and approach-avoidance behaviors with respect to "nonsocial" objects are also mediated by personal-affective experiences. To the extent that these conceptualizations are accurate, it would be expected in the present investigation that evaluations of personal feelings (F_1 and F_2), interpersonal attraction, and evaluations of nonsocial objects such as the experimental room and experiment would be positively related. Table 3 shows the correlations among semantic-differential ratings of the experimental room and experiment, F_1 and F_2, and attraction responses. It is apparent that ratings of personal affective experience (F_1 and F_2), social-affective responses (attraction), and nonsocial affective ratings (room and experiment) are positively related.

DISCUSSION

Under conditions of high temperature and high population density, personal-affective, social-affective, and non-social-affective responses were found to be significantly more

TABLE 3

INTERCORRELATIONS AMONG RESPONSE VARIABLES

Variable	F_1	F_2	Attraction
Room			
Good–bad	.24**	.17*	.19*
Pleasant–unpleasant	.52***	.51***	.19*
Comfortable–uncomfortable	.58***	.63***	.22*
Experiment			
Pleasant–unpleasant	.70***	.70***	.21*
Attraction	.19*	.26**	

* $p < .05$.
** $p < .01$.
*** $p < .001$.

negative than under conditions of comfortable temperature and low population density. The significant temperature effect provides a replication of a previous finding (Griffitt, 1970), while the "crowding" effect has not previously been demonstrated in humans.

With the absence of systematic data concerning human behavior, investigators have been forced to speculate concerning the influences of high population density or "overcrowding" on social behaviors (United States Riot Commission, 1968). The findings of the present experimental investigation, however, support the hypothesis that extremely crowded conditions do, in fact, influence social behaviors in a negative fashion. The parameters of overcrowding in humans are, if at all, only vaguely defined. The question of at what points on the density dimension do humans experience feelings of crowding which are initially unpleasant, then intolerable, is not answered by the present factorial investigation. Few would disagree, however, that human density conditions as they exist in the major American ghettos are subjectively evaluated as overcrowded and unpleasant. Hall (1966) has pointed out the difficulties in attempting to establish maximum, minimum, and optimum densities of human populations. It is clear, however, as pointed out by Carter (1969) that "the concentration of people in the larger urban areas, especially those of the Northeast, California, and the Great Lakes states, is making many Americans uneasy about the chamber of commerce belief that bigger means better [p. 722]."

The many factors potentially capable of altering the density-affect relationship have yet to be investigated. Using the present investigation as a model, for example, it might be expected that several factors would be effective in either intensifying or mitigating the relationship. The subjects of the present experiment were all run in same-sex groups, and it might be expected that heterosexual groups would have experienced the crowded situation as being somewhat more positive than did the present groups. It might be speculated that variations in the seating configuration such that face-to-face orientations

are necessary would make the situation even more unpleasant. As a final example, the friendship relationships within a high-density group would be expected to influence the perceived pleasantness of the experience with "friendly" groups responding more positively than "unfriendly" groups.

REFERENCES

Byrne, D. Attitudes and attraction. In L. Berkowitz (Ed.), *Advances in experimental social psychology*. Vol. 4. New York: Academic Press, 1969.

Byrne, D., & Griffitt, W. Similarity and awareness of similarity of personality characteristics as determinants of attraction. *Journal of Experimental Research in Personality*, 1969, 3, 179–186.

Byrne, D., & Nelson, D. Attraction as a linear function of proportion of positive reinforcements. *Journal of Personality and Social Psychology*, 1965, 1, 659–663.

Calhoun, J. B. Population density and social pathology. *Scientific American*, 1962, 206, 139–148.

Carter, L. J. The population crisis: Rising concern at home. *Science*, 1969, 166, 722–726.

Christian, J. J. The pathology of overpopulation. *Military Medicine*, 1963, 128, 571–603.

Clore, G. L., & Byrne, D. The process of personality interaction. In R. B. Cattel (Ed.), *Handbook of modern personality theory*. Chicago: Aldine, in press.

Glass, D. C., Singer, J. E., & Friedman, L. N. Psychic cost of adaptation to an environmental stressor. *Journal of Personality and Social Psychology*, 1969, 12, 200–210.

Greenberg, G. The effects of ambient temperature and population density on aggression in two strains of mice. Unpublished doctoral dissertation, Kansas State University, 1969.

Griffitt, W. Environmental effects on interpersonal affective behavior: Ambient effective temperature and attraction. *Journal of Personality and Social Psychology*, 1970, 15, 240–244.

Griffitt, W., & Byrne, D. Procedures in the paradigmatic study of attitude similarity and attraction. *Representative Research in Social Psychology*, 1970, 1, 33–48.

Griffitt, W., & Guay, P. "Object" evaluation and conditioned affect. *Journal of Experimental Research in Personality*, 1969, 4, 1–8.

Guhl, A. M. The social environment and behavior. In E. S. E. Hafez (Ed.), *The behavior of domestic animals*. Baltimore: Williams & Wilkins, 1962.

Hall, E. T. *The hidden dimension*. New York: Doubleday, 1966.

Little, K. B. Personal space. *Journal of Experimental Social Psychology*, 1965, 1, 237–247.

Nevins, R. G., Roiiles, F. H., Springer, W. E., & Feyerherm, A. M. Temperature-humidity chart for thermal comfort of seated persons. Paper presented at the American Society of Heating, Refrigerating, and Air-Conditioning Engineers semiannual meetings, Houston, January 1966.

Nowlis, V. Research with the Mood Adjective Check List. In S. Tomkins & C. Izard (Eds.), *Affect, cognition, and personality*. New York: Springer, 1965.

Rohles, F. H. Environmental psychology: A bucket of worms. *Psychology Today*, 1967, 1, 55–63.

Rohles, F. H. Psychological aspects of thermal comfort. Paper presented at the American Society of Heating, Refrigerating, and Air-Conditioning Engineers semiannual meetings, Denver, July 1969.

Sommer, R. Small group ecology. *Psychological Bulletin*, 1967, 67, 145–152.

Terris, W., & Rahhal, D. K. Generalized resistance to the effects of psychological stressors. *Journal of Personality and Social Psychology*, 1969, 13, 93–97.

Thiessen, D. D. Role of physical injury in the physiological effects of population density in mice. *Journal of Comparative and Physiological Psychology*, 1966, 62, 322–324.

United States Riot Commission. *Report of the National Advisory Commission on civil disorders*. New York: Bantam Books, 1968.

Wilkinson, R. Some factors influencing the effect of environmental stressors upon performance. *Psychological Bulletin*, 1969, 72, 26–272.

The Effect of Crowding on Human Task Performance[1]

Jonathan L. Freedman,   Simon Klevansky,
and Paul R. Ehrlich

In a series of three experiments, groups of people performed tasks under varying conditions of density. The tasks ranged from very simple to complex, from rote memory to a test of creativity. Subjects worked on the tasks for 4 hours at a time for two or three successive days. There were no significant effects of density on performance, nor any consistent trends.

The number of human beings on earth is huge and is increasing at an accelerating rate. There are currently about 3.5 billion humans; and at the current rate of growth, there will be twice that many in 35 years. No one will deny that this great population of humans presents many difficulties. It is now and will become increasingly difficult to feed them all adequately. Even if enough food were available, which is questionable, the logistics of supply are staggering. These billions of humans consume enormous quantities of resources, many of which cannot be replaced and which will, accordingly, become more and more scarce in the future. More immediately, this consumption produces waste that threatens to pollute our environment. Finally, because there is a shortage of some resources, particularly land (or at least good land), there is inevitably competition that produces tension and conflict (as was seen most clearly recently in the "war" between Honduras and El Salvador, which may well be the first conflict fought almost entirely because of overpopulation). It is impossible to deny that our huge population is a matter of grave concern that threatens the peace, stability, and happiness of the whole world.

However, it is exceedingly important to separate the kinds of problems we have just mentioned from the effect of population density per se. Many of those

[1] This research was supported in part by a grant from the Ford Foundation. We are grateful to David Campisi and Michael Katz for assisting in the running of parts of these studies and to Elizabeth Yates for doing much of the painstaking tabulation and analysis of the data.

JOURNAL OF APPLIED SOCIAL PSYCHOLOGY, 1971, Vol. 1, pp. 7-25.

who are worried about overpopulation and recognize the problems it is causing have tended to attribute negative effects to the mere presence of many people. They have, for example, assumed that high population density itself causes aggressiveness, conflict, breakdown in morality, mental illness, and so on. Some writers have attributed virtually all the ills of the world and, in particular, the ills of our urban centers to population density. Although there is no question that the presence of many people in a small area causes problems in terms of logistics, noise, food supply, and so on, it is entirely an open question whether high concentrations of humans are inherently harmful. The fact is that we do not know what effect population density per se has on human beings. Since we are going to have high concentrations of people for the foreseeable future, and since social planning could conceivably either encourage or discourage such concentrations, it is extremely important that we begin to find out.

The amount of research on this vital problem is, to put it generously, less than might be expected. There is some research on nonhumans. In a continuing series of studies, Calhoun and his associates (Calhoun, 1962; Marsden, 1970) have placed a small number of rats or mice in an enclosed area, provided them with sufficient food and water, and allowed them to reproduce with a minimum of restrictions. Under these benign conditions, the population of the colonies increased rapidly and eventually reached a point of density much greater than would occur in a natural environment. Dramatic negative effects were associated with these high densities. Social behavior broke down. Some males became uncontrollably aggressive while others became totally passive; individual nests were invaded by marauding males; and females did not build adequate nests. Perhaps because of this breakdown, infant mortality rose sharply, as did the rate of unsuccessful pregnancies. These severe effects did not apply to all animals in the colonies. Some males managed to occupy and defend their own areas and thus prevented extreme density in those areas. Within these areas more or less normal behavior occurred. But for the great majority of the animals, the high density had extremely negative effects that threatened their survival and eventually the survival of the colony as a whole.

Similar although less dramatic effects of high population density have been observed by Christian, Flyger, and Davis (1960) in a natural environment among deer that were confined to a small island. In this natural environment, high density also led to a marked decrease in reproductivity. Equivalent results have been reported by a number of other authors on a variety of species. This research is impressive and provocative, but its relevance for humans is questionable. It is always difficult to generalize from studies of nonhumans to humans, and it is particularly so in this context. As Rene Dubos has pointed out, "The readiness with which man adapts to potentially dangerous situations makes it unwise to apply directly to human life the results of experiments designed to test the acute effects of crowding on animals" (1970, p. 207). We can use this animal work as a starting point and source of ideas, but must turn to work on humans to answer our original question.

Unfortunately, there is very little such work. There have been several attempts to assess the effects of population density in a broad natural setting. The basic approach was to obtain a measure of population density in various areas of a city and correlate it with indicators of social or individual breakdown. Schmitt (1957) computed five different measures of population density for the 29 census tracts in Honolulu and correlated these five measures with the rates of juvenile delinquency and adult crime for these tracts. The five measures used were: population per acre; number of dwelling units with 1.51 or more persons per room; average household size; married couples without their own household and therefore doubled up or living in a rooming house; and dwelling units in structures with five or more units. Although these measures are obviously quite diverse, they all correlated quite strongly with juvenile delinquency or adult crime rate.

A second study by Schmitt (1966) was more extensive. The same five measures of population density were correlated with the following nine indicators: death rate, infant mortality, suicide rate, tuberculosis rate, venereal disease, admissions to mental hospitals, illegitimate births, juvenile delinquency, and adult crime rate. Except for household size, all measures of density had positive correlations with all measures of social, physical, and mental breakdown. Partial correlations holding the various density measures constant indicated that population per acre correlates much more strongly with the nine breakdown measures than do any of the other indicators of density.

A study by Winsborough (1965) produced similar results. He correlated population density per acre in the city of Chicago with measures of infant mortality, death rate, tuberculosis rate, public assistance rate, and public assistance to persons under 18. He found high correlations with all five measures. Thus, all three studies demonstrated that in urban settings, density is highly associated with a variety of measures of morbidity and social and individual breakdowns.

However, density is also correlated with many other social factors, the most obvious of which are income and educational level. Socioeconomic class is highly associated with rates of mental illness (at least reported to public hospitals), death rate, infant mortality, and crime and juvenile delinquency; therefore, in order to make any statement about the relationship of density per se to these measures, it is crucial to control for these other variables. Unless that is done, the high correlation between density and, for example, death rate, tells us nothing about the effect of density since the effect could easily be due to these other factors. Both Schmitt and Winsborough attempted to control the effects of these other factors by performing partial correlations. Schmitt (1966) partialled out measures of education and income and still found a strong correlation between population per acre and all of his measures except suicide rate and infant mortality. Unfortunately, the measures of education and income he used were somewhat questionable. Education was measured as the percentage of persons 25 years or older with 12 or more years of schooling. This obviously divides the population into those well educated and those not well educated, but provides no indication of how many had very little schooling. Since the major effects of education on crime, for example, probably occur at the relatively low end of the continuum, this is a rather poor measure for these purposes. Similarly, the measure of income is the percentage earning $3,000 or more per family. Since Honolulu is one of the wealthiest cities in the country, this line of demarcation probably splits the areas into lower class and the rest, rather than providing distinctions between groups. It seems likely that both measures, while providing some indication of education and income, are inadequate as a means of controlling for these two variables; and the partial correlations between population density and crime rate, etc. should not be interpreted as being totally independent of income and education. That is, these correlations do not demonstrate unequivocal relationships with density per se.

Winsborough (1965) also used partial correlations to control for various factors that were themselves correlated with density and had much more sensitive measures for his control factors. He partialled out many different factors including percent of workers in professional, technical, and kindred professions; median income of families; median years of school completed; percent of the population foreign born; median age; median rent; percent of dwellings with no water, with no bath, or dilapidated. With these partialled out, the correlations with density changed dramatically. He still found a positive correlation with infant mortality (.33), but total death rate, tuberculosis rate, and public assistance rate all became negatively correlated with density (-.62, -.67, and -.39, respectively). In other words, with economic, education, and migration levels partialled out, density actually is associated with less morbidity, disease, and need for public assistance. This result is unfortunately just as questionable as Schmitt's. Whereas Schmitt did not control well enough, it seems likely that Winsborough controlled too well. Partial correlations with more than one factor removed are often difficult to interpret. Since each of the factors correlates with density and with each other, there is the possibility that the effect of, say, economic level is, in a sense, being removed more than once. This seems likely in this instance since the negative correlations between density and death rate and tuberculosis rate are implausible. The results suggest that holding economic level constant, there is less tuberculosis under crowded than under noncrowded conditions. While this is not impossible, given the fact that tuberculosis is highly contagious, it seems unlikely. In any case, neither Schmitt nor Winsborough controlled effectively for contaminating variables in their assessment of the effects of population density. Therefore, at the present time, there is no definitive or even straightforward study. along these lines. This approach is very promising and should be pursued with even larger areas considered and with more sophisticated statistical techniques.

In addition to this survey work, there are a few (very few) studies under relatively controlled conditions. Ittelson, Proshansky, and Rivlin (1970) observed patterns of behavior in psychiatric wards and attempted to assess the effect of size of bedrooms on behavior. They report that a higher percentage of passive (i.e., nonsocial) behavior occurred in larger than in smaller rooms. This type of observational work in a natural setting has the advantage of dealing with "real" people in real situations. Unfortunately, it has the great disadvantage of lack of control of the crucial variables, and even more important, lack of random assignment of subjects to the various conditions. In this case, patients are assigned to bedrooms at least in part on the basis of their illness and their ability to pay. Those in the smaller rooms are accordingly different from those in the larger rooms on a number of unknown dimensions. In addition, the variable of density is not pure. Larger rooms generally also have more patients. Thus, although these observations are interesting and provocative, they are difficult to interpret because of the many uncontrolled factors. Perhaps more important for our purposes, it seems likely that the effects (if they are real and not due to subject differences) are due to the number of patients in the room rather than to the population density.

Similar difficulties beset a study by Hutt and Vaizey (1966). They observed children at free play in either small or large groups, and found that normal children were more aggressive and less social in larger groups. They interpret this result in terms of density, but once again a simpler explanation is in terms of the number of individuals present. Since the room in which the children played did not vary, and since the number of play objects presumably also did not vary, it hardly seems surprising that there was more competition and aggression when there were more children. In addition, the number of children studied was very small, the statistical analyses are questionable, and in general the experimental design is weak. Nevertheless, as with the other research, this study is on the right track; the results do suggest that density may lead to increased aggressiveness.

In addition to this work, there is a considerable body of research on humans' use of space and their reactions to it. Hall (1966, etc.) and Sommer (1969, etc.) have been concerned with how people use a given amount of space, how close they stand to each other, whether or not they will move away from each other, and what effects space has on social interaction. This work has not involved conditions that would ordinarily be considered "crowded," but it is certainly relevant to our concerns. Its major implication for the study of crowding seems to be that people are aware of and respond to the amount of space that is available and that, accordingly, there is reason to believe that removing space by increasing density will have appreciable effects on human behavior.

192

With the animal work, the few human studies, and the work of Hall and Sommer as background, we set out to investigate the effect of population density on human behavior. Although we had no firm theory, we did have some hypotheses that we used as starting points. The first notion, and perhaps the simplest, is that population density is a variable much like any other strong stimulus: that at sufficient intensity it produces stress and that the effects of density on humans can be conceptualized and explained as reactions to stress. Or, to put it another way, high density is an aversive stimulus, raises drive level, and produces the same effects that any other aversive stimulus would.

This formulation is consistent with most of the previous findings, although it is by no means the only one that would be. Animals that are crowded go beserk because crowding is exceedingly unpleasant and stressful. The particular types of breakdown may be due to the particular type of stress, but actually so many different types of breakdown occur that this is hard to argue. It could even be argued that similar breakdown could be caused by any other strong pressure such as continual noise, heat, lack of food, etc. Thus, the simplest possible approach is to think of crowding as a stressful situation.

This line of reasoning draws some support from the extensive literature on so-called social facilitation or coaction. There have been many experiments assessing the effect on performance of the presence of other individuals. Much early research (e.g., Allport, 1924) suggested that a subject working alone in a room performed considerably less well than he did if someone else was in the room, even if the other person were working on an entirely different task and were in no way related to the first subject. Further research, however, indicated that the effect of the presence of others was not always beneficial. On some tasks it facilitated performance; on some it interfered. In a thorough review of this literature, Zajonc (1965) argued convincingly that the other people arouse motivation and thereby raise drive. Regardless of the particular motive that is aroused, the evidence indicates that other people do raise drive level and that the effects of their presence can be explained in those terms. As with any other drive, performance on simple, well-learned tasks is facilitated by the presence of others; while performance on complex or not-well-learned tasks is interfered with. It should be noted that these effects are quite strong—the presence of others has a substantial (not just significant) effect on task performance.

If the presence of others has these effects as a result of an increase in drive level, it seems plausible that similar effects could be caused by the presence of "too many" others in too small a space—that high density would magnify this effect of others and serve to increase drive still further. Or, to state it differently, if others serve as a stimulus to increase drive, a formulation in terms of drive for the variable of population density makes sense. Once again, it is not by any means required by this previous research. Rather, in seeking for research on which to base this work, the social facilitation literature is obviously relevant and suggests that density may function as an aversive stimulus to arouse drive.

If high density does function as an aversive stimulus, it should produce certain familiar effects. Performance on a variety of tasks is affected by aversive stimulation and by high drive. In particular, there should be a decrement in performance on all complex tasks and on tasks that are not well learned. Any task that involves competing responses, creative thinking, flexible manipulation of material, or the learning of new material should be interfered with. The situation with very simple tasks is less clear since it depends on the base level of drive. If the initial level is low, increasing drive should facilitate performance; if the base level is already high, increasing it further should produce a decrement even on simple tasks as long as there are any competing responses.

The duration of the stimulation is also an important variable. It has been demonstrated that humans are able to adapt to extremely aversive stimulation. For example, Broadbent (1957) and Glass, Singer, and Friedman (1969) have shown that humans can adapt to high levels of noise, although the latter study suggests that this adaptation involves some psychological costs that may show up later. This work does indicate that initially, at least, noise produces decrements that disappear only after the subject has time to adapt to the aversive stimulation. On the other hand, it is also possible that less intense stimulation may produce an effect only after it has had time to build up. That is, a short exposure to a mildly aversive stimulus (and even high density may be relatively mild compared to 100 dB white noise or electric shock) may not produce an effect, but continued exposure may become increasingly aversive and eventually produce an effect on performance. Since both formulations are plausible, it is important to have comparisons of the effect after a short time and after a longer time, and to look at the relationship. Therefore, our investigation of the effects of crowding on human task performance attempted to answer two questions:

1. What effect does density have on performance on simple and complex tasks?
2. What role do temporal factors play?

We should make it clear that this research was designed to investigate the effects of high density per se, and not the effect of other factors that tend to go along with high density. We did not want to study the effects of lack of air, physical discomfort, restriction on movement, high temperature, odors, or any of the other typical consequences of high density among humans. Rather, we were interested in the individual's reactions to the high density itself, to their feelings of being crowded when these other variables were eliminated or controlled. The reason for this was that these other variables are largely nonpsychological, their effects are to some extent trivial and, perhaps most important, they can conceivably be eliminated in the real world. It is possible to

194

have a very large number of people in a room and yet not have physical discomfort, lack of air, too much noise, or any other such factor. If the population of the world continues to increase, the cities of the future could still conceivably control these consequences of overcrowding. It is important to know how crowding itself affects human behavior, because nothing short of a decrease in population will eliminate the high density of human beings. Thus, all this research was designed to eliminate or control the physical effects of high density, including noise, temperature, odors, physical discomfort, and so on. As much as possible, we were trying to assess the effects of level of density itself.

METHOD

We chose the straightforward method of putting subjects in rooms that varied considerably in size and presenting them with tasks to perform. In the first study, density was varied by using rooms of 160, 80, and 35 square feet, and placing either nine or five subjects in each room. It is, of course, not possible to specify *a priori* what level of density should be considered crowded for any given subject or group of subjects, but our assumptions seem *prima facie* to be reasonable.

Subjects were all seated on reasonably comfortable wooden chairs with a desk-type arm that they could write on. In the smallest room the chairs were arranged in the only way that was possible, back against all of the walls in roughly an oval shape. With nine chairs in the room and a water cooler provided for comfort, there was no room for an additional chair. The chairs themselves were hardly spacious; therefore, it is safe to say that the level of density in the room was as great as it could possibly have been and still allowed the subjects to sit without touching each other but with a place to write. Let us remember that one decision we made was to eliminate all obvious physical discomfort or lack of freedom of movement so that the use of smaller chairs or benches was really not possible. The subjects did not quite touch each other, but it would have been difficult to imagine anyone else in the room with them.

The largest room was obviously not particularly crowded; there was considerable space between each of the subjects; there was room for them to move around; and two or three times as many subjects could fit in the room without interfering with each other's movements. It seems reasonable to call this an uncrowded situation.

Whether the moderate-sized room with nine people was crowded cannot be determined, but those of us who were involved in the research considered it unpleasantly crowded ourselves. The specific choice of rooms and the number of subjects and the particular chairs used were, of course, arbitrary, but it seems unlikely that different results would have been obtained using other rooms or chairs or numbers of subjects as long as the basic conditions of high and low density and lack of physical discomfort were met.

The basic notion was that nine subjects would be extremely crowded in the smallest room, still somewhat crowded in the moderate-sized room, but not crowded in the large room; whereas five subjects would be crowded in the smallest room, but not crowded in either of the other rooms. If we found that groups of nine in the small and moderate rooms differed from the way they behaved in the large room and groups of five differed in the smallest room from the way they behaved in the other two rooms, we could conclude with some confidence that the effect was due to crowding. It would not be due to the number of subjects since that was controlled for, nor would it be due to the specific rooms used, since the moderate-sized room would produce the effect in one case and not in the other. Although this design does provide a very strong test of the interpretation in terms of crowding, in subsequent studies only the smallest and the largest rooms were used because, as will be seen, we were then simply trying to get some kind of effect and were less worried about eliminating alternative explanations.

As much as possible, we wanted to place the groups in the rooms and maintain the level of density in the room. Thus, we tried to minimize leaving or entering the room, the opening of doors, and anything else that would detract from or interfere with the level of density in that room. The rooms' were equipped with air conditioning that was generally adequate to keep the temperatures constant, they had good rugs and quite good sound insulation so that the rooms were fairly quiet, they had a water cooler so that subjects could get drinks if they wanted to, and the rooms were equipped with microphones and speakers so that communication to and from the rooms from outside was possible without entering the rooms. All instructions were taped and were delivered to the rooms simultaneously, and thus all subjects in all conditions received identical instructions that were received at exactly the same time. In the first study, experimenters did enter the room at the end of each task to collect the answer sheets; this produced a considerable amount of intrusion. In all later studies, experimenters entered the rooms at most once or twice in the course of the 4-hour study. Although the subjects were, of course, allowed to use the bathroom facilities if they had to, this was not mentioned; generally, subjects stayed in the room for the full time.

In all studies to be described here, each subject was in all conditions of density. This was accomplished by placing the subjects in one room on one day and different rooms on succeeding days. The order in which this was done was counterbalanced to control for order effects, and all subjects were randomly assigned to conditions. This design allows both within- and between-subject comparisons. It is possible to compare a given subject's performance under the different levels of density, and it is also possible to compare the different groups of subjects on the first day.

EXPERIMENT I

The subjects were 84 boys and 42 girls from high schools in the vicinity of Palo Alto, California. They were recruited through an ad in the local newspaper that offered them $1.75 an hour to take part in a psychology study that would last 10 hours. A total of 18 groups was run. Twelve had all males, 6 all females; half had five and half had nine subjects. Except for an attempt to separate friends, subjects were randomly assigned to conditions before they arrived.

There were four sessions. First there was a short briefing session on Monday at which Ss were told that they had to attend three more sessions and that they would be performing a variety of tasks as part of a continuing study of group performance; then three experimental sessions were held on the following days. Each group came separately for the briefing sessions and met in a large waiting room. At the first experimental session, three groups of the same size and sex arrived and were placed in one of the three experimental rooms to which they had previously been randomly assigned. On succeeding days, each group was assigned to one of the other rooms so that over the 3 days all groups were in each of the rooms.

An experimental session consisted of a number of separate tasks.

1. A group discussion of a current problem (e.g., What can be done to reduce highway accidents?). The group discussed this for 20 minutes and then wrote their proposed solutions, indicating those three ideas they considered best.
2. A crossing-out task. Each S was given a sheet containing random numbers and was told to cross out all of a particular number that he could find. They did this for 10 minutes.
3. Forming words task. The group was read six letters and told to form as many different English words as they could from these letters. Each S worked separately on this task. They were given two different sets of letters and worked on each for 8 minutes.
4. Object uses. A common object is described (e.g., a 10-gallon metal barrel) and each S suggests as many different unique uses for it as he can. This has been considered a measure of divergent or creative thinking (10 minutes).
5. Memory task. Twelve common words are read aloud at the rate of 1 per second and S has to write down as many as he can remember after the reading is completed. Eight such lists were read, with a 30-second pause between lists.
6. A concentration task. Clicks are sounded at the rate of about 3 per second, but not at a fixed rhythm. The number ranged from 15 to 57 and

S had merely to count them. This turns out to be quite a difficult task, requiring strict concentration.

7. The object-uses task again, this time with the whole group working on it together.

This series of tasks was followed by a 10-minute break, and then the complete series was repeated with, of course, different materials. Finally, at the end of the last session, a questionnaire covering biographical information and S's reactions to the study was given.

Results and Discussion

The design of the study allows both within and between comparisons, and both were done. In addition, we considered the first day by itself in case subsequent days were for some reason invalidated by the previous experience, and sequence effects across days in case the effect of density appeared only as a result of a shift from one size room to another. Finally, within each day, we assessed the effect of time by comparing performance on the first and second presentations of a task. All analyses were done by group, but the results do not change even if we use the more generous degrees of freedom allowed by considering the subjects individually.

TABLE 1

DENSITY AND TASK PERFORMANCE IN EXPERIMENT I

Task	Best performance for each group[a]		
	Small room	Medium room	Large room
Crossing-out	6	7	5
Forming words	8	4	6
Object uses	5	6	8
Memory	4	9	5
Concentration	6	6	6
Object uses (group)	7	7	4

[a]Entries represent the number of groups for which the best performance occurred in that size room.

Table 1 presents the results as a function of density. The data are summarized in terms of the number of times each level of density produced the best performance on a task. This is done for convenience because of the large amount of data, but group means show the same lack of trends. In addition, if any pair of two rooms is considered alone, the same pattern emerges.

The results can be summarized by saying that there were no effects of any kind attributable to the level of density in the rooms. The rooms did not differ appreciably on any task or group of tasks. This was true of small groups and large groups, of male and female groups. There were no effects at the beginning of the session, none at the end, and none in terms of changes from beginning to end. Regardless of the task, when it was performed, whether it was first or second time, whether it was group or individual, whether it was first, second or third day, there were no effects of density.

Nor were there any noticeable trends. If we look simply at the direction of difference, there is no consistency. The small rooms do better almost exactly as often as they do worse; they do better on simple tasks as often as they do worse; on complex tasks as often as they do worse.

We also considered the possibility that some Ss react favorably to crowding and others unfavorably. If this were true, one might expect greater variance within crowded rooms than in uncrowded rooms. There were, however, no differences in variance as a function of room size.

We should perhaps add that other types of differences did emerge. The "typical" sex differences appeared, with girls performing better on concentration and memory tasks and less well on the more "creative" tasks. There was also a consistent tendency for all groups to perform better the second time they took a test than the first, and to continue to improve somewhat over subsequent presentations on following days. This was true for all tasks, but was most marked on the forming words and concentration tasks.

In other words, although some expected and familiar effects appeared, no appreciable differences could be attributed to density. Subjects did as well when they were crowded as when they were not: high density neither facilitated nor interfered with their performance on either simple or complex tasks, and there was no indication that density produced greater effects over time.

EXPERIMENT II

The lack of effect of density in Experiment I was somewhat surprising. If density is an aversive stimulus that arouses drive, clearly there should have been some effect on performance. Even if humans are able to adapt quickly, the effect should appear at some point—either at the very beginning of the study or later, or perhaps in terms of change from beginning to later in the same session. But none of these effects appeared. Since a lack of effect is always questionable, we decided to try again with slightly different procedures.

The major change in the second experiment concerned the number of tasks that were performed. One plausible explanation of the lack of results in experiment I was that with so many tasks the Ss were not given time to get bored or oppressed by any one task, that they were continually interested, and that their high motivation and high level of interest obscured any negative effects that might otherwise have appeared. Accordingly, we attempted to remove this criticism by using fewer tasks and by manipulating motivation level directly. In experiment II, Ss performed only three tasks—crossing out numbers, forming words, and anagrams. The first was very tedious and boring and required little creativity; the others were more interesting, more complex, and somewhat creative. They worked on each for long enough to produce boredom, to reduce motivation, and to maximize any effects of stress.

Method

The Ss were 306 high school students, divided into 34 groups of 7 to 9 each. Eighteen of the groups were all male, 16 all female. Each group took part in two sessions. At the first session they were in either the large or small room (the moderate-sized room was not used) and were in the other room for the second session.

The procedure was similar to the first experiment except that only three tasks were used and they were each given only once. Ss were given 12 sheets of random numbers. The experimenter told them which number to cross out on the first sheet; they worked for 10 minutes, then turned to the next sheet and were told which number to cross out there. The numbers to be crossed out were chosen randomly, except that the first four were the same as the last four. This was done because we had found some systematic differences between numbers on this task and we wanted exact comparisons of the first and last third. This arrangement allowed us to measure exactly how each Ss performed during each 10-minute period and to compare his early and late performance.

Then the group worked together on a forming-words task for 10 minutes—5 minutes for each of two words. After working on this task, subjects were given the anagram task, which consisted of sets of five letters that could be rearranged to spell an English word (e.g., awret=water). Each S was given two sheets containing 20 such words each and was given 50 minutes to work on them, stopping after the first 25 minutes to turn to the second page. The anagrams were difficult enough so that no one completed all on either page.

Manipulation of Motivation

Although the study was designed to minimize motivation, we also included a manipulation that would experimentally vary how motivated the subjects were. Half the subjects were told that if they did well on the tasks and got a lot done, they would be given a large bonus. Half of the subjects were told nothing about the bonus. Since all subjects would receive their basic pay regardless of how much work they did, and since the tasks, particularly the crossing-out task, were tedious and obviously not very meaningful, we assumed that motivation would be quite low for the nonbonus subjects. Just how much higher motivation would

200

be when students were working for bonuses was not clear, but we did assume that it would be somewhat higher since all of these students were working primarily to earn money and an additional $7.50 (i.e., an additional 40%) was a substantial sum of money.

TABLE 2

DENSITY AND TASK PERFORMANCE FOR EXPERIMENT II

Task	Superior performance for each group[a]	
	Small room	Large room
Crossing-out	16	18
Forming words	18	16
Anagrams	14	20

[a]Entries represent the number of groups for which the better performance occurred in that size room.

Results

As in the first study, typical effects did appear. There were the usual sex differences and temporal effects. In addition, the high motivation condition did more work on the crossing-out task and was slightly inferior on the more creative forming-words and anagram tasks.

Table 2 summarizes the overall results of density. Clearly there are no significant effects or trends in these data. A more detailed analysis in terms of individual days and sections of each task revealed one slight trend. On the first day, groups in the smaller room did somewhat worse on the first half of the anagram task than did groups in the larger room. This difference is not significant, is considerably smaller on the second half of the task, and disappears entirely by the second day. Obviously, one slight trend chosen from a large number of possible effects cannot be given much weight, but it was the first hint of an effect and therefore perhaps worth mentioning. Other than this, the internal analyses revealed no trends. Once more, density did not affect performance.

EXPERIMENT III

One more experiment was conducted to make certain that the lack of effect was not due to something as trivial as the particular population of subjects we had chosen. It could be argued, and in fact many of us did argue, that high school students are a very special type of subject for this particular kind of experiment. High school students are, after all, young, generally adaptable, and probably better than average at enduring stress, at least for a limited period of time. More important, they are quite accustomed to working on tasks in a crowded situation. Many high school rooms are crowded (although obviously not as crowded as our rooms) and students often take tests, have to learn material, study, and even have to think creatively under conditions of very high density. They are probably more accustomed to performing the kind of task we asked of them under crowded conditions than are most people. They may previously have adapted to and learned to ignore the crowding while doing this kind of task.

In addition, most of these subjects took part in the study partly because they wanted the money and partly because they were bored during the summer and had nothing else to do. They were probably more highly motivated than most subjects who take part in psychology studies. Most of them were planning to go to college, the whole idea of psychology was interesting to them, and taking part in the study provided relief and a change from a summer that, in general, was not full of many activities. This may be overstating it somewhat, but it did seem as if most of them were highly motivated and more interested in the study than might be expected, given the boring nature of some of the tasks.

In any case, whoever the population had been, it would be desirable to check the result using a different population. This seemed particularly true given that we had performed the first studies using high school students. Therefore, the study was repeated with a sample of 180 women between the ages of 25 and 60 who were recruited through a temporary employment agency. These women had no special skills and very few of them had any college education. In addition, they had relatively little motivation because they were assured of payment regardless of how hard they worked, they knew that we were not sending reports to the agency, and in general, it would seem that their motivation would be low. Also, they had little experience, at least in recent years, in taking tests of the kind we gave them, especially under crowded conditions. Thus, although they came from the same community as the high school students, they were in many ways about as different from them as they could have been.

Method

The procedure was identical to experiment II. The Ss were run in groups of nine. Two groups were run simultaneously—one in the large and one in the small room. Each group participated for 2 days and was in different rooms on the successive days, and each session took about 4 hours.

As shown in Table 3, once again there were no effects of any kind of density on performance. There were no main effects nor were there any interactions between density and any temporal measures that we looked at. The large room did as well as the small room at all points, both in amount of work and number

TABLE 3

DENSITY AND TASK PERFORMANCE FOR EXPERIMENT III

| Task | Superior performance for each group[a] | |
	Small room	Large room
Crossing-out	12	8
Forming words	9	11
Anagrams	11	9

[a]Entries represent the number of groups for which the better performance occurred in that size room.

of errors. This finding seems reliable, at least for the conditions we have employed.

Discussion

What can we say about these results? The first question is whether we should believe them. It is always difficult to be convinced by negative results. Perhaps the experimenters were sloppy, perhaps the tasks were poorly chosen, or the measures insensitive, or there was too much noise from other unspecified variables, or the subject population was one that would be unlikely to show the effect, or the manipulation was too weak. Perhaps. But there is no obvious error in design or procedure, we used a wide variety of tasks, our measures were certainly sensitive enough to pick up effects of reasonable strength, and we used two very different subject populations. As far as other variables obscuring the effect, all that can be done is to specify them and demonstrate that the effect does or does not then appear. We cannot think of any that seem convincing.

The issue of the strength of the manipulation or nature of the manipulation is more substantive. As we stated at the beginning of the paper, our procedure was limited. The length of time during which Ss were crowded was only 4 hours, and Ss knew that it was limited. Perhaps effects appear only with much greater duration or only if S is not aware that eventually he will be less crowded.

The level of density seems to us to be ample. It is literally true that no more Ss could have been in the small room and still had a seat to themselves. Although density was not as great as occurs in some natural settings such as the New York subway at rush hour, it was greater than ordinarily occurs for this length of time. People may occasionally be packed like sardines in a subway car, in a crowded store or on a line rushing to get into a movie or out of a stadium, but this is usually temporary—a matter of minutes rather than hours. In contrast, the level of density that occurs in working or living situations is almost always considerably less than the 4 square feet per person that we used. In other words, the level of density per se (without for the moment considering the type of activity) is certainly high. It is probably as great as could be achieved without causing real physical discomfort.

This leads to the more crucial issue—the situation itself. It is relatively formal and structured. Each Ss has his own chair, there are specific tasks to work on, the verbal interactions are largely in terms of the task. In addition, the Ss are more or less strangers and have no anticipation of a long term relationship. Perhaps most important, the activity does not involve much if any physical movement. The participants do not get in each other's way, they do not interfere physically with each other's work, and more generally do not have to use the available space for moving around. It could be argued that any or all of these characteristics of the situation are crucial—that changing any of them would produce a dramatic effect of density. This is certainly possible. We have not demonstrated that density *never* has an effect on performance—only that it has no effect under the particular conditions we employed. Of course this limitation applies to all research, whether it produces negative or positive effects. All one can ever say is that under the specified conditions the results are as shown. Someone can always suggest that changing a particular variable would change the results, increase or decrease them or even reverse them. But until that notion is tested, there are only the current data and the problem is how to interpret them.

The first point we would make is that in a sense, the lack of effect is more interesting than a small, negative effect would have been. It would seem that being a very crowded room should, if anything, be aversive and should produce a decrement in performance, at least on complex tasks. If we had found a slight decrement, no one would have been surprised or for that matter even particularly interested. Obviously if you make a situation aversive enough, you can eventually produce a decrement in performance; and we could have increased the level of density to that point by, for example, using exceedingly small chairs and packing the subjects in, or dispensing with chairs entirely and putting dozens of people in the small room. But with the high density we used, we did not get such an effect. If we are to believe this result and generalize it to more extended periods of crowding, it means that even very high density is not an aversive stimulus in the usual sense, that it does not produce arousal, and that it does not affect people's ability to work at simple tasks, to learn, to concentrate or even to think creatively.

The findings should be considered in the light of research on social facilitation that was mentioned earlier. The presence of one other individual produces an appreciable effect on performance. It is not necessary to compare someone alone with someone in the presence of dozens of others—the simple expedient of bringing one other person into the room produces an effect on performance. Similarly, other variables such as anxiety level manipulated in simple ways, moderate increases in fear, moderate increases in motivation to succeed and so on, produce sizeable and highly reliable effects on performance. Thus, the lack of effect of density is not because it is difficult to produce such effects nor because enormously powerful manipulations are necessary. If density does arouse drive, if it is an aversive stimulus, if it has any of these properties, it would have been expected to produce an effect in the setting we used—and it did not.

Thus, we feel that there is good reason to interpret the present findings as demonstrating that density per se does not function as an ordinary aversive, arousing stimulus as does, say, electric shock or loud noise. Density may function this way under some as yet unspecified conditions; but it not a simple, aversive stimulus in the usual sense. It is not even a question of people adapting to it, because there is no effect at any stage of exposure. Whatever other effects density may have, however else people react to it, it should not be conceptualized, as many writers tend to, as a drive-inducing stimulus.

This suggests that any effects high density does produce will turn out to be quite complicated. To begin with, it seems highly likely that, being a social stimulus, it will affect primarily social behaviors. We have already collected some evidence to support this (Freedman, Levy, Price, Welte, Katz, & Ehrlich, 1971). Whatever effects density has will be largely on interactions among people, rather than on the performance of individuals working alone or even in groups. In addition, it seems likely that the effects will not be simple ones. Its effects will probably be determined by the particular conditions, by differences in individual reactions, and by other complicated factors such as set, initial relations among the individuals involved, and so on.

The larger implication of this work is that density should not be viewed as necessarily a social evil. Although having many people in a small area presents great problems in logistics, organization, potential pollution, noise, etc., it may not automatically have a negative effect on the people involved. Density per se is not a simple negative, aversive stimulus; and more particularly, there is no evidence that it produces a decrement in performance. High density should be considered in terms of the problems it presents, but should, for the moment, not be considered inherently evil. Thus, if the problems of a logistical nature can be solved, it may be that we will want to encourage or at least allow high density rather than discourage it. This is not to say that we want to allow or encourage population growth; but given a particular population, we may want to encourage concentration rather than, as is the fashion now, rail against the evils of urban concentrations and blame them on negative effects of density per se. This is, of course, all speculative; but for the moment, this research indicates that density per se is not inherently evil. That is all we know for the moment.

REFERENCES

Allport, F. H. *Social psychology*. Cambridge, Mass.: Riverside Press, 1924.

Calhoun, J. B. Population density and social pathology. *Scientific American*, 1962, **206**, 139-148.

Christian, J. J., Flyger, V., & Davis, D. C. Factors in the mass mortality of a herd of sika deer *Cervus nippon. Chesapeake Science*, 1960, **1**, 79-95.

Dubos, R. The social environment. In H. Proshansky, W. Ittelson, and L. Rivlin (Eds.), *Environmental psychology*. New York: Holt, 1970.

Freedman, J. L., Levy, A., Price, J., Welte, R., Katz, M., & Ehrlich, P. The effect of density on human aggression and affective reactions. In preparation, 1971.

Hall, E. T. *The hidden dimension*. Garden City, N. Y.: Doubleday, 1966.

Hutt, C., & Vaizey, M. J. Differential effects of group density on social behavior. *Nature*, 1966, **209**, 1371-1372.

Ittelson, W. H., Proshansky, H. M., & Rivlin, L. G. The environmental psychology of the psychiatric ward. In H. Proshansky, W. Ittelson, and L. Rivlin (Eds.), *Environmental psychology*. New York: Holt, 1970.

Marsden, H. M. Crowding and animal behavior. Paper presented at American Psychological Association annual meeting, 1970.

Schmitt, R. C. Density, delinquency, and crime in Honolulu. *Sociology and Social Research*, 1957, **41**, 274-276.

Schmitt, R. C. Density, health, and social disorganization. *Journal of American Institute of Planners*, 1966, **32**, 38-40.

Sommer, R. *Personal space: The behavioral basis of design*. Englewood Cliffs, N. J.: Prentice-Hall, 1969.

Winsborough, H. H. The social consequences of high population density. *Law and Contemporary Problems*, 1955, **30**, 120-126.

Zajonc, R. B. Social facilitation. *Science*, 1965, **149**, 269-274.

AFFECT, FACIAL REGARD, AND REACTIONS TO CROWDING[1]

MICHAEL ROSS[2]

BRUCE LAYTON, BONNIE ERICKSON, AND JOHN SCHOPLER

The purpose of this experiment was to examine some of the consequences of crowding on human behavior. Male or female groups of eight subjects each were confined in a crowded (small) room or an uncrowded (large) room for either 5 or 20 minutes. During this period they discussed a series of "choice-dilemma" problems. Affective dependent measures revealed consistent Room Size × Sex of Subject interactions. Males rated themselves and others more positively in the uncrowded condition; females evaluated themselves and others more favorably in the crowded than in the uncrowded condition. Similarly, males tended to gaze at others' faces more often in the uncrowded room, while females tended to engage in more facial regard in the crowded room than in the uncrowded room.

Research on the effects of crowding has generally pointed to a variety of deleterious consequences. Studies on animals (e.g., Calhoun, 1962; Marsden, 1971) have found increases in aggression, infant mortality, sexual perversion, and cannibalism. Survey research on humans (e.g., Schmitt, 1957; Winsborough, 1965) has indicated that increasing population density is positively associated with crime rates, suicide rates, and the frequency of various diseases. As Freedman, Klevansky, and Ehrlich (1971) have noted, however, the data from these surveys are ambiguous since controls for such confounding factors as education and socioeconomic status are usually inadequate. Consequently, a causal link between crowding and pathology has not yet been unequivocally demonstrated in human populations (cf. Galle, Grove, & McPherson, 1972).

In an attempt to overcome the problems associated with survey methodology, Freedman et al. (1971) conducted a series of laboratory experiments in which crowding was manipulated by varying the size of the room in which the experimental session occurred. Possible confounding factors such as group size and the temperature and comfort of the rooms were controlled. Though subjects remained in the experiment for periods up to 4 hours, their performance at a series of simple and complex tasks did not appear to be affected by the crowding manipulation.

The present research employed a methodology similar to that of Freedman et al. to study the effect of crowding upon group members' affective feelings for each other. It was hypothesized that crowding would negatively influence subjects' evaluations of their fellow group members. In addition to the survey and animal research already noted, three recent studies on group size have produced results consistent with this hypothesis. It has been found that patients in the more populous wards of a psychiatric hospital engaged in more asocial behavior than patients in less populous wards (Ittelson, Proshansky, & Rivlin, 1970); that children manifested more aggressive and asocial behavior when playing in larger groups (Hutt & Vaizey, 1966); and that subjects in more numerous all-male and all-female groups showed less liking for an anonymous stranger when compared to subjects in less numerous groups (Griffitt & Veitch, 1971). It should be noted that these studies on group size are only indirectly relevant to crowding because the findings could be attributed to differences in the number of persons in the group, rather than to variations in the space allocated to each member.

Another line of research is related to the

[1] This research was supported in part by assistance from the Carolina Population Center.

[2] Requests for reprints should be sent to Michael Ross, Department of Psychology, University of Waterloo, Waterloo, Ontario, Canada.

JOURNAL OF PERSONALITY AND SOCIAL PSYCHOLOGY, 1973, Vol. 28, No. 1, pp. 69-76.

207

general hypothesis guiding the present study. When crowding is defined in terms of density, it inherently involves a manipulation of intramember spatial distances. Sommer's (1969) research on the concept of personal space (the normative expectation held by an individual about the appropriate intramember distance in any given interaction) suggests that any person experiences considerable discomfort when his personal space is violated. Strangers in a densely occupied room should thus experience anxiety and wish to escape the crowding. If physical withdrawal is not possible, however, individuals may cope with their anxiety by a different means. For example, they may attempt to increase the psychological distance between each other by reducing the frequency of eye contact. Argyle and Dean (1965) and Goldberg, Kiesler, and Collins (1969) found that amount of eye contact between two persons was reduced as the distance between them decreased. On the basis of this research it was predicted, in the present study, that subjects in a crowded room would be less likely to gaze at another's face (facial regard) than would subjects in an uncrowded room.

Research on personal space also indicates that sex of the subject may be an important factor. Sommer (1969) has observed that females choose to sit closer to other females than males do to other males. Leibman (1970) suggested that this difference is a result of the socialization process: Women are trained to be dependent and to express love and affection openly for each other; males are trained to be independent and not to express warmth for, or be intimate with, other males. The significance of these observations is that females in all-female groups may find crowding less upsetting than do males in all-male groups. If this reasoning is valid, females in the present experiment should be less likely than males to reduce facial regard and to show derogation in the crowded room.

To this point, we have not considered the effect of temporal factors on reactions to crowding. If crowding produces anxiety its effects may be cumulative such that longer exposure periods would be more debilitating. On the other hand, human beings have demonstrated considerable capacity to adapt to and cope with their environment. It is possible, then, that in longer time periods individuals decrease for themselves the negative impact of crowding. In the current experiment half of the subjects were exposed to crowded conditions for only 5 minutes, while the others remained in the situation for 20 minutes. At the end of the exposure time, subjects were asked how crowded they found the room and whether or not they and the others were upset by the experience. Thus it was possible to determine the degree to which subjects perceived the crowded room to be more or less upsetting over time.

A final word about our definition of crowding and our orientation to this experiment is in order. The present study conceptualized crowding in terms of population density and manipulated crowding by varying room size while holding group size constant, as in Freedman et al. (1971). While it would perhaps be more appropriate to define crowding as a subjective reaction to spatial restrictions, a reaction that is determined by density in interaction with personal and social factors (cf. Stokols, 1972), the manipulation of density appears justified as a starting point for a study of crowding. It was also our intention to study crowding per se, devoid of concomitant variations in other factors frequently accompanying crowding in natural settings. It is obvious, albeit not very illuminating, that aversive effects of crowding can be induced if crowding creates noxious physical effects or inadequate space to perform requisite responses. An effort was made, therefore, to hold constant the temperature of the room, the physical discomfort, etc., between the crowded and uncrowded conditions.

In summary, the study used a $2 \times 2 \times 2$ experimental design. Subjects in groups of eight were seated in a small (crowded condition) or large (uncrowded condition) room. They remained in the room for either a 5- or a 20-minute discussion period. Each group was composed of either males or females. Three major dependent variables were assessed: the amount of facial regard between subjects, the subjects' evaluations of both themselves and the others in the room, and the subjects' reactions to the experimental session itself.

Subjects

The subjects were paid volunteers recruited from the summer school population at the University of North Carolina at Chapel Hill. Individuals were approached on campus and asked if they would be interested in participating in a "group process" experiment which would last approximately an hour. They were informed that they would receive $2.00 for their participation. No other information was given. If the individual agreed, he or she was assigned to a group, with the restriction that all eight group members be unacquainted. In all, 12 male and 12 female groups participated in the experiment. Three experimenters, two males and one female, conducted the experiment. One third of the groups in each condition was run by one of the three experimenters.

Experimental Situation

The experiment was conducted in a large rectangular space containing a one-way mirror at one end. The small and large discussion rooms were created around the same one-way mirror by the location of a movable wooden partition, which was 8 feet high (2.44 meters). The large discussion room was produced by using the partition as one wall and was 9 feet 11 inches wide (3.02 meters), 13 feet 6 inches long (4.11 meters) and 8 feet high (2.44 meters). The small discussion room was formed by bending the partition to make two walls, which resulted in a room 5 feet 7 inches wide (1.70 meters), 8 feet 1 inch long (2.46 meters), and 8 feet high (2.44 meters). The partition had been constructed to reach a square neon light suspended 2 feet 4 inches (.71 meters) from the ceiling. The resultant opening above the partition permitted fresh air from the large, rectagular space to circulate into the discussion room under both experimental arrangements. This represented an attempt to control temperature differences between the two rooms without sacrificing the subjective feeling of being in a solid room. The seating arrangements were similar in the small and large room. Eight molded plastic chairs, without arms, were arranged in a rectangular U-shaped formation with the open end facing the one-way mirror. In the small room each chair touched the one next to it. There was about 5.84 square feet (.54 square meter) of space for each subject. In the large room there was a distance of 15.5 inches (.39 meter) between all adjacent chairs and about 16.8 square feet (1.56 square meters) of space for each subject. In the small room there was a distance of 16 inches (.41 meter) from the front of one chair to the front of the chair directly opposite. This distance was increased to 5 feet 1 inch (.55 meter) in the large room.

Procedure

When the eight subjects had arrived for the experiment, they were ushered into several small rooms that isolated them from one another. Each subject completed an "opinion questionnaire" consisting of twelve choice-dilemma problems (see Kogan & Wallach, 1964, for the complete instrument), in which a protagonist must choose between two courses of action that differ in their attractiveness. For each situation subjects were instructed to indicate the minimum likelihood of success they would demand for the more attractive alternative before recommending that it be chosen.

When everyone was finished, the questionnaires were collected, and the subjects were taken into either the small or large discussion room. After the subjects were seated, the experimenter passed out new "opinion questionnaire" booklets containing the same items as before. The task of the group now was to discuss each problem in turn and arrive at a unanimous decision on each.

The experimenter concluded by saying:

> Because we are interested in studying the development of group processes over time, the group discussion will be monitored by observers behind the one-way mirror. Begin when I leave the room. When I reenter the room, the discussion phase of the experiment will be over. Remember: Discuss each problem in turn and arrive at a unanimous decision on each. Do not shuffle your chairs about. You may begin.

The discussion began when the experimenter left the room and was terminated either 5 or 20 minutes later by the return of the experimenter. The subjects then returned to their original isolation rooms where they were given a series of questionnaires to answer. Finally, the subjects were completely debriefed and were paid the $2.00 that had been promised them.

Dependent Variables

During the discussion period itself, the amount of facial regard in each group was recorded by a trained observer from behind the one-way mirror. Facial regard was defined as an individual's looking at the face of another. The observer followed a fixed schedule, watching a different subject every 10 seconds throughout the entire discussion period. Thus each subject was observed once in a period of 80 seconds. The observer was not aware of the experimental hypotheses.

The second dependent measure, administered immediately upon the subjects' return to the isolation rooms, was a six-item questionnaire requiring subjects to indicate their reactions to both the discussion room and the discussion. Subjects rated their impressions of the temperature of the discussion room, its stuffiness, and their physical discomfort during the discussion on five 9-point scales. Subjects were also asked to estimate on 9-point scales the personal upset they experienced while in the room and the degree of upset of the others in the group. A final question asked them to estimate the length of the discussion period. Subjects were told that they were being asked these and subsequent questions so that the experimenter could assess what effect

209

TABLE 1
MEAN AFFECTIVE RATINGS

Rating	Male		Female	
	Small room	Large room	Small room	Large room
Self-rating				
Unlikable	3.57	2.85	3.30	3.57
Bad	3.50	2.96	3.34	3.75
Rating by others				
Unlikable	4.02	3.76	3.70	3.84
Bad	4.18	4.20	3.68	4.20
Unselfish	5.16	5.29	5.79	5.35
Calm	5.37	5.55	5.90	5.50

Note. Larger means indicate higher ratings on the attribute listed.

their feelings and reactions might have had on "group processes."

This questionnaire was followed by a set of assessments which involved the subjects' making detailed evaluations of both themselves and the other members of the group. Each subject was required to rate himself, on 9-point scales, on a series of semantic differential items assessing intelligence, likability, imagination, nervousness, patience, selfishness, warmth, and goodness. Subjects then rated each member of their group on the same scales. If a subject could not remember one or more of the other group members, he was instructed to guess. The remaining assessment was inserted at the end of the rating booklet. At that point subjects were asked to indicate on a scale running from "very crowded" to "not at all crowded" their impression of how crowded the discussion room had been.

RESULTS

Since data from members of the same group cannot be treated as independent observations, the mean response in each group served as the unit of measurement. The results were not influenced when experimenter was introduced as a factor and the statistical analyses are therefore reported with this factor collapsed.

Perceptions of Crowding and Discussion Length

The degree of crowding present in the discussion room was assessed on a 9-point scale with lower numbers indicating more crowding. An analysis of variance indicated a significant main effect for the manipulation of room size on perceived crowding ($F = 60.9$, $df = 1/16$, $p < .001$). Subjects rated the small room ($\bar{X} = 3.50$) as being more crowded than the large

room ($\bar{X} = 6.72$). On the perceived-crowding measure the absence of significant effects for sex of subject ($F = 1.1$ $df = 1/16$, $p < .31$) and the absence of a Room Size × Sex of Subject interaction ($F = 1.71$, $df = 1/16$, $p < .21$) eliminated the possibility of differential perception of crowding by males and females.

An analysis of variance conducted upon the estimates of length of the discussion period showed a significant main effect for time ($F = 122.67$, $df = 1/16$, $p < .001$). Subjects in the 5-minute condition perceived the discussion time to be shorter ($\bar{X} = 8.36$) than subjects in the 20-minute condition ($\bar{X} = 20.8$). Estimates of time were not affected by sex of subject or the room size manipulation (all $Fs < 1$).

Self-Ratings

Room Size × Sex of Subject interaction effects were found on the self-rating scales of likable–unlikable ($F = 6.50$ $df = 1/16$, $p < .02$) and good–bad ($F = 6.53$, $df = 1/16$, $p < .03$). Mean ratings on these scales (Table 1) revealed that males who had been in the small room tended to rate themselves as less likable and less good than did males in the large room. Conversely, females tended to rate themselves as more likable and good if they had been in the small room. No other main effects or interactions were significant on self-ratings.

Ratings by Others

The Room Size × Sex of Subject interaction obtained on self-ratings was also present in the subjects' ratings by the other group members. Each person in the group was rated by his seven fellow group members. A significant Room Size × Sex of Subject interaction was obtained on ratings of good–bad ($F = 4.97$, $df = 1/16$, $p < .041$) and similar trends were obtained for nervous–calm ($F = 3.89$, $df = 1/16$, $p < .066$), likable–unlikable ($F = 2.67$, $df = 1/16$, $p < .112$), and selfish–unselfish ($F = 2.47$, $df = 1/16$, $p < .135$).[3] Inspection of

[3] When the individual serves as the unit of analysis these interactions become highly significant. For example, selfish–unselfish was significant at $p < .001$ ($F = 10.82$, $df = 1/68$). For these, and subsequent re-

210

the means for these interactions (Table 1) reveals that females who had been in the small room were rated more positively by other group members than females who had been in the large room. As on self-ratings, the responses of male subjects showed the reverse pattern to that of females, except on ratings of good–bad. Males in the large room tended to be rated more positively on the likable–unlikable, selfish–unselfish, and nervous–calm dimensions than did males in the small room. Finally, it should be noted that the discussion-length manipulation did not interact significantly with room size on any of the ratings of others, and that the one significant main effect for room size (good–bad, $F = 5.93$, $df = 1/16$, $p < .02$) was qualified by the Room Size × Sex of Subject interaction.

Facial Regard

Because each subject was observed once every 80 seconds, the maximum facial-regard score for a subject in the 5-minute groups would be 4, while the maximum score would be 15 in the 20-minute groups. An analysis of variance on the total facial-regard scores for the first 5 minutes of the discussion showed no significant main effects or interactions. A second analysis was conducted on total facial-regard scores in the groups that had remained in the discussion room for 20 minutes.[4] The main effects for room size and for sex of subject did not approach significance. There was, however, a marginally significant Room Size × Sex of Subject interaction ($F = 4.55$, $df = 1/7$ $p < .07$). Females in the small room tended to engage in more facial regard ($\bar{X} = 10.17$) than females in the large room ($\bar{X} = 8.50$). This pattern was reversed for male subjects who were more likely to gaze at others' faces in the large room ($\bar{X} = 8.96$) than in the small room ($\bar{X} = 7.69$). Converting these figures to percentages, it was found that females in the small room

sults, the individual analyses always produced more robust significance levels. Hence the weakness of the group results possibly is due to the small number of groups run in each condition ($N = 3$), rather than to variation between groups.

[4] Because one of the 20-minute groups finished its discussion in 15 minutes, data from this group were not included in the analyses of eye contact.

TABLE 2
MEAN RATINGS OF OWN AND OTHER UPSET WHILE IN THE DISCUSSION ROOM

Item	Small room		Large room	
	5 minutes	20 minutes	5 minutes	20 minutes
Own upset	1.33	2.00	1.98	1.57
Other upset	2.02	2.85	2.92	2.37

Note. Higher numbers indicate greater upset.

looked at others on 68% of the observation periods, while females in the large room looked at others on 57% of the periods. The corresponding percentages for males were 51% in the small room and 60% in the large room. These results parallel the relationship found for self-ratings and ratings of others.

Reactions to Experimental Setting

One of the purposes of the present experiment was to determine whether or not subjects adapted over time to crowded conditions. An analysis of variance conducted upon ratings of own upset showed a marginally significant Room Size × Length of Discussion interaction ($F = 3.20$, $df = 1/16$, $p < .09$). The means in Table 2 indicate that subjects reported being more upset in the small room over time and less upset in the large room over time. The Room Size × Discussion Length interaction upon ratings of upset of others was also marginally significant ($F = 3.21$, $df = 1/16$, $p < .09$). The pattern of means shown in Table 2 is similar to that obtained on self-ratings. In the small room others were perceived as more upset in the longer time period, while in the large room greater upset was associated with the shorter period. No other main effects or interactions approached significance on these variables.

Physical Comfort

Ratings of physical comfort were not affected by the crowding manipulation ($F = 1.63$, $df = 1/16$, $p < .22$). The Sex × Room Size interaction was also nonsignificant ($F < 1$). These results indicate that, as expected, increased density was not confounded by greater physical discomfort. However, subjects in the small room did rate the discussion room as warmer ($F = 8.08$, $df = 1/16$, $p < .01$) and more stuffy ($F = 9.37$, $df = 1/16$, $p < .01$) than subjects in the large room. Nevertheless, since these effects were obtained for both males and females, it is unlikely that variations in temperature or stuffiness contributed to the significant interactions obtained on the major dependent variables.[5]

DISCUSSION

The purpose of the present experiment was to examine some of the consequences of confining human subjects in a crowded room. The assessment of the room-size manipulation indicated that subjects did indeed feel crowded in the small room. This was true for females as well as for males, and for both the 5- and 20-minute groups. Although subjects perceived the crowded room to be warmer and stuffier than the uncrowded room, there were no differences with respect to rated physical discomfort, which apparently was minimal. The latter finding is also reflected in the magnitude of the means for warmth and stuffiness. Temperature was assessed on a 9-point scale with end anchor points of "very cold" and "very warm," and with the three midpoints of the scale anchored by "comfortable." The temperature means, which ranged 5.1–5.7, fall well within the "comfortable" range. Furthermore, all the means for stuffy fall toward the end of the 9-point scale labeled "not stuffy."

Main effects of room size upon perceived warmth and stuffiness would have clouded the interpretation of the predicted main effects for self and other ratings, but the predicted main effects were not found. Instead, both sets of ratings showed consistent Room Size × Sex of Subject interactions. Ratings of self and ratings of individuals by others were more positive in the large room than the small room for male subjects; female subjects, how-

ever, evaluated themselves and the other group members more favorably in the small room than in the large room. Moreover, even though females showed a slight tendency to perceive the small room as warmer, they were more positive about themselves and the other group members in the small than in the large room.

It is evident that the sex composition of the group mediates the affective consequences of crowding. The present data suggest several possibilities concerning the nature of this mediation. It might be thought that fixed, intramember distances imply different degrees of crowding for males than for females. Recall, however, that females did not differ from males in the amount of crowding ascribed to the small room. Although the perception of being crowded is the same for males and females, the subjective meaning of this experience apparently differs for males and females. In fact, females in the small room of the present experiment not only reflected more positive feelings than did males in the small room, but the pattern also indicated that females in the small room gave more positive evaluations than did *females* in the large room.

What are the specific ways in which crowding is differentially interpreted? It seems evident, within the confines of a discussion-group setting, that crowding does not induce feelings of sufficient intensity to warrant the label of anxiety. Ratings of personal and other upset were confined to the lower-third range (not upset) of the scale. The most salient aspect of the crowding manipulation seems to have been the induction of violations of personal space. Males appear to have found the interpersonal distance in the small room too close for comfortable interaction, while females apparently found the interpersonal space in the large room to be too distant. A similar sex difference is implied in Sommer's (1969) observation that females chose to sit closer to other females than males did to other males. It thus may be that the violation of interpersonal space produced discomfort which resulted in lower affective ratings: For males this violation was experienced in the crowded circumstance, while for females it occurred when there was ample space.

It is recalled that the facial-regard data

---

[5] Although irrelevant to the purposes of the experiment, subjects' responses to the choice-dilemma problems were analyzed by subtracting a group's consensus score from the average prediscussion score for that group. Despite the presence of an overall significant shift toward risk ($F = 34.10$, $df = 1/16$, $p < .001$), there were no significant differential effects between experimental conditions.

were congruent with this speculation. Males tended to engaged in more facial regard in the large room than in the small room. Females tended to engage in more facial regard in the small room than in the large room; *within* the large room, the pattern shows that females engaged in less facial regard than the males. It may be that this overall pattern of results could account for the more favorable affective ratings obtained from females in the small room and from males in the large room. Several authors have observed the importance of mutual glances in social interaction. According to Goffman (1959), for example, mutual glances are likely to make participants feel accepted and close to each other. In addition, experimental evidence points to a relation between eye contact and affect. Winer and Mehrabian (reported in Argyle & Kendon, 1967, p. 74) conducted an experiment in which an interviewer spoke to two persons simultaneously, but spent more time looking at one of them. Subsequent ratings showed that the person who was looked at more often judged the interviewer to be more positive toward her than did the person who was looked at less. Exline and Winters (1965) found that subjects increased eye contact with an interviewer who evaluated them positively and decreased eye contact with a critical interviewer. Finally, Ellsworth and Carlsmith (1968) observed that increased eye contact led to increased liking when the content of the discussion was positive. It should be emphasized, however, that establishing a causal relation between facial regard and affective reactions to crowding awaits further research.

It has been suggested that while the crowding manipulation violated personal space expectations, albeit differentially for males and females, it induced only mild stress. This interpretation can be extended to fit the Freedman et al. (1971) results if it is assumed that personal space violations do not affect the members' task productivity. This assumption appears to be particularly warranted for tasks requiring individual performance or minimal interdependence. A personal-space-violation interpretation is also in keeping with the present results, which showed a lack of any adaptation over time for the affective ratings. Since personal-space expectations are learned throughout a lifetime of personal experiences, they may continue to be salient for interactions lasting only 20 minutes, several hours, or even a few days.

To say that personal-space expectations do not adapt quickly does not mean that the duration of the crowding experience is irrelevant. In the present study, a marginally significant Duration × Room Size interaction was found. In general, subjects were more upset in the small room over time, but less upset in the large room over time, though all of these ratings were of low magnitude. It is likely that in some circumstances crowding induces other sources of stress which will accumulate over time. It is our final speculation, however, that any aversive effects of crowding may be contingent upon the group's lack of ability to evolve viable mechanisms to deal with the consequences of crowding. For example, crowding could increase the difficulty of coordinating the members' responses. Tasks that require a high degree of member coordination (a class of tasks which has not yet been used in crowding research) should be more vulnerable to the effects of crowding than tasks that do not contain this requirement. A particular group's ability to evolve a viable structure, for example, by developing clear norms, would still be critical in mitigating the potentially aversive consequences.

REFERENCES

Argyle, M., & Dean, J. Eye-contact, distance, and affiliation. *Sociometry*, 1965, **28**, 289–304.

Argyle, M., & Kendon, A. Experimental analysis of social performance. In L. Berkowitz (Ed.), *Advances in experimental social psychology*. Vol. 3. New York: Academic Press, 1967.

Calhoun, J. B. Population density and social pathology. *Scientific American*, 1962, **206**(2), 139–150.

Ellsworth, P. C., & Carlsmith, J. M. Effects of eye contact and verbal content on affective responses to a dyadic interaction. *Journal of Personality and Social Psychology*, 1968, **10**, 15–20.

Exline, R. Y., & Winters, L. C. Affective relations and mutual glances in dyads. In S. S. Tomkins & C. E. Izard (Eds.), *Affect, cognition, and personality*. New York: Springer, 1965.

Freedman, J. L., Klevansky, S., & Ehrlich, P. R. Effect of crowding on human task performance. *Journal of Applied Social Psychology*, 1971, **1**, 7–25.

GALLE, O. R., GROVE, W. R., & McPHERSON, J. M. Population density and pathology: What are the relations for man? *Science*, 1972, 176(4030), 23–30.

GOFFMAN, E. *Presentation of self in everyday life.* Garden City, N. Y.: Doubleday, 1959.

GOLDBERG, G. N., KIESLER, C., & COLLINS, B. Visual behavior and face-to-face distance during interaction. *Sociometry*, 1969, 32, 43–53.

GRIFFITT, W., & VEITCH, R. Hot and crowded: Influences of population density and temperature on interpersonal affective behavior. *Journal of Personality and Social Psychology*, 1971, 17, 92–98.

HUTT, C., & VAIZEY, M. J. Differential effects of group density on social behavior. *Nature*, 1966, 209, 1371–1372.

ITTELSON, W. H., PROSHANSKY, H. M., & RIVLIN, L. G. The environmental psychology of the psychiatric ward. In H. Proshansky, W. Ittelson, & L. Rivlin (Eds.), *Environmental psychology.* New York: Holt, 1970.

KOGAN, N., & WALLACH, M. A. *Risk taking: A study in cognition and personality.* New York: Holt, 1964.

LEIBMAN, M. The effects of sex and race norms on personal space. *Environment and Behavior*, 1970, 2, 208–246.

MARSDEN, H. M. Crowding and animal behavior. Paper presented at the annual meeting of the American Psychological Association, Washington, D.C., September 1971.

SCHMITT, R. C. Density, delinquency, and crime in Honolulu. *Sociology and Social Research*, 1957, 41, 274–276.

SOMMER, R. *Personal space: The behavioral basis of design.* Englewood Cliffs, N.J.: Prentice-Hall, 1969.

STOKOLS, D. On the distinction between density and crowding: Some implications for future research. *Psychological Review*, 1972, 79, 275–277.

WINSBOROUGH, H. H. The social consequences of high population density. *Law and Contemporary Problems*, 1965, 30, 120–126.

SIZE OF CHURCH MEMBERSHIP AND MEMBERS' SUPPORT OF CHURCH BEHAVIOR SETTINGS [1]

ALLAN W. WICKER [2]

Complete lists of all organized group activities occurring ɪ five Methodist churches were compiled for a 1-year period. In the five churches, the members/ activities ratio consistently increased with church size, suggesting that activities in small churches are relatively undermanned. A comparison of members of a small church (338 members, sample $n = 30$) and members of a comparable large church (1599 members, $n = 34$) revealed that small church members participated in more different kinds of activities, had more leadership positions and spent more time in the activities, attended church more often, and contributed more money. Members of the small church were also more approving of high levels of support for church activities. Archival data on 104 churches also showed a negative relationship between church size and several indexes of support for church activities. The findings support Barker's behavior setting theory.

According to behavior setting theory (Barker, 1960, 1968), the behaviors of members of a voluntary organization are greatly influenced by the number of people available to support the organization's activities. When the manpower supply is low, members expend more effort to maintain the activities than when participants are abundant. Undermanning induces members to assume positions of greater responsibility and importance, to engage in a wider range of supportive behaviors, and to recruit others to participate.

The theory has been tested in a series of investigations of students' behaviors in extracurricular activities of large and small high schools (Barker & Gump, 1964; Wicker, 1968, 1969; Willems, 1965, 1967). The activities studied included such events as theatrical productions, organization meetings, and athletic contests. All activities were identified and selected according to the standard procedure for identifying behavior settings. The behavior setting is an ecobehavioral unit whose attributes include occurrence at a specifiable time and place, and systematic arrangement of people, other physical objects, and certain behavior patterns (Barker, 1968; Barker & Wright, 1955). Organized group activities within institutions are behavior settings.

Barker and his colleagues have shown that while the number of school behavior settings increases with school size, the rate of increase is not as great as the increase in number of students. To illustrate, a small school had 21 juniors (eleventh grade) and 54 behavior settings, or expressed as a ratio, .4 student per setting. If the same students/behavior settings ratio held in a large school having 794 juniors, there would have been over 2,000 behavior settings. Actually there were 189, and the ratio was 4.2 (Gump & Friesen, 1964a). Comparable data on a number of schools show that the students/behavior settings ratio increases with school size, suggesting that on the average, behavior settings in

[1] A grant from the Graduate School of the University of Wisconsin-Milwaukee supported the research. Use of University of Wisconsin computing facilities was made possible through support from the National Science Foundation, other United States Government agencies, and the Wisconsin Alumni Research Foundation (WARF) through the University of Wisconsin Research Committee. The writer is indebted to Anne Mehler for valuable technical assistance during all stages of this research. The cooperation of church members participating in the study, and the help of The Reverends Earl Allen, Roger Becker, Clifford Fritz, Richard Jones, William Morton, Marvin Schilling, Lee Smith, Martin Thomas, and John Thompson are also gratefully acknowledged. Thanks are due to Anne Mehler, W. D. Claus, and L. B. Kornreich for helpful comments on the manuscript and to Michael Mertz and Michael Becker for assistance on computer analyses.

[2] Requests for reprints should be sent to the author, who is now at the Department of Psychology, University of Illinois, Urbana, Illinois 61801.

JOURNAL OF PERSONALITY AND SOCIAL PSYCHOLOGY, 1969, Vol. 13, No. 3, pp. 278-288.

215

small schools are undermanned relative to those in large schools (Barker & Barker, 1964). Thus the behaviors of students from large and small schools were expected to differ in ways specified by behavior setting theory. Gump and Friesen (1964a) reported that although the students of large and small schools did not differ in number of extracurricular behavior settings entered, the small-school students had more positions of responsibility in settings they entered. The settings entered by small-school students were also more heterogeneous than those entered by large-school students. These findings have been confirmed by Wicker (1969) and Willems (1965).

The primary aim of the present study is to test the generality of the above findings supporting behavior setting theory by studying churches differing in number of members. However, the study is not merely a replication of the earlier research. It is rather an important test of the theory, in that several presumably noncrucial aspects of the earlier studies are varied while allowing the hypothesized relationship between variables to obtain. Lykken (1968) considered such "constructive replications" to be more critical in the evaluation of postulated relationships than levels of significance of findings.

Differences between the earlier research and the present study include the following: (a) Churches, rather than schools, are the institution studied. Gregory (1952) has urged social psychologists and others to "study objectively this vast institutional field [of religion and churches] where there is waiting a richness of material still unexamined [p. 258]." (b) Subjects in the present study are middle-aged adults, rather than adolescent students. Smart (1966) has recently documented the fact that psychological research has almost totally ignored "nonschool and adult noncollege populations." (c) Data on members' overt behaviors were not solely obtained from self-report measures, but included contributions and attendance figures taken from church records. Webb, Campbell, Schwartz, and Sechrest (1966) have urged investigators to employ such unobtrusive measures in conjunction with more traditional methods. (See Barker,

Barker, & Ragle, 1967, for another study of churches which includes a broad population and employs nonreactive measures.) (d) The large and small churches in the present study were located in the same urban area, whereas in the school research, school size varied with community size. Deutsch (1968) has suggested that rural-urban differences offer an alternative explanation to Barker and Gump's (1964) findings in schools.

A second major purpose of the present study is to examine a previously untested derivation from behavior setting theory: members of organizations whose behavior settings tend to be relatively overmanned, that is, large organizations, have different social norms regarding members' support of the behavior settings of the organization than members of organizations whose behavior settings tend to be relatively undermanned, that is, small organizations. More specifically, it is expected that members of small churches, compared to members of large churches, will be more approving of high levels of support of church behavior settings, and less approving of low levels of support. Support would include such behaviors as attendance, active participation, and contributions. Barker (1963, 1968) stated that occupants of undermanned settings, under pressure to maintain the settings when people are scarce, employ "deviation-countering" feedback to influence members to contribute to the settings. Such feedback could include both encouragement of high levels of support and discouragement of low levels of support.

The present expectations are represented in Figure 1 in terms of Jackson's *return potential model* of norms (Jackson, 1965, 1966). The points along the abscissa represent possible behaviors of church members. These behaviors differ in degree of support given to church behavior settings. For example, the set of behaviors could represent the number of hours per week spent in church activities and could range from 0 hours (low support) to 30 hours (high support). The ordinate represents the average evaluation (degree of approval or disapproval) of each of the behaviors, as rated by church members. For example, the members might give an average

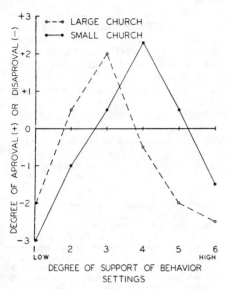

FIG. 1. Hypothetical return potential curves for members of large and small churches.

evaluation of −2 or −3 to the behavior of spending no hours per week in church activities. The curve connecting average ratings for each degree of support is the *return potential curve;* it indicates the possible positive or negative feedback to a member at each support level.

The return potential curves for large and small churches given in Figure 1 are hypothetical. They illustrate the expectations that (*a*) the behavior most approved by members of large churches will be lower in degree of support than the behavior most approved by members of small churches, and (*b*) the behaviors lower in degree of support will be evaluated more highly by members of large churches than by members of small churches, while the converse will be true for behaviors higher in degree of support.

Surveys of Behavior Settings in Five Churches

In order to test behavior setting theory in large and small churches, it was first necessary to obtain evidence that churches of different membership size also differ in degree

of undermanning of their settings. Following the earlier research, the ratio of members to behavior settings was employed as an index of degree of undermanning. For each of five Methodist churches in metropolitan Milwaukee, Wisconsin, complete lists were compiled of the behavior settings occurring in a 1-year period. The churches selected were, in the opinion of knowledgeable church officials, "typical" churches having memberships roughly comparable in socioeconomic class. The churches ranged in membership from 127 to 1,599.

For each church, lists were drawn up on the basis of information from Sunday church bulletins, church newsletters, calendars of pastors and church secretaries, and interviews with pastors and members. According to the standard procedures for identifying behavior settings (Barker, 1968; Barker & Wright, 1953), a group activity which meets at regular intervals, such as the women's organization, is counted as a single setting. In an effort to obtain a measure of the total frequency of behavior settings, the number of occurrences of each setting was also determined. Although space limitations do not permit the presentation of even one complete behavior settings list,[2] the brief list given in Table 1 is illustrative.

[2] Complete behavior setting lists for the five churches have been deposited with the National Auxiliary Publications Service. Order Document No. 00519 from National Auxiliary Publications Service of the American Society for Information Science, c/o CCM Information Services, Inc., 909 3rd Avenue, New York, New York 10022. Remit in advance $3.00 for photocopies or $1.00 for microfiche and make checks payable to: Research and Microfilm Publications, Inc.

TABLE 1

Illustrative Items from a List of Church Behavior Settings

Behavior setting	No. occurrences
Commission on Missions meeting	5
Grade 4 church school class 9:00 A.M.	45
Men's team dartball game	32
Methodist Mates Club bowling party	1
Nursery during 11:00 A.M. church service	45
Thanksgiving Eve Holy Communion	1
Training session for church school teachers	4
Women's Society of Christian Service monthly meeting	10

TABLE 2

SUMMARY DATA FROM BEHAVIOR SETTINGS
LISTS OF FIVE CHURCHES

Church	Members	Behavior settings	Occur-rences of behavior settings	Mem-bers/ settings ratio	Mem-bers/ occur-rences ratio
A	127	84	1,251	1.51	.10
B	338	118	1,602	2.86	.21
C	546	139	1,888	3.92	.29
D	961	139	2,242	6.91	.43
E	1,599	205	3,551	7.80	.45

Data from the behavior settings lists of the five churches are summarized in Table 2. Consistent with the findings in schools, the number of behavior settings increased with church size, but at a slower rate than the increase in number of members. The largest church had 12.6 times as many members as the smallest church, but only 2.4 times as many behavior settings. The ratio of members to settings increased progressively with increases in church membership, from 1.51 in the smallest church to 7.80 in the largest church.

The data on number of occurrences of behavior settings give essentially the same picture. There were 10 members per 100 occurrences in the smallest church, compared to 45 members per 100 occurrences in the largest church.

These figures thus suggest that church behavior settings are increasingly overmanned as church size increases. In the larger churches there are more people available to carry out the activities of settings, and so presumably the demands or claims upon the average member to support the settings are fewer and weaker. And lesser demands on members should result in lower levels of support for church activities by church members, and perhaps different social norms regarding such support. These questions are examined in the following section.

MEMBERS' NORMS AND BEHAVIORS IN
SUPPORT OF CHURCH BEHAVIOR SETTINGS

Data on members' support of church behavior settings and their social norms regarding such support were obtained from members of a small church (338 members) and a large church (1,599 members). (These are Churches B and E in Table 2.) In the judgment of three pastors familiar with all Methodist churches in the Milwaukee area, the two churches provided the best match of a large and a small church, in that they were comparable on factors which affect member participation: age, sex, and social class distribution of the members (Argyle, 1958). Also, both churches were located in stable, rather than "transitional," urban areas, and had popular pastors of approximately the same age.

Method

Subjects. Membership records of each church were examined to identify persons whose spouses were also members and whose youngest children were between 5 and 14 years old. These selection criteria were employed in an attempt to provide relatively homogeneous and comparable samples. There were 37 couples meeting the criteria in the small church and 143 in the large church. In order to reduce the large church sample to a manageable size, 99 of the 143 couples were eliminated by a random procedure, leaving 44 couples. A further restriction was that only one spouse per couple (half husbands, half wives) was asked to participate in the study.

Subjects were contacted by a personal letter from their pastor. The letter, which was the same for both pastors, introduced the study as dealing with "differences and similarities of churches of different sizes," and asked the recipient to attend one of two evening sessions in his church to fill out questionnaires. Every subject who did not appear at an evening session was later contacted by phone to schedule an individual session if possible. In the small church 30 out of 37 subjects contacted completed questionnaires (81%), compared to 34 out of 44 (77%) in the large church. This difference in participation is not significant ($\chi^2 = .18$); neither is the sex distribution of the participating subjects different for the two churches (46% males in each sample).

Questionnaire materials. Questionnaires were used to measure subjects' social norms regarding support of church activities, and their own level of participation in church activities.

Separate norm measures were obtained for three different ways of supporting church activities: frequency of attendance at Sunday worship service, hours spent in church activities, and amount of money contributed to the church. For each of the above categories, six levels of support were described: attending Sunday worship service fewer than 26 times a year (Level 1) to attending 52 times a year (Level 6), spending less than 1 hour per week in church activities (Level 1) to spending more than 30 hours (Level 6), and contributing less than

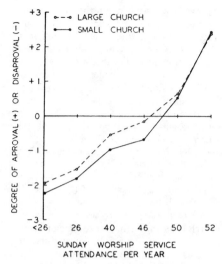

FIG. 2. Attendance at Sunday worship service return potential curves for members of a large and a small church.

.3% of one's annual income to the church per year (that is, less than 1 day's income, Level 1) to contributing more than 8% (that is, more than 1 month's income, Level 6). Subjects indicated on a 7-point scale their degree of approval or disapproval of behavior at each level by "a church member such as yourself."

The questionnaire on participation in church behavior settings consisted of a list of all the church's settings which had occurred during the 3½-month period immediately preceding the testing sessions. Subjects indicated whether they had attended each setting, and if so, the approximate number of hours they spent and whether they were a "member," "worker," or "leader" in the setting. The three role categories were defined for the subjects as, respectively, attending but having no particular job or responsibility (for example, sitting in the congregation at Sunday worship service), having an assignment which contributed to the setting, but which did not involve the main activity (for example, ushering at Sunday worship service), and having a position of control and authority in the main activity of the setting (for example, directing the choir at Sunday worship service). These categories are adapted from Barker and Wright (1955) and Gump and Friesen (1964a).

Numbers, rather than names, were employed for subject identification on the questionnaires. While subjects did give their names together with the identification number, names were obtained only once on individual cards. Subjects were assured they would remain anonymous, in that only group data such as

averages would be reported back to pastors and other church officials, and none of the clerical workers on the project would have access to the names.

Data from church records. Data on members' Sunday worship service attendance, and on their pledges and contributions of money to the church, were obtained from church records. Both churches determine attendance by passing sign-up sheets along the pews during each Sunday worship service. Also, at the beginning of each fiscal year, members are asked to indicate or pledge whatever amount of money they are willing to give to the church during the next year. Contributions are placed in an envelope having an identifying number, and a record is kept of the contributions. Members who do not make pledges are also requested to use envelopes when making contributions. In practice, pledges and contributions are made by the family, rather than by the husband or wife independently. Data to be reported were thus necessarily on the subject's family.

Results

Members' norms regarding support of church behavior settings. Figures 2, 3, and 4 show return potential curves for Sunday worship service attendance, time spent in church activities, and contributions to the church, as determined from responses by members of the two churches. Comparison of these figures with Figure 1 reveals no support for the hypothesis that the most approved behavior for

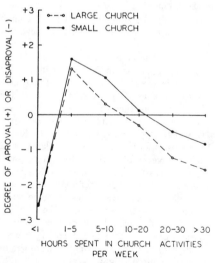

FIG. 3. Time spent in church activities return potential curves for members of a large and a small church.

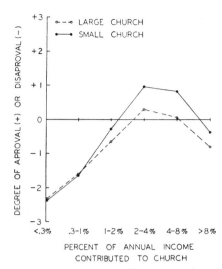

FIG. 4. Contributions to the church return potential curves for members of a large and a small church.

the small church is higher in degree of support for church behavior settings than the most approved behavior for the large church. Rather, for each of the categories of behavior, the most approved level of support is the same for both churches.

It was also hypothesized that small church members are less approving of lower levels of support, and more approving of higher levels of support, than large church members. If low levels of support are arbitrarily defined as all levels below the most approved level, and high levels defined as the most approved level and all higher levels, then the curves for the three categories of behavior reveal a coherent pattern which supports the hypothesis. In Figure 2 the most approved level of attendance is 52 times per year; at each of the levels lower than 52 times per year, that is, the low levels according to the above definition, the average degree of approval is less for the small church than for the large church. In Figure 3 each of the five high levels of time spent in church activities (levels of 1–5 hours per week and higher) is more approved by members of the small church. Figure 4 also reveals that high levels of contributions to the church (levels of 2–4% and higher) are also more

approved by members of the small church. Over all six levels of support in three figures, there is only one direct contradiction to the hypothesis: members of small churches are more approving of contributing 1–2% of one's income, a level below the most approved level.

The preceding discussion has been based upon inspection of the patterns of responses of members of large and small churches. In one sense, Figures 2, 3, and 4 represent three separate replications of the same hypothesis, and each replication is consistent with the expectation. For some, such data may be more convincing than citing probability levels. Results of statistical analyses of the norms data are given below.

For each of the three ways of supporting church behavior settings, a two-factor (church size, levels of support) repeated-measures analysis of variance was computed. These analyses revealed that (a) although the average approval rating over the five Sunday worship service attendance levels below 52 times per year (the low levels) is higher for the large church ($-.7$ versus -1.0), this difference is not significant ($F = 1.42$, $df = 1/62$, $p < .25$); (b) the difference between mean approval ratings by members of the large and the small church over the five high levels of time spent in church activities is highly significant (small church $\bar{X} = .3$, large church $\bar{X} = -.3$; $F = 5.38$, $df = 1/62$, $p < .025$); (c) the difference between mean approval ratings of the two churches over the three high levels of contribution is of borderline significance (small church $\bar{X} = .5$, large church $\bar{X} = -.1$; $F = 3.39$, $df = 1/61$, $p < .08$). All p levels are for the two-tailed test. It can be seen in Figures 2, 3, and 4 that the two church samples do not differ in their mean approval ratings of the high level of attendance, the low level of time spent in church activities, or the low levels of contributions.

Members' behaviors in support of church behavior settings. Table 3 reports means for behaviors by members of the large church and the small church,[3] and t's and probability

[3] Actually, two separate analyses were computed for each behavioral measure taken from church records: one included the entire sample originally asked to participate in the study, and the other in-

TABLE 3

BEHAVIORS IN SUPPORT OF CHURCH BEHAVIOR SETTINGS

Behavior	Large church (n = 34)	Small church (n = 30)	
Sunday worship service attendance	15.8	24.8	3.30****
No. behavior settings entered	7.4	9.2	1.11
No. kinds of behavior settings entered	4.6	6.2	1.81**
No. behavior settings in which S was a worker or leader	2.6	4.0	1.35*
No. behavior settings in which S was a leader	.2	1.1	3.00****
No. hours spent in behavior settings	29.2	43.5	1.90**
Amount of money pledged, 1966–1967	$128	$214	2.92****
Amount of money given, 1966–1967	$111	$187	2.53***
Amount of money pledged, 1967–1968	$137	$255	2.83****

Note.—All t tests are one-tailed. The time periods for the above behaviors were as follows: Sunday worship service attendance, September 1966, through May 1967 (39 Sundays); participation in church behavior settings, January 1, 1967, through Apri 15, 1967 (15 weeks); contributions to the church, June 1, 1966, through May 31, 1967 (52 weeks).
   * $p < .10$.
   ** $p < .05$.
   *** $p < .01$.
   **** $p < .005$.

levels associated with the differences in the means. As expected, for each of the behaviors, the mean level of support is lower for the large church than for the small church; seven of the nine differences are significant beyond the .05 probability level.

The data on participation in church behavior settings in Table 3 are quite similar to the findings by Gump and Friesen (1964a) in high schools. In both studies, members of small organizations, when compared with members of large organizations, (a) did not differ significantly in number of behavior settings entered, (b) entered more different kinds of behavior settings (criteria for grouping behavior settings into kinds, or *genotypes*, are described by Barker, 1968), (c) had more positions of responsibility (worker and leader levels combined), and (d) had many more high level positions of responsibility (leader level).

The present results also suggest that members of the small church attend Sunday worship service more frequently, spend more hours in church behavior settings, and pledge and contribute more money to the church than members of the large church.

cluded only those persons who completed questionnaires. Since probability levels were the same for both analyses, only data for the subjects who completed questionnaires are given in Table 3.

Discussion

The present findings offer strong support for behavior setting theory. Derivations from the theory have now been supported in two different kinds of social organization, with subjects of different ages, and from different geographical areas. The question of generality of the findings may still be raised, however, due to the fact that both the research in schools and the present study involved very small samples of organizations. Baird (1969), addressing himself to the generality question, has replicated Barker and Gump's (1964) findings in a national sample of high school students.

The generality of behavior setting theory would be further demonstrated if it were shown in a broader sample of churches that support for church behavior settings varies as a function of church size. In the following section, relevant data are presented for more than 100 churches ranging widely in membership. A word of caution should be advanced concerning these data. The two churches for which members' norms and behaviors have been reported were selected because they were comparable on a number of variables known to influence members' participation. In contrast, the selection of all the Methodist churches within a geographical area admits many other variables which influence members' support of church behavior settings.

Therefore it may be expected that the influence of church size, while still operating, may be somewhat attenuated in the unselected sample of churches.

BEHAVIORS IN SUPPORT OF CHURCH BEHAVIOR SETTINGS: DATA ON A LARGE NUMBER OF CHURCHES

Method

Each year, the East Wisconsin Conference of the Methodist Church publishes a *Year Book and Journal*, which includes statistical data on membership, attendance, and contributions for all Methodist churches within the jurisdiction of the Conference. Separate analyses were computed on all churches located in two subdivisions of the Conference, one predominately urban and the other predominately rural. Nearly all of the 47 churches in the Milwaukee district are located in metropolitan Milwaukee. These churches have an average of 533 members, with the range from 47 to 2,402. Many of the 57 churches in the Green Bay district are located in small towns. The average membership of these churches is 306, with the range from 23 to 1,596.

The following statistics reflecting support for church activities were selected from the *Year Book and Journal* (East Wisconsin Conference, 1967) for analysis: (a) average attendance at Sunday worship service, (b) average attendance at church school (c) number of church school officers and teachers, (d) women's organization membership, (e) monetary contributions of the women's organization for benevolence projects and local church expenses, and (f) members' contributions to the church. In order to obtain a measure reflecting average degree of support by church members, for each church the above figures were divided by the number of church members to yield percentage of members attending Sunday worship service, percentage of members who are church school officers and teachers, average contribution per member, and so on. These quotients were then correlated with church membership to test the hypothesis that support for church behavior settings is negatively related to church size.

Results

Product-moment correlation coefficients relating each of the indexes of support with church size were computed separately for the two districts, and then with the combined data. As shown in Table 4, five of the six indexes show the expected negative relationship, whether churches are located in predominately urban or predominately rural areas. As church size increases, there are significant decreases in the percentage attendance at Sunday worship service and church school, the

TABLE 4

CORRELATION COEFFICIENTS RELATING SUPPORT FOR CHURCH BEHAVIOR SETTINGS AND CHURCH SIZE

Index of support	Milwaukee district ($n = 47$)	Green Bay district ($n = 57$)	Two districts combined ($n = 104$)
Worship service attendance	−.44**	−.39**	−.43**
Church school attendance	−.29*	−.32*	−.25*
Church school officers and teachers	−.28	−.24	−.21*
Women's organization membership	−.42**	−.46**	−.45**
Women's organization contributions	−.23	−.32*	−.28**
Members' contributions	.12	.24	.19

* $p < .05$.
** $p < .01$.

percentage of members who have responsible positions in the church school, the percentage of members belonging to the women's organization, and the average contribution per church member by the women's organization.

The coefficients relating members' contributions and church size show an unexpected positive relationship, although the r's are not significant. A number of factors may contribute to this finding. In most cases, churches having fewer than 250 members do not support a full-time pastor, but have part-time pastors shared with other nearby churches. Thus the amount of money needed for this purpose is less. Also, large churches tend to have more prestige and to attract wealthier members than small churches. Furthermore, small churches include both rural and urban populations, while large churches are almost exclusively urban, so that rural-urban differences in wealth may be a factor. (In the Green Bay district, which is predominately rural, the relatively few large churches are in cities.)

An Additional Analysis

Since only the data on contributions did not follow predictions based on behavior setting theory, an attempt was made to examine the relation of church size and contributions when some of the above factors were eliminated. The five churches in Table 2 all supported one or more full-time pastors; none of the churches had a reputation for being particularly high in prestige; and all were located in urban areas with memberships roughly comparable in socioeconomic status.

Data on pledges and contributions of comparable samples of members from the five churches were obtained. Sampling procedures were identical to those for selecting subjects from Churches B and E. To assure comparability, data from all persons in Churches B and E who were asked to participate were included, whether or not they completed questionnaires. Members of Churches A, C, and D were not contacted; their contributions were obtained directly from church records. The average pledges for the samples were: A, $280; B, $196, C, $193; D, $168, and E, $131. Average contributions were: A, $282; B, $166; C, $174; D, $84; E, $107. The product-moment correlation coefficient relating church size and average pledge is $-.885$ ($p < .05$, $df = 3$), and for church size and contributions, $-.791$ (ns), providing at least some evidence that monetary support of church behavior settings is also related to number of church members.

DISCUSSION

According to behavior setting theory, the degree of responsibility felt and actually taken by occupants of behavior settings varies inversely with the number of people available to carry out the setting's activities. When people are sparse, members sense that the fate of the setting depends upon them; responsibility cannot be easily shifted to others. But when people are plentiful, demands on the average member are less; other people are available to carry on the setting's activities, so felt responsibility and actual support for behavior settings are not so great.

The present findings provide strong support for the theory and for the generality of Barker and Gump's (1964) findings in high schools. Degree of undermanning, as measured by the members/behavior settings ratio, increases as church size and school size decrease. Members of small churches and schools, compared with members of large churches and schools, enter a wider range of behavior settings, and have more responsible positions in the settings entered.

It may be argued that there is a natural selection process by which members consciously select churches of the size which make demands compatible with their willingness to expend effort. Obviously, however, such a process cannot be the sole factor operating, since there are wide ranges of member support within churches of all sizes. And when persons do not have a choice of size of organization with which to affiliate, the same results are obtained as when they do. Thus the same relationships between member behaviors and size occur in schools, where selectivity of affiliation is not a factor, and in churches, where selectivity might occur. Also, selection of a church on the basis of size would be easier in urban than in rural areas, but the relationship between church size and support for church activities is no stronger in the urban district than in the rural district (Table 4).

The present findings in churches are consistent with organizational research in industry. Reviews of the literature by Porter and Lawler (1965) and Willems (1964b) indicate that small organizational units have lower absence and turnover rates than large units. The small units are also characterized by higher productivity and higher job satisfaction.

The present results are also consistent with another line of research which relates group size and assumption of responsibility. Latané and his associates (Darley & Latané, 1968a, 1968b, Latané & Rodin, 1969) have found that the likelihood that a person will come to the aid of another person in distress is greater the smaller the number of persons present. Darley and Latané (1968a, 1968b) also pointed out that the behaviors of others in such a situaiton may serve as cues for how the individual should react. And Bryan and Test (1967) have shown in field experiments that the presence or absence of a helping model influences observers' helping behaviors. A similar phenomenon probably occurs in behavior settings (Barker, 1968, p. 175). Occupants of undermanned settings, when they perceive that certain satisfactions may no longer be forthcoming because a setting is in jeopardy, expend greater effort in support of the settings. They not only directly contribute to the setting, but they also provide models for others in the setting. Presumably, the greater the percentage of hard-working persons (models) in a situation, the greater the pressure on others present also to work hard.

Future research on behavior setting theory might take a number of directions. One question is whether the relationship between organization size and support for organization activities is best represented by a linear function. For example, there may be a point beyond which increases in membership have little or no effect on members' supportive behaviors. An increase in membership by a given amount may have greater consequences, in terms of member support, for a small organization than for a large one. Research in progress is attempting to assess the impact of a merger of a large and small church upon the behaviors of members from each church.

Another approach would be to test the theory's predictions regarding subjective experiences of members of large and small churches and other organizations. Differences in feelings about participation in activities of large and small schools have been reported by Gump and Friesen (1964b), Wicker (1968), and Willems (1964a, 1967). Research might also focus upon new members of large and small organizations. In small organizations where manpower is needed, new members would be expected to be drawn into activities more quickly, and to have more experiences of involvement in activities than would be the case in large organizations. And additional constructive replications are needed in churches of other denominations and faiths, and in other kinds of social organizations, such as civic clubs.

Finally, some aspects of the theory might be tested experimentally by creating work groups of different size and measuring group-related experiences and behaviors. For example, it might be possible to divide a large college class into discussion groups of various sizes and to assign to each group one or more course-related projects to be completed during the semester. The influence of group size on attendance at group meetings, overall quality of work on the project, members' assumption of responsibility, and their satisfactions could be determined.

REFERENCES

ARGYLE, M. *Religious behaviour.* London: Routledge & Kegan Paul, 1968.

BAIRD, L. L. Big school, small school: A critical examination of the hypothesis. *Journal of Educational Psychology,* 1969, in press.

BARKER, R. G. Ecology and motivation. *Nebraska Symposium on Motivation,* 1960, 8, 1–50.

BARKER, R. G. *Ecological psychology: Concepts and methods for studying the environment of human behavior.* Stanford, Calif.: Stanford University Press, 1968.

BARKER, R. G., & BARKER, L. S. Structural characteristics. In R. G. Barker & P. V. Gump (Eds.), *Big school, small school: High school size and student behavior.* Stanford, Calif.: Stanford University Press, 1964.

BARKER, R. G., BARKER, L. S., & RAGLE, D. D. M. The churches of Midwest, Kansas, and Yoredale, Yorkshire: Their contributions to the environments of the towns. In W. Gore & L. Hodapp (Eds.), *Change in the small community.* New York: Friendship Press, 1967.

BARKER, R. G., & GUMP, P. V. (Eds.) *Big school, small school: High school size and student behavior.* Stanford, Calif.: Stanford University Press, 1964.

BARKER, R. G., & WRIGHT, H. F. *Midwest and its children: The psychological ecology of an American town.* New York: Row, Peterson, 1955.

BRYAN, J. H., & TEST, M. A. Models and helping: Naturalistic studies in aiding behavior. *Journal of Personality and Social Psychology,* 1967, 6, 400–407.

DARLEY, J. M., & LATANÉ, B. Bystander intervention in emergencies: Diffusion of responsibility. *Journal of Personality and Social Psychology,* 1968, 8, 377–383. (a)

DARLEY, J. M., & LATANÉ, B. When will people help in a crisis? *Psychology Today,* 1968, 2(7), 54–57. (b)

DEUTSCH, M. Field theory in social psychology. In G. Lindzey & E. Aronson (Eds.), *The handbook of social psychology.* Vol. 1. *Historical introduction/systematic positions.* (2nd ed.) Reading, Mass.: Addison-Wesley, 1968.

EAST WISCONSIN ANNUAL CONFERENCE OF THE METHODIST CHURCH. *Year book and journal.* Kenosha, Wis.: William V. Stevens, 1967.

GREGORY, W. E. The psychology of religion: Some suggested areas of research to psychology. *Journal of Abnormal and Social Psychology,* 1952, 47, 256–258.

GUMP, P. V., & FRIESEN, W. V. Participation in nonclass settings. In R. G. Barker & P. V. Gump (Eds.), *Big school, small school: High school size and student behavior.* Stanford, Calif.: Stanford University Press, 1964. (a)

GUMP, P. V., & FRIESEN, W. V. Satisfactions derived from nonclass settings. In R. G. Barker & P. V. Gump (Eds.), *Big school, small school: High* school size and student behavior. Stanford, Calif.: Stanford University Press, 1964. (b)

JACKSON, J. Structural characteristics of norms. In I. D. Steiner & M. Fishbein (Eds.), *Current studies in social psychology*. New York: Holt, Rinehart & Winston, 1965.

JACKSON, J. A conceptual and measurement model for norms and roles. *Pacific Sociological Review*, 1966, 9, 35–47.

LATANÉ, B., & RODIN, J. A lady in distress: The effects of friends and strangers on bystander intervention. *Journal of Experimental Social Psychology*, 1969, 5, 189–202.

LYKKEN, D. T. Statistical significance in psychological research. *Psychological Bulletin*, 1968, 70, 151–159.

PORTER, L. W., & LAWLER, E. E. Properties of organization structure in relation to job attitudes and job behavior. *Psychological Bulletin*, 1965, 64, 23–51.

SMART, R. G. Subject selection bias in psychological research. *Canadian Psychologist*, 1966, 7, 115–121.

WEBB, E. J., CAMPBELL, D. T., SCHWARTZ, R. D., & SECHREST, L. *Unobtrusive measures: Nonreactive research in the social sciences*. Chicago: Rand McNally, 1966.

WICKER, A. W. Undermanning, performances, and students' subjective experiences in behavior settings of large and small high schools. *Journal of Personality and Social Psychology*, 1968, 10, 255–261.

WICKER, A. W. Cognitive complexity, school size, and participation in school behavior settings: A test of the frequency of interaction hypothesis. *Journal of Educational Psychology*, 1969, 60, 200–203.

WILLEMS, E. P. Forces toward participation in behavior settings. In R. G. Barker & P. V. Gump (Eds.), *Big school, small school: High school size and student behavior*. Stanford, Calif.: Stanford University Press, 1964. (a)

WILLEMS, E. P. Review of research. In R. G. Barker & P. V. Gump (Eds.), *Big school, small school: High school size and student behavior*. Stanford, Calif.: Stanford University Press, 1964. (b)

WILLEMS, E. P. *Participation in behavior settings in relation to three variables: Size of behavior settings, marginality of persons, and sensitivity to audiences*. (Doctoral dissertation, University of Kansas) Ann Arbor, Mich.: University Microfilms, 1965. No. 66–6060.

WILLEMS, E. P. Sense of obligation to high school activities as related to school size and marginality of student. *Child Development*, 1967, 38, 1247–1260.

Crowding among Hunter-Gatherers: The !Kung Bushmen

Patricia Draper

Abstract. *Highly crowded living conditions exist among the !Kung Bushmen, hunter-gatherers who live on the edges of the Kalahari Desert in Botswana and South-West Africa. The !Kung appear to be crowded by choice, and biological indicators of stress are absent. Data indicate that residential crowding alone does not produce symptoms of pathological stress.*

Recent studies of crowding among nonhuman primates and other mammals suggest that various biological and social pathologies are associated with abnormally increased population. density (1). The effects of density, however, vary among different species; while speculations are increasing in the popular literature about the deleterious effects of crowding on humans (2), in fact, the evidence for the effect of crowding is equivocal. An article by Galle *et al.* (3) reviewed the problem of interpreting the possible significance to man of density effects observed in other mammals and suggest refinements of the concept of density with reference to human (particularly urban) populations. The authors recommended specifying separate components of density (the number of persons per room, the number of rooms per housing unit, the number of housing units per structure, the number of residential structures per acre) instead of relying on an overall measure of population density in terms of numbers of people per unit area. The authors suggested that for certain pathologies the most important components of density are those related to "interpersonal press," such as the number of persons per room and number of housing units per structure. Most investigators agree that the overcrowding in certain areas of cities and among particular ethnic groups contributes to poor public health, although the parameters of density and their individual and multiple relations to pathology are only beginning to be studied (4).

In this report I will present data which show that intense interpersonal press exists among a people whose population density [approximately one person per 10 square miles (5)] is among the lowest in the world—the !Kung Bushmen of Ngamiland, Botswana and northeastern Namibia (South-West Africa). However, in their camp settlements these people experience extreme crowding without any conceivable economic or ecological constraint which might produce it. The !Kung are free of biological indicators thought to be indicative of high stress. For example, blood pressures are low and do not rise with age, and serum cholesterol levels are among the lowest in the world (6). The !Kung are unfazed by the press and are able to maintain a multi-sensory, diffuse contact with each other that is supportive rather than stressful.

The !Kung are well described in the anthropological literature, notably by members of the Marshall family (7) and by members of the Harvard Kala-

Table 1. Occupation density of four !Kung camps.

Date	Place	People in camp (No.)	Camp area (square feet)	Square feet per person
July 1969	≠ To//gana	17	698	42
August 1969	≠ To//gana Fence	28	4419	158
September 1969	≠ To//gana Tsi N!	40	7079	176
October 1969.	≠ To//gana Fence	24	8343	348
				Average 181

hari Project (8). The !Kung are of interest since their way of life preserves an adaptation thought to be characteristic of most of man's evolutionary history. Students of these and other contemporary hunter-gatherers hope that understanding the social organization and economy of living hunters and gatherers can lead to an understanding of our own evolutionary heritage.

The !Kung group which was studied is a population of about 150 people who, in 1968 and 1969, were living on the border between Botswana and South-West Africa, approximately 100 miles north of Ghanzi, Botswana. They lived wholly by hunting and gathering and were not associated with or dependent upon Bantu pastoralists. They lived in kin-based groups averaging 30 to 40 people. The group composition was not stable over time, nor territorial, nor organized by any rigid kinship criterion. Instead, group size and mobility were determined by availability of water, game, and bush food and the wishes of individuals to visit other groups (9).

The !Kung settlement pattern ensures that coresidents are maximally close together. The area of village occupation is small, compact, and densely settled. Table 1 gives information on the size and number of inhabitants of four !Kung camps. The average density of

occupation of these camps (based on diagrams made over a 4-month period) was 188 square feet per person. This compares with 350 square feet per person which was set as the desirable standard by the American Public Health Association (10). Not only are people closely packed in (arbitrarily) limited space, but the organization of the interior space in each settlement increases the exposure of each individual to another. !Kung women build small grass huts, one per family, and locate them at the outer edges of a circular village space. The inner area is carefully denuded of grass, bushes, saplings, or anything which might provide shade or privacy or screen one part of the village from another. The huts themselves do not break up the inner space or create micro-neighborhoods. People do not live in the huts or go into them for rest or privacy; rather the huts are used for dry storage of food, skins, and tools. Each hut, with its own hearth, is a marker signifying the residence of one nuclear family. Typically huts are so close that people sitting at different hearths can hand items back and forth without getting up. Often people sitting around various fires will carry on long discussions without raising their voices above normal conversational levels.

In addition to high per person density per unit area, and the absence of rooms, walls, or other architectural features which limit access by one person to another, !Kung camps are well staffed during the day. One might expect, for example, that camps would be deserted during the day, with people dispersed into the bush in search of game, bush food, and water. In fact, the organization of work and leisure is such that during an average day about 65 percent of the camp residents are at home in the settlement. Children under age 14, adolescents, and old people contribute little or nothing to the work of food collecting. The day-to-day life is not arduous, despite the inhospitable environment and the simple technology with which the !Kung are equipped. Able-bodied adults hunt and gather on an average of about 3 days per week. The !Kung are not unique among hunter-gatherers in their modest work effort; recent studies by students of living hunter-gatherers are correcting an earlier widespread notion of privation among hunter-gatherers (*11*).

The !Kung live in sufficient abundance that they do not require work from children and the nature of adult work is such that children cannot easily be incorporated into it. The scarcity of water is the chief limiting factor. Much of the year there is no standing water, and, for children to work with their parents, additional water would have to be brought from camp for them. Men and women both prefer to leave children at camp in order to travel lighter and work more efficiently. Children are well supervised by the remaining adults at camp—the elderly or the men and women who are not working for the day.

In the matter of adult supervision of children, the !Kung are unlike crowded urban populations, where parents are unable to control the movements, associations, and activities of their children.

Perhaps the single most striking feature of !Kung childhood is the extraordinarily close association between children and adults. Children living in these small band encampments have virtually no place where they can go, such as a public gathering place, or a field where animals are pastured or crops are tended. There is only the camp space; beyond that stretches the Kalahari bush, which from a child's vantage point is vast, undifferentiated, and unsocialized. Children spend most of their time within the circle of huts, although both age and sex influence the extent to which children use the bush near the campsite.

Field research was focused on child life and behavior, but the small size of !Kung living groups meant that most aspects of life and individuals of all ages could be readily observed. The data gathered consisted mainly of timed, randomized, and written observations of the natural behavior of children. Data from spot observations of each subject child included such information as date, time of day, child's identification number, his whereabouts in space (inside or outside the circle of huts), and the number, names, and identification numbers of other people (if any) in his immediate group of interactants. Also noted in the spot observation were such particulars as whether or not other people were nearby (but not in his immediate group of interactants), where his mother and father were at that moment in time, and whether the child was in physical contact with another person at the moment of the spot observation. The observations were carried out at different times during the daylight hours in order to sample evenly throughout the day of each child. As a research tool, the spot observation has many advantages: information can be gath-

228

ered quickly, and observations can be made repeatedly of all the children of a group for many days in succession.

In a series of 165 systematically collected, randomized spot observations of 30 children living in the bush, girls (14 years and under) showed an average score of .77 on being inside the circle of huts. (In this usage, a "score" for each child is the proportion of spot observations during which the given behavior was observed.) Boys of the same age range had an average score of .50 on being inside the circle. One or more adults (for reasons already stated) was always present with the children within the village circle. At other times, children played in the bush adjacent to the camp circle but generally were still within eye or ear contact with adults in camp. As might be expected, older children used the near bush more frequently than young children.

!Kung children spent a minor portion of their time in children-only play groups; typically they were found in informal interactive clusters which included one or more adults. Girls had an average score of .77 on being in face-to-face clusters which included one or more adults. The average score for boys on this measure was .66.

The human press in !Kung camps is clearly extreme. The campsites themselves are tightly packed, and the absence of physical barriers combined with the circular arrangement of inward-facing huts means, effectively, that approximately 30 people are living in a single room. The !Kung apparently like to be close together, even touching. As people sit in camp, resting, talking, and doing chores, they prefer to gather in knots or clumps, leaning against each other, their arms brushing, their crossed legs overlapping. Physical contact reaches its highest expression among children. Girls showed an average of .57 on being in physical contact with at least one other person. The average score for boys was .35.

Refinements of the concept of density may improve our grasp of the relationship between space and the quality of human life. In the !Kung example their are several conditions which may facilitate accommodation to close interpersonal press in daily life. Individuals or families have the culturally acceptable option of moving from one camp to another. Band fission seems to be a time-honored technique which band-level peoples employ to resolve conflict. !Kung bands are in a more or less continuous state of flux, largely in response to changes in food and water supplies, although personal conflict also motivates changes in group membership. In contrast, individuals living in modern urban ghettos probably lack this mobility option. Moving in itself may be expensive, work may not be available elsewhere, the social networks linking friends and relatives who can lend economic support are likely to be severely truncated in comparison with those which link individuals in a small, kin-based society such as the !Kung.

A !Kung family can move and thereby escape social tensions and effect a change of faces. However, the new camp will be very similar in settlement pattern and in density of occupation, and it will be staffed, not with strangers with whom a person can make a new start, but with relatives and acquaintances who are known to the individual through years of intermittent coresidence.

Another condition which may facilitate accommodation to close interpersonal press may derive from the fact that the camp settlement, although densely packed, is well separated from others like it. In the area in which this study was carried out, groups with an average size of 30 to 40 people were typically separated by 15 or more miles. This uninhabited area minimized both visiting and chance encounter with strangers. It is possible that stranger density is an important component of modern urban stress. !Kung rarely encounter strangers, and when such meetings do occur, the parties can readily establish a basis for cooperation by establishing a genealogical connection.

Whatever may be the ameliorating conditions, it is clear that the !Kung are crowded, yet the absence of presumably stress-related diseases suggests that residential crowding is not necessarily related to social pathology.

References and Notes

1. J. Calhoun. *Sci. Amer.* **206**, 139 (Feb. 1962); V. Wynne-Edwards, *Animal Dispersion in Relation to Social Behavior* (Oliver & Boyd, London, 1962); R. Snyder, in *Progress in Physiological Psychology*, E. Stellar and J. Sprague, Eds. (Academic Press, New York, 1968), pp. 119-160.
2. R. Ardrey, *African Genesis* (Atheneum, New York, 1961); *The Territorial Imperative* (Atheneum, New York, 1966); D. Morris, *The Naked Ape* (McGraw-Hill, New York, 1967).
3. O. R. Galle, W. R. Gove, J. M. McPherson, *Science* **176**, 23 (1972).
4. R. E. Mitchell, *Amer. Soc. Rev.* **36**, 18 (1971).
5. Approximate conversion factors are: 1 square mile = 2.590 square kilometers; 1 mile = 1.609 kilometers; 1 square foot = 0.093 square meter.
6. A. S. Truswell and J. D. L. Hansen, *S. Afr. Med. J.* **42**, 1338 (1968); *Lancet* 1968-II, 684 (1968); B. M. Kennelly *et al.*, *S. Afr. Med. J.*, in press.
7. J. Marshall, thesis, Harvard University (1957); *Natur. Hist.* **67**, 291 (1958); *ibid.*, p. 376; L. Marshall, *Africa* **29**, 335 (1959); *ibid.* **27**, 1 (1957); *ibid.* **30**, 325 (1960); *ibid.* **31**, 231 (1961); *ibid.* **32**, 221 (1962); E. M. Thomas, *The Harmless People* (Knopf, New York, 1959).
8. R. B. Lee, thesis, University of California (1965); in *Man the Hunter*, R. B. Lee and I. DeVore, Eds. (Aldine, Chicago, 1968), pp. 30-48; *Natur. Hist.* **28**, 14 (1969); *ibid.*, p. 60; in *Ecological Essays*, D. Damas, Ed. (National Museum of Canada, Ottawa, 1969), pp. 73-94; H. Harpending and J. Yellen, *World Archaeology*, in press; P. Draper Harpending, thesis, Harvard University (1972).
9. R. B. Lee, in preparation.
10. American Public Health Association, Committee on Hygiene of Housing, *Planning the Home for Occupancy* (Public Administration Service, Chicago, 1950).
11. R. B. Lee, in *Man the Hunter*, R. B. Lee and I. DeVore, Eds. (Aldine, Chicago, 1968); M. Sahlins, in *ibid.*, pp. 85-89; J. Woodburn, in *ibid.*, pp. 49-55.
12. This work was supported by NIH grant MH 13611 to Irven DeVore and Richard B. Lee. Fieldwork was done in 1968 and 1969 for 22 months.

PERSONAL SPACE

Body-Buffer Zone in Violent Prisoners

BY AUGUSTUS F. KINZEL, M.D.

Comparative measurement of the body-buffer zones of eight violent and six nonviolent prisoners showed the zones of the violent group to be almost four times larger. In the violent group the rear zones were larger than the front zones; in the nonviolent group the front zones were larger. The large zones of the violent group may reflect a pathological body image state. The author discusses potential application of body-buffer zone measurements in the detection, treatment, and prognosis of individuals predisposed to violent behavior.

ARE VIOLENT INDIVIDUALS provoked simply by physical closeness to others? Daily clinical observations of prisoners at the U. S. Medical Center for Federal Prisoners suggested that physical proximity to another inmate was at least as powerful a trigger of violence as were threats, thefts, or other more overt provocations. The violent episodes were usually abrupt and not premeditated. Violent inmates spoke of their victims as "messing with me" or "getting up in my face" when they were actually at conversational distances. Many preferred to keep themselves at great distances during weekly standing therapeutic interviews. Often the physical closeness of "horseplaying" was only briefly tolerated before violence erupted. Many spoke of homosexual provocations by their victims when none had actually occurred. This hypersensitivity to physical closeness appeared quite similar to what ethologists refer to as reaction distance and what psychiatrists refer to as body image disturbance.

Ardrey(1) points out that many animals normally maintain invariable interspecies distances. Hediger(2) has quantified reaction distances in many species. Violation of these distances results in sham or actual violence. Hall(3) has delineated intimate, personal, social, and public distances in different cultures. Horowitz, Duff, and Stratton have measured the closest distances tolerated by schizophrenic and nonschizophrenic subjects. They identified the "body-buffer zone" as the area around a person within which anxiety is produced if another enters. They define it as ". . . an area surrounding each individual which represents the boundaries to what is felt as 'inner' versus what is felt as 'outer' "(4).

This concept showed promise in elucidating the apparent hypersensitivity to physical closeness in violent prisoners. Accordingly, a preliminary experiment was undertaken to try to answer the following questions:

1. Do violent prisoners have larger body-buffer zones than nonviolent prisoners?

2. Do the zones of violent prisoners have a different shape from those of nonviolent prisoners?

3. Do the size and shape of the zones change in either group over repeated determinations?

Method

Inmates were screened for histories of violent behavior by means of a questionnaire, psychiatric interview, and criminal record. Violence, for the purposes of this study, was defined as a physical assault on another person producing tissue injury. Of 15 inmates reported for assault or fighting in prison in 1967, eight were chosen who had life histories of the most frequent violent behavior. Of 14 inmates classified as

Read at the 125th anniversary meeting of the American Psychiatric Association, Miami Beach, Fla., May 5-9, 1969.

Dr. Kinzel currently is attending psychiatrist, New York State Psychiatric Institute, 722 West 168th St., New York, N. Y. 10032. At the time this paper was written, he was a career teacher, department of psychiatry, College of Physicians and Surgeons, Columbia University; he is now instructor in psychiatry.

The author wishes to thank J. Fleiss and J. Tanur of Biometrics Research, New York State Department of Mental Hygiene, for their assistance in the statistical analysis of the data.

THE AMERICAN JOURNAL OF PSYCHIATRY, Vol. 127, 1970, pp. 59-64. Copyright 1970, the American Psychiatric Association.

requiring minimum security, six were selected who gave histories of the least frequent violent behavior.

Factors found most frequently in the violent group and least frequently in the nonviolent group were: history of repeated violent behavior with little provocation, frequent necessity for forcible restraint, use of weapons in fights, carrying weapons for prolonged periods for protection, history of violence between parents, serious self-perpetrated accidents, bisexual and hypersexual behavior, hypersensitivity to name-calling, and history of violence to domestic animals. A general profile of the violent and nonviolent experimental groups is given in table 1.

Inmates who were acutely psychotic or were unable to participate for the duration of the experiment were excluded. Each inmate was told that the purpose of the experiment was to see if people differed in how close they would let another come before feeling uncomfortable. Participation was voluntary, and each subject was told that nothing could be offered in return for his cooperation.

Procedure

Following the screening interview, the subject (S) was taken by the experimenter (E) into a bare 20 foot by 20 foot room and was told to stand in the center. He was instructed to say "Stop" when he felt E had approached "too close." Starting eight feet in front of S, E inquired, "Here?", waited two to three seconds for a response, took a step toward S, repeated the inquiry, and proceeded in like fashion until S indicated he should stop. At this point the distance between E's toes and the center of the room was recorded. E then made similar approaches from seven more directions around S. S was first instructed not to look at E and to respond only to his voice when E made the rear approaches. E then made a second series of rear approaches, instructing S to look at him without turning his trunk. Because there was no consistent difference in either group in the distances tolerated in the looking and not-looking situations, only the data from the looking responses were used.

The area within the eight closest distances

TABLE 1
Demography of Experimental Groups

FACTOR	VIOLENT	NONVIOLENT
Total Subjects	8	6
Age	28	34
Height (inches)	70	71
Weight (pounds)	167	153
IQ	91	114
Race		
White	4	4
Negro	4	2
Offense		
Second-degree murder	1	0
Assault with dangerous weapon	1	0
Threatening U. S. President		
(by mail)	0	1
Bank robbery	3	1
Car theft (interstate)	3	2
Illegal dispensing of narcotics	0	1
Passing false securities (interstate)	0	1
Sentence (years)	9	5.5
Psychiatric diagnosis		
Schizophrenia (in remission)	3	2
Sociopathic personality	4	1
Passive-aggressive personality	1	3

tolerated by S was taken as his body-buffer zone. A typical zone plot is illustrated in figure 1. The area of each zone was calculated by summing the areas of the eight triangles formed by the radial distances measured. The procedure was repeated on each S, at approximately weekly intervals, for 12 weeks. After each determination, S was asked to verbalize what he felt when he said "Stop."

FIGURE 1
Plot of Zone

○━━━○ Subject looking
○━━━○ Subject not looking

Results

1. *Difference in Size of Zone*

The body-buffer zones were almost all larger in the violent group. Figure 2 repre-

233

sents the area of each zone for each subject over 12 weeks. Figure 3 represents a composite comparison of the average zone (mean of the individual means) for each group. The average zone area for the vio-

FIGURE 2
Measured Zones

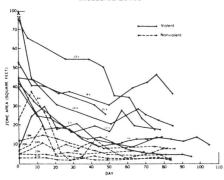

FIGURE 2
Measured Zones

lent group was 29.3 square feet. The average zone area for the nonviolent group was 7.0 square feet. The difference between groups was 22.3 square feet [± 17.2 square feet[1] (ϵ = .73)[2]]. The ratio of violent to

nonviolent zones was 3.8,[3] based on eight consecutive measurements for each subject.

2. Difference in Shape of Zone

The rear zones were larger than the front zones in the violent group. By contrast, there was a tendency for the front zones to be larger than the rear zones in the nonviolent group (with one exception). There was a significant difference in front-rear proportions between the two groups. Figure 4 illustrates these different front-rear proportions. Table 2 shows the magnitude of these differences in zone shape.

3. Change in Size and Shape of Zone Over Repeated Determinations

The area of the zones tended to decrease in both groups over 12 weeks. Figure 5 shows that the decrease was initially rapid and then leveled off in the violent group and was irregular in the nonviolent group. Comparison of the average zones for weeks 0, 1, and 2 with those of weeks 10, 11, and 12 revealed a decrease in area of approximately 50 percent in both groups by the end of the experiment.

The shape of the violent zones changed on repeated determinations. In the violent group the size of the rear zone relative to the front zone diminished abruptly in the first three weeks. There was no such con-

FIGURE 3
Average Body-Buffer Zones

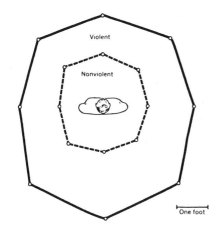

FIGURE 4
Average Front Minus Rear Zones

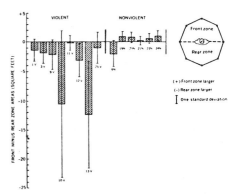

---

[1] 99 percent confidence interval.
[2] Epsilon is a measure of the degree of association between group membership (violent or nonviolent) and the dependent variable (zone area); it is interpretable as a correlation coefficient(5).

[3] 95 percent confidence that violent zones were at least twice as large as nonviolent zones.

TABLE 2
Comparison of Zone Shape

ZONE	AREA
1. Front-rear (violent)	−4.9 sq. ft.
	p < .05 (one-tailed t-test)
2. Front-rear (nonviolent)	+0.2 sq. ft.
	p not significant from
	zero (one-tailed t-test)
3. Front-rear (violent) minus front-rear (nonviolent)	+5.0 sq. ft.
	p < .025 (one-tailed t-test)

sistent change in shape in the nonviolent group. Figure 6 illustrates these trends.

Comments

The behavior and comments of the subjects after the procedures supported the

FIGURE 5
Weekly Comparison of Violent and Nonviolent Zones

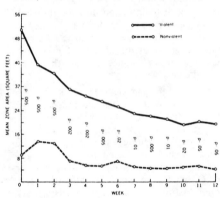

clinical observation that violent individuals tend to perceive nonthreatening intrusion as attack. Violent subjects frequently reported misperceiving the experimenter as "looming" or "rushing" at the subjects. Several mentioned that this was very much like the sensation they had had prior to assaults. In view of the experimental design, which permitted a violent subject to "fake good" if he wished to be seen as nonviolent and not sensitive to physical closeness, the frequency of these comments was surprising.

One subject (12-V) repeatedly said nothing but moved from the center of the room with clenched fists each time he felt the ex-

perimenter was too close. Two subjects (10-V, 12-V) could not tolerate the experimenter behind them at any distance without looking at him for the first three trials. Another subject (11-V) said, "If I didn't know you I might be ready for anything." By contrast, the nonviolent group let the experimenter approach closer than ordinary conversational distances and did not report the "looming" or "rushing" sensations.

FIGURE 6
Weekly Comparison of Front Minus Rear Zones

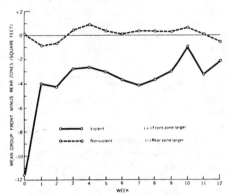

The violent group appeared to react differently from the nonviolent group when approached from the rear. Not only were they less able to tolerate closeness in the rear than in the front, but many also experienced tingling or goose pimples across their shoulders and backs. Their hypersensitivity to approach from the rear, combined with their tendency to perceive passive intrusion as homosexual provocation, their frequent history of homosexual contact and hypersexuality, their denial of being homosexual, and their strong stated aversion to the feminine homosexual role, reported elsewhere(6), were strongly suggestive of a high level of homosexual anxiety. By contrast, the nonviolent group showed a tendency toward greater sensitivity to approach from the front than from the rear. This suggested that they perceived the rear surface of their bodies as a protective barrier, whereas the violent group perceived it as a vulnerable body area.

One subject (12-V) showed a relative increase in his rear zone despite a decreasing front zone and total zone between the third and eighth trials. After the third trial he reported the following dream: "I dreamed that animals and people were coming up close to me, and I wasn't afraid. Then I saw a snake and couldn't see if it was moving. I got very scared."

Up to the eighth trial he appeared increasingly anxious. After the eighth trial he related that he had been upset over repeated homosexual propositioning by another inmate. After the ninth trial he said, "I got out of it," and his previously increasing rear zone abruptly decreased 4.3 square feet. This man may have been experiencing a homosexual panic during the experiment. It is possible that the large rear zone measurements were actually reflecting the degree of his homosexual anxiety all along. If so, this would appear to be the first time that a difference between homosexual and signal anxiety has been concretely demonstrated.

The decrease in the size of the zones over 12 weeks in both groups suggests adaptation to the procedure, but several of the violent subjects spoke of the experiment as "Doc's treatment" and indicated an improved sense of well-being and less predisposition to violence at the end of the experiment. The experimenter did not consciously intend to give treatment.

Despite the decrease in the size of the zones, the violent group maintained larger zones even at 12 weeks. They maintained these larger zones despite the fact that the intruder had clearly come to be perceived more as friend than foe. This finding suggests that many repeatedly violent individuals have a permanent abnormality of body image. They behave as if their bodies are extended farther into the space around them. Thus to intrude on their personal space is to intrude on their bodies. It is unclear whether this is due to a breakdown in their perception of their skin barrier, such that the sense of "inner" and "outer" is poorly delineated, or whether they erect a kind of body shell around themselves as a primitive defense against touching.

Unfortunately, little information was available regarding the earlier development of the violent subjects. Most spoke as if their sensitivity to closeness had been lifelong,

but there was no way of checking how much and what kind of constitutional or environmental factors may have produced their large body-buffer zones. Further research involving zone measurements on children with long-term follow-up will be necessary before any reasonable inferences can be made regarding such influences.

The data reported were subject to the limitations of the experimental design. The samples were small, the sampling and procedures were done by the same person (the author), and the zone thresholds were measured by subjective response only. Unfortunately, a more rigorous design was not possible due to time and personnel limitations. The data do suggest, however, that one might be able to distinguish violent from nonviolent individuals by body-buffer zone measurements alone. A predictive study using larger samples, double-blind technique, and some physiological means of measuring the response to intrusion on zone threshold is now being planned in order to further define the correlation between large zones and violence. It is possible that large rear zones may have more diagnostic value than large overall zones.

Body-buffer zone measurements may also be of value in the treatment and prognosis of individuals showing a predisposition to violent behavior. Periodic zone measurements might document the effect of psychotropic medications, need for incarceration, and improvement. Such information is urgently needed by courts, staffs of correctional institutions, and psychiatrists working with violent individuals, who now have to make such distinctions on impressionistic bases. It is probable that many people could be freed or diverted from incarceration if a more definitive measure of violent potential were available.

This study emphasizes the view that violent behavior may be one sign of a distinct psychopathological complex that includes, among other factors, a marked disturbance in personal space. It is hoped that further studies based on this view will help determine why only a few individuals behave violently, when so many more have been subjected to the same life frustrations.

236

REFERENCES

1. Ardrey R: The Territorial Imperative. New York, Dell Publishing Co, 1966
2. Hediger H: Studies of Psychology and Behavior of Captive Animals in Zoos and Circuses. New York, Criterion Books, 1955
3. Hall ET: The Hidden Dimension. New York, Doubleday & Co, 1966
4. Horowitz MJ, Duff D, Stratton L: The body buffer zone: an exploration of personal space. Arch Gen Psychiat 11: 651-656, 1964
5. Spitzer R, Cohen J: Common errors in quantitative psychiatric research. Int J Psychiat 6:109-118, 1968
6. Kinzel AF: Violent behavior in prisons, read at a divisional meeting of the American Psychiatric Association, Chicago, Ill, November 15-17, 1968

SEATING ARRANGEMENTS AND STATUS [1]

DALE F. LOTT AND ROBERT SOMMER

3 questionnaire and 1 experimental study were designed to explore the connection between location and status. The question in each case was how the S would locate himself vis-à-vis a person of higher, lower, or equal status. The first 2 studies employing paper-and-pencil diagrams of rectangular tables showed a clear association of the head position with the higher status figure. The 3rd questionnaire study using square tables where all positions were equal suggested that the people sat further from *both* high- and low-status individuals than they did from their peers. The 4th study involved an experimental test of these findings, in which an S was asked to go into a room and sit at a table containing a surrogate of a high-, low- or equal-status individual. The results showed that Ss sat further from higher- and lower-status individuals than they did from peers.

Social orders in the animal kingdom are most frequently constructed on the basis of territoriality and dominance behavior. In the first instance, each animal knows where he belongs spatially, and in the second, socially. Experiments by Shoemaker (1939) and Davis (1959) suggest that territoriality and dominance behavior are two end points of a single continuum. Territoriality represents a dominance order where each individual is at the apex. When animals are crowded, such as chickens in a coop, individual territories will be difficult to mark out and maintain, as well as being relatively nonfunctional since separate nesting areas are provided, and a dominance order will emerge. Both territoriality and dominance behavior serve to limit aggression, since an individual either refrains from going where he is likely to become involved in disputes or knows who is above him and below him, and is able to engage in ritualized dominance and subordination behavior.

Since there exists an intimate connection between the functions served by social orders and spatial orders, we should expect to find spatial correlates of status levels and, conversely, social correlates of spatial positions. The first hypothesis raises the question of whether people of different status would choose different locations with varying amounts of space. In small-group work, rank is associated with differential space usage as indicated by the tendency of leaders to gravitate to the head position at tables, to

sit at the front of the room, for people to face the leader, etc. (Hall, 1959; Sommer, 1961; Strodtbeck & Hook, 1961).

The obverse question, the way an individual's location influences status, has been the subject of less research, perhaps because experimentation requires conditions that are not often found in nature. Typically, status and location are confounded in that prestigious individuals occupy the best places. An exception to this can occur in artificial communities or total institutions when space usage is decided on the basis of arbitrary or random criteria. Though spatial segregation prevails in isolated service communities in the far north and in army towns, it is still possible to find instances where several status levels share space. Madge and Madge (1965), who studied housing for married noncommissioned officers in several British army stations, found that a difference of more than one step in rank decreased contact between neighbors.

This article presents several studies of the relation between status and seating arrangements.

METHOD

Before beginning the study the authors needed some indication of status levels for the subjects (college students) they would be using. To this end, 103 students in an upper-division psychology class, which draws students from all departments, were given the following instructions:

Please draw your subjective dominance hierarchy here on campus. Draw diagrams showing who is above you, who is below you, and who is on the same level with you.

[1] This study was supported in part by a grant from the United States Office of Education (6-1121). The authors are grateful to Marina Estabrook for her assistance.

JOURNAL OF PERSONALITY AND SOCIAL PSYCHOLOGY, 1967, Vol. 7, No. 1, pp. 90-95.

The question was deliberately vague and all queries from the students were answered, "Just do the best you can, draw a dominance hierarchy as you see it." Ten papers had to be discarded because no hierarchy could be drawn or the student's diagram was undecipherable. Usable dominance hierarchies were obtained from 93 students, 64 females and 29 males. Many girls put their boyfriends or husbands above them on the hierarchy, but no male ever put a girlfriend or wife above him. Janitors and maintenance employees on campus were omitted from the diagrams. Rather than their being below the students as one might have supposed, they are non-persons. The only group that a sizable number of students placed below themselves were lower classmen, particularly females, and students doing poorly in school. The only group that was consistently placed above the students were professors. The chancellor, regents, and dean of students were always above the students when they were included, but only a minority of diagrams actually contained these categories. On the basis of these hierarchies, the authors decided to use as the higher status figure "a professor," and as the lowest of the low, "a freshman who is doing poorly in school." As someone of equal status they used the category "another student in your class." [2]

The subjects were 813 students in psychology and physical education classes at the University of California at Davis. No subject was used in more than a single procedure. The first three studies used paper-and-pencil diagrams in which a subject indicated where he would sit vis-à-vis another person whose status and gender were indicated in the instructions. All the paper-and-pencil diagrams involved a table and chairs in the student-union cafeteria between classes, which was actually used for studying and conversation by students, administrative employees, and faculty between meals.

Questionnaire Form A

Two hundred and twenty-four students were asked where they would sit if they were to meet another person at the student cafeteria between classes. There were six different versions of the questionnaire, consisting of three status levels of male and female stimulus persons. The status levels were derived from the dominance study mentioned previously. Some respondents were to meet "Professor" Henry or Susan Smith, others were to meet fellow students named "Henry" or "Susan Smith," while others met "a freshman who wasn't doing well in school" named Henry or Susan Smith. To insure that the freshman was actually beneath the respondent, the authors drew their subjects from upper-division

[2] A similar status differentiation was used by Brehm and Cole (1966), who had students fill out questionnaires for either "an undergraduate student in sociology who is doing a class project" or "Professor Terrel who had just received a large grant from the National Science Foundation to support his research."

TABLE 1
SEAT CHOSEN BY SUBJECT WHO ARRIVES FIRST

Other person's status	No. Ss placing themselves at:		
	Head	End	Center
High	10	54	11
Equal	5	52	20
Low	8	50	14
Total	23	156	45

classes. The six versions of the questionnaire were passed out randomly during the class session, so that a person filled out one form and no more. This random distribution meant one could not control the exact number of males or females who received each version. The questionnaire showed a rectangular table with one chair at the head and one at the foot of the table, and three chairs at each side, with the following instructions:

You are to meet ——————— at the student cafeteria at 10:00 a.m. (between meals and most of the tables are empty). You arrive there first. Where at the table would you sit? Please indicate the chair you'd probably occupy by placing an A in the appropriate circle in the table diagram below.

Now where do you think ——————— would sit when (he) (she) arrived. Place a B in the circle to indicate the chair (he'd) (she'd) occupy.

RESULTS

The first question is where the respondent sat while waiting for the other person to arrive. Table 1 shows that two-thirds of the respondents placed themselves in one of the end chairs.[3] This trend obtained regardless of the status level or sex of the other person or sex of the respondent. This preference is interesting in its own right. In a later survey the subjects were asked why they chose each chair, and the major reasons given were that this choice gave the next person at the table a wide choice of seats and permitted easy access and egress.

Table 2 shows that the seat chosen for the second person varied with the status of the other person ($x^2 = 13.77$, $df = 4$, $p < .01$). Professors Henry and Susan Smith were placed at

[3] For the description of the data the chairs are designated as follows: the two chairs at the head and foot of the table are called head chairs. Of the three chairs placed along each side of the table the center one is called the center chair and the remaining two chairs on each side are called end chairs. Thus, of the eight chairs around each table there are two head chairs, two center chairs and four end chairs.

TABLE 2

SEAT CHOSEN BY OTHER PERSON WITH SUBJECT
ALREADY SEATED

Other perons's status	No. Ss placing other person at:		
	Head	End	Center
High	37	26	12
Equal	20	35	22
Low	19	38	15
Total	76	99	49

TABLE 4

SEAT CHOSEN BY OTHER PERSON WHO ARRIVES FIRST

Other person's status	No. Ss placing the other person at:		
	Head	End	Center
High	23	55	14
Equal	4	67	16
Low	10	63	16
Total	37	185	46

the head position, a finding which is in line with previous observational, questionnaire, and experimental studies of leadership ecology in this culture (Sommer, 1961; Strodtbeck & Hook, 1961).

Table 3 shows that the status relationship between the subject and the stimulus person has a significant effect on their arrangement ($x^2 = 18.89$, $df = 4$, $p < .001$). With a high-status person, the corner arrangement was most popular with very little use of side-by-side seating. With equal- or low-status stimulus persons, there was no single preferred arrangement. The predominance of corner seating with high-status persons can be explained by the more frequent use of the head chair by the authority figure. When one person sits in a head chair, the only close arrangement is corner to corner. There are certain other trends that appear with close inspection of the data. Approximately twice as many females as males sat side by side, and this is more frequent vis-à-vis a low-status than a high-status person.

Questionnaire Form B

The same situation as before was described to the respondent, except that the person he was to meet arrived at the table first. The subject was asked where the other person would sit and then where he would sit himself when he arrived

later. The six versions of the questionnaire (Three Status Levels × Sex) were distributed to 139 males and 131 females in various psychology and physical education classes.

Table 4 shows where the other person sat when he arrived at the table before the respondent. There was a strong tendency to place all other persons at an end chair, and this tendency was significantly greater ($x^2 = 14.11$, $df = 4$, $p < .01$), for a high-status *male* authority figure, Professor Henry Smith, than for the other persons.

Table 5 shows where the subject sat when he arrived at the table later. Slightly more than half the subjects chose an end chair. There was a linear relationship ($p < .01$) between status and use of the head chair. More than twice as many respondents chose the head chair vis-à-vis the flunking freshman than chose it vis-à-vis a professor. It is also interesting that 37 subjects chose the head chair for themselves vis-à-vis Professor Susan Smith while half that number chose it vis-à-vis Professor Henry Smith.

Table 6 shows that most of the pairs sat across from one another or corner to corner, a finding consistent with actual observations of conversing groups in situations like those described (Sommer, 1965). The figures deviate significantly from chance ($x^2 = 13.0$, $df = 6$, $p < .05$) due mainly to the greater use of side seating between peers. There is an interesting

TABLE 3

ARRANGEMENT OF PAIR WHEN SUBJECT ARRIVED FIRST

Other person's status	No. pairs placed			
	Corner to corner	Side by side	Across	Distant
High	44	5	22	4
Equal	25	21	30	1
Low	27	20	24	1
Total	96	46	76	6

TABLE 5

SEAT CHOSEN BY SUBJECT WITH OTHER
PERSON ALREADY SEATED

Other person's status	No. Ss placing themselves at:		
	Head	End	Center
High	12	64	16
Equal	19	41	27
Low	25	44	20
Total	56	149	63

240

| TABLE 6 |
| ARRANGEMENT OF PAIR WHEN OTHER PERSON ARRIVED FIRST |

Other person's status	No. pairs placed			
	Corner to corner	Side by side	Across	Distant
High	29	5	48	10
Equal	23	21	40	4
Low	30	14	36	10
Total	82	40	124	24

| TABLE 7 |
| ARRANGEMENT OF PAIR AT SQUARE TABLE |

Other person's status	No. pairs placed	
	Corner to corner	Opposite
High	39	61
Equal	60	40
Low	32	64
Total	131	165

trend for distant arrangements to be used more frequently with higher or lower status persons than with peers.

Finally, one can compare the results from Questionnaires A and B by asking if it made a difference which person arrived at the table first, the respondent or the stimulus person. The answer is decidedly affirmative, as can be seen in a comparison of Tables 3 and 6. When the respondent arrived first, he was most likely to end up in a corner-to-corner arrangement. This was produced by his selecting an end chair and the other person sitting in the head chair, particularly if he were of higher status. On the other hand, when the other person arrived first, there was greatest likelihood that the pair would sit opposite one another. This was produced by the other person overwhelmingly being placed in an end chair, and the respondent selecting an end chair himself directly opposite the other person.

Questionnaire Form C

The previous results make it apparent that the identification of the head position with authority has confused the status-distance relationship. One cannot clearly speak of trends in *relational space* when certain *fixed spaces* are associated with particular status levels. For this reason, a third study was undertaken involving a diagram of a small square table with one chair to a side. It does not matter where the other person is placed, since all chairs are functionally equivalent, and the second person can sit either corner to corner or directly opposite the first. A questionnaire containing the diagram of a small square table surrounded by four chairs was administered to 296 students in several psychology and physical education classes. The same three status levels (professor, classmate, freshman doing poorly in school), along with the sex of the respondent and stimulus-person, provided a 12-cell matrix.

Table 7 shows that students chose to sit opposite the flunking freshman and the professor, but corner to corner with their classmates. Assuming that the corner arrangement is psychologically closer than the across arrangement (Felipe, 1966; Sommer, 1965), the students put more distance between themselves and those above or below them than between themselves and their peers. The absence of a head position at the small square tables yields results that suggest a simpler model of social and physical distance than the authors had anticipated. In this situation, social distance per se results in physical distance, and it does not seem to matter whether the distance is above or below the respondent's own status. A further analysis of the 12-cell matrix showed that there was more likelihood of corner seating if the other person were female than if he were male, but this was significant at only the .10 level.

Experimental Study

At this point it was felt that a change from a questionnaire to an experimental approach was warranted. The authors are in agreement with Webb, Campbell, Schwartz, and Sechrist (1966) in that the use of several complementary methods is superior to reliance on a single approach. They therefore attempted to develop an experimental analogue to the questionnaire situation of two individuals of varying status seated at a table.

All sessions were held in a small conference room in a university building, which contained a rectangular table with three chairs at each long side and one chair at each end. Instead of a live person of a particular status the authors used a surrogate in the form of a lady's sweater placed around a chair in front of a notebook placed on the table.[4] Pilot work has revealed that the person's location with respect to the door was quite significant, since with certain locations there was very little variability in where the subjects sat. The room was rectangular, large enough to hold the table and

[4] A pilot study by Lee Mohr in the library showed that a jacket placed over a chair protected the seat even under conditions of high room density.

241

TABLE 8

ARRANGEMENT VIS-À-VIS STIMULUS PERSON
IN EXPERIMENT

Other person's status	No. Ss sitting			
	Corner to corner	Side by side	Across	Distant
High	1	1	5	3
Equal	2	7	2	2
Low	2	2	4	0

chairs comfortably, but with little space to spare. The only door was in one of the shorter walls, near a corner. The sweater was on the end chair furthest from the door. The subjects, who were all female undergraduate students, were ushered to the door of the room by a female experimenter and told that they would be interviewed by ——————, and that they should go in the room and sit down since —————— would be along shortly. Although nothing was said on this point directly, the sweater and the notebook were intended to indicate the chair that —————— would occupy. Subsequent interviewing revealed that the subjects accepted the sweater and notebook as indicating where the other person would sit when she returned. Depending on the status condition involved in the experimental plan, the other person was either "Professor Susan Davidson," "Susan Davidson, a freshman in introductory psychology who didn't do well on the last exam and is doing this as a remedial project," or "Susan Davidson, a student from your psychology class."

RESULTS

Table 8 shows how the subjects sat vis-à-vis the high-, low-, and equal-status persons. The results parallel those from the questionnaire studies, where social distance per se is related to physical distance, and it is of less import whether the distance is up or down than that the distance exists at all.[5]

DISCUSSION

These results indicate that there is a connection between status and location which is determined both by fixed and relational aspects of the environment, the identification of certain table positions with status levels, as well as the loca-

[5] The fact that the subjects were to be interviewed by the other person probably accounts for the high frequency of distant arrangements in Table 8. A pilot study in which a subject was asked to enter a room and "converse" with a classmate showed almost no distant seating. However, the authors felt that a task set of "conversation" would be highly artificial when the other person was a professor.

tion of another person already seated. The symbolic significance of the head position at a rectangular table confounds any attempt to relate status to physical distance. For this, one must turn to the undifferentiated square tables where the sides have equal symbolic significance. Here, as in the experimental study, we find that peers are arranged closer together than individuals of disparate status. Although this relationship comes out clearly in the data, the authors feel that a more detailed analysis, using angle of orientation, eye contact, and distance, would disclose that there is a difference in how one sits vis-à-vis a high- and a low-status individual.

A major goal of the study had been to learn the connection between eye contact, dominance, and spatial arrangement. The authors hoped to determine if the relationship between eye contact and dominance-subordination behavior would also exist in table positions. They imagined that people would avoid sitting opposite a dominant individual, but might seek direct eye contact with a subordinate individual. During the course of the study it became apparent that in studying spatial arrangements around tables, the authors were not dealing directly with eye contact. For one thing, the special significance of table positions introduces a variable irrelevant to the eye-contact hypothesis. It may be that leaders are placed at the head positions because they have visual access to the whole group (and vice versa), but this identification of the head chair with authority is now so much a matter of custom and tradition that the quest for direct eye contact or avoidance of eye contact does not seem of great relevance. At the square tables, physical distance is confounded with angle of orientation. Corner seating not only brings the participants closer than opposite seating, but has a smaller angle of visual regard. Regretfully, the authors came to the conclusion that to study eye contact between individuals one had to approach the matter directly, that is, actually measuring the amount of eye contact following the methods used by Exline (1963) and Argyle and Dean (1965), rather than studying it indirectly using seating position or body orientation.

REFERENCES

ARGYLE, M., & DEAN, J. Eye-contact, distance, and affiliation. *Sociometry*, 1965, 28, 289–304.
BREHM, J. W., & COLE, A. H. Effect of a favor which reduces freedom. *Journal of Personality and Social Psychology*, 1966, 3, 420–426.
DAVIS, D. E. Territorial rank in starlings. *Animal Behaviour*, 1959, 7, 214–221.

EXLINE, R. V. Explorations in the process of person perception. *Journal of Personality*, 1963, 31, 1–20.

FELIPE, N. Interpersonal distance and small group interaction. *Cornell Journal of Social Relations*, 1966, 1, 59–64.

HALL, E. T. *The silent language.* Garden City, N. Y.: Doubleday, 1959.

MADGE, J., & MADGE, J. *Survey of new army married quarters.* London: Ministry of Public Buildings & Works, 1965.

SHOEMAKER, H. Social hierarchy in flocks of the canary. *The Auk*, 1939, 56, 381–406.

SOMMER, R. Leadership and group geography. *Sociometry*, 1961, 24, 99–110.

SOMMER, R. Further studies of small group ecology. *Sociometry*, 1965, 28, 337–348.

STRODTBECK, F. L., & HOOK, L. H. The social dimensions of a twelve-man jury table. *Sociometry*, 1961, 24, 397–415.

WEBB, E. J., CAMPBELL, D. T., SCHWARTZ, R. D., & SECHRIST, L. *Unobtrusive measures: nonreactive research in the social sciences.* Chicago: Rand McNally, 1966.

SHAPE-OF-THE-TABLE NEGOTIATIONS AT THE PARIS PEACE TALKS ON VIETNAM

Allen H. Kitchens, Department of State

In a series of talks held periodically in Paris between May and October 1968, U.S. and North Vietnamese representatives agreed that a meeting should be convened in the same city to discuss a peaceful settlement in Vietnam. During the May-October talks the U.S. negotiators made clear that the holding of such a meeting would not be possible unless South Vietnam participated as a separate delegation, forming with the United States one side in the meeting. North Vietnam accepted this proposal and indicated that the National Liberation Front would also be included in the sessions. North Vietnam viewed the forthcoming talks not as two-sided, however, but as four-sided, to be attended by four independent delegations.

These divergent concepts complicated subsequent negotiations on procedural arrangements for the meeting, especially with regard to the seating plan and the shape of the table. The United States and South Vietnam viewed the NLF as a creation of North Vietnam and wanted to avoid a seating arrangement which would implicitly recognize the NLF as an independent military and political force and as one of the parties to the talks. On the other hand, North Vietnam and the NLF argued that the Saigon Government was a puppet of the United States, but they were willing to meet with delegates from South Vietnam so long as the NLF had full delegate status.

The United States initially proposed two long rectangular tables facing each other, leaving each side to organize itself as it wished. The North Vietnamese countered by proposing several alternatives: a single four-sided conference table; four separate tables arranged in a square pattern; four separate tables arranged in either a circular or diamond pattern; or one round table with the delegations seated in such a manner that there would be visible, distant, and equal spaces between the four delegations. Because of the differing two-side/four-side concepts, none of these proposals were acceptable to both sides.

The United States made further proposals designed to define clearly the two sides: two separate arcs of an oval; two separate semi-circles facing each other; or two separate semi-circles facing each other with two rectangular working tables in the spaces between the two semi-circles and a space on each side of the rectangular tables. The United States revised slightly the last of these proposals by suggesting that the space between the two semi-circles and the two working tables be eliminated, i.e., the two semi-circles would be moved up against the two working tables.

The North Vietnamese rejected these proposals because they were based on the U.S. conception of a two-sided conference; they in turn proposed that the semi-circles not be split. The North Vietnamese delegation would occupy one-quarter of the table and the NLF one-quarter, with the two delegations seated side by side. On the other half of the table the U.S. and South Vietnamese delegations could arrange themselves as they wished. The North Vietnamese proposal was rejected because it called for a four-side arrangement which would give the NLF equality with South Vietnam.

The U.S. delegation made a number of additional proposals which were rejected by North Vietnam, before proposing a table arrangement which North Vietnam did accept. The rejected proposals included the following: (1) an oval table with a rectangular working area cut from its center; (2) two parallel tables with half circles at each end, forming a continuous table, the two arcs to be occupied by staff or left vacant; (3) a doughnut-shaped table with a single retangular table inside it; (4) a doughnut-shaped table with two small sunken working areas at opposite points of the circle; (5) a doughnut-shaped table with two small secretarial tables placed against it at opposite points of the circle; (6) a solid round table bisected by a strip of baize, separating the sides; and (7) a doughnut-shaped table with narrow strips of baize or with narrow painted or scratched lines, separating the ring into two sides. The table arrangement which North Vietnam accepted on January 15, 1969, was a revision by the United States of number (5)--a solid round table, with two separate rectangular tables placed at right angles to the round table at opposite points of the circle, thus giving the appearance of a separation of two sides: each rectangular table would be separated from the round table enough to permit walking between it and the round table. The side tables would be used for secretarial purposes. On January 16, the United States and North Vietnam announced agreement on the shape of the table and other procedural matters. The first substantive session of the Vietnam peace talks took place in Paris on January 25th.